INSIDE INTERNATIONAL FINANCE

For my parents,
Veronica and Ben

Inside International Finance

....

**A CITIZEN'S GUIDE TO THE WORLD'S
FINANCIAL MARKETS, INSTITUTIONS
AND KEY PLAYERS**

Richard Roberts

ORION
BUSINESS
BOOKS

The right of Richard Roberts to be identified as the
author of this work has been asserted by him in accordance with the
Copyright, Designs and Patents Act 1988.

This edition first published in Great Britain in 1998 by
Orion Business
An imprint of The Orion Publishing Group Ltd
Orion House, 5 Upper St Martin's Lane,
London WC2H 9EA

A CIP catalogue record for this book
is available from the British Library.

ISBN 0–75281–047–2

Typeset by Deltatype Ltd, Birkenhead, Merseyside
Printed in Great Britain by
Butler & Tanner Ltd, Frome and London

CONTENTS

PREFACE AND ACKNOWLEDGEMENTS

International finance is rarely out of the news these days. The aim of this book is to provide an accessible and up-to-date guide to this vital and dynamic subject for students, trainees, practitioners and interested laymen.

Many people have helped with the preparation of *Inside International Finance*. In particular, I would like to thank Rosi Bachmann, Philip Davis, Dr Marc Flandreau, Sue Gamble, Professor Yassi Hamada, Professor Y. C. Jao, Dr David Kynaston, Pierre de Longuemar, Barney Reynolds, Professor Gail Triner, Professor Toshio Suzuki, and Robin Woodhead. I am also most grateful to officials of the stock exchanges, futures exchanges, central banks and other financial institutions in Amsterdam, Basle, Chicago, Frankfurt, Hong Kong, London, Luxembourg, New York, Paris, Singapore, Tokyo and Zurich, and to corporate communications staff at numerous international banks. Special thanks are due to Martin Liu, publishing director at Orion Business Books, and editors Clare Christian and Liz Coghill.

Richard Roberts
March 1998.

CHAPTER 1

The International Financial System

INTRODUCTION

The international financial system is the framework of agreements, rules conventions and institutions within which international markets and firms operate. The evolution of the international financial system in the twentieth century has seen three major phases: the gold standard, the Bretton Woods system, and floating exchange rates. Today's era of global financial markets began in the 1970s; international financial flows are nowadays unprecedented in scale and scope, and they are growing relentlessly.

FUNCTIONING OF THE INTERNATIONAL FINANCE SYSTEM

A financial system performs three functions:

- it makes payments to cover transactions
- it provides a stable unit of value
- it furnishes a standard for deferred payments

In the case of an international financial system, payments are made across borders, usually involving a foreign currency transaction. Foreign currency transactions go through the foreign exchange market, which is an important component of the international financial system.

International trade and cross-border capital movements generate currency transactions, since participants usually require payment in their own national currency. National currencies that are acceptable to residents of other countries are known as 'international money'. Buying and selling foreign currency is the business of the foreign-exchange market (see Chapter 2). Determination of the price at which currencies trade against each other in the foreign-exchange market – the exchange rate – depends on the functioning of the international financial system.

For the international financial system to operate smoothly, there are three requirements:

- an effective adjustment mechanism
- adequate liquidity
- confidence in the system

An adjustment mechanism

The adjustment mechanism is the means by which payments imbalances between countries are rectified. The global balance of payments between countries must always sum to zero, but individual countries have surpluses or deficits. There comes a point at which persistent imbalances become unsustainable and potentially disruptive, and must be reduced. A realignment of the exchange rate of a country's currency against other currencies is one possible adjustment mechanism; alternatively, governments can adopt domestic economic policies that unilaterally adjust the payments balance, but such actions may be unpopular and politically problematical. Or governments may seek adjustment through co-ordinated currency management with other countries.

Liquidity

Liquidity means adequate availability of international money. A shortage of international money will constrain trade and capital transfers.

Confidence

Confidence in the stability of the system as a whole, and of key components such as the value of a leading currency, encourages participation in international transactions. Lack of confidence leads to wariness of involvement and thus diminishes international transactions and global prosperity. *Unwillingness to trade.*

EXCHANGE-RATE SYSTEMS

Economists identify four possible types of exchange-rate system:

- automatic exchange-rate systems

- (N–1) exchange-rate system
- multilateral exchange-rate management
- monetary union

Automatic exchange-rate systems

There are two types of automatic exchange-rate system: a fixed commodity standard system; and a freely floating exchange-rate system. They have very different adjustment mechanisms.

Under a fixed commodity standard, all countries in the system set a fixed price between their national currencies and a commodity – in practice, gold or silver – thereby also fixing their exchange rates *vis-à-vis* each other. Each national currency is backed by a fixed ratio of reserves of the commodity, and is freely convertible into the commodity. With fixed exchange rates, balance-of-payments imbalances are eliminated by international transfers of the commodity. This has the effect of increasing or decreasing a country's money supply, causing shifts in the respective price levels. Adjustment of price levels in turn increases or decreases competitiveness, thereby automatically bringing the balance of payments back into equilibrium.

Under a freely floating exchange-rate system, any balance of payments imbalance is automatically eliminated by adjustment of exchange rates.

(N–1) exchange-rate system

One country – called the Nth country, in a system of N countries – fixes its currency in terms of a commodity – gold, for instance – while the other countries fix theirs in terms of the Nth country's currency. In this system there are $N-1$ exchange rates, hence the name.

The $N-1$ exchange-rate system is a variant of the commodity standard system discussed above, but there is no automatic connection between the money supply in a particular country and the commodity backing the Nth currency. For the system to function, participants with balance-of-payments imbalances must adopt domestic economic policies that achieve adjustment. In practice, adjustment may be politically difficult for both deficit and surplus countries. This is a source of weakness.

The Nth country occupies a special position, which may also present problems. Its currency is the foremost international money, the principal international means of settlement and form of reserves. For other countries to hold adequate amounts of this key currency, the Nth country has to run balance-of-payments deficits. But if its deficits become too large, foreign holders will begin to lose confidence in the Nth currency.

Loss of confidence in the key currency will undermine confidence in the system itself.

Multilateral exchange-rate management

Multilateral exchange rate management is a form of floating exchange-rate regime. In practice, governments are unwilling to allow exchange rates to fluctuate entirely freely because of economic and political costs. They prefer to try to manage the process of adjustment, which is done through multilateral policy co-ordination and multilateral arrangements in order to help countries cope with short-term imbalances. But the growth in scale of the international financial markets since the 1970s has undermined the ability of governments to manipulate exchange rates, obliging them to adopt economic policies that prioritise the avoidance of exchange-rate adjustment problems.

Monetary union

The ultimate way of avoiding exchange-rate adjustment problems is the adoption of a common currency. This confers the benefits of eliminating uncertainty and transaction costs in relation to other participants. But balance-of-payments imbalances do not disappear, but instead become regional problems requiring other adjustment solutions such as labour mobility, flexible wage rates and social transfers (see Chapter 9).

THE GOLD STANDARD, 1816–1933

The 'gold standard' was a fixed commodity standard system, the commodity of course being gold. Participating countries fixed a physical weight of gold into which their currency was freely convertible, the central bank being obliged to provide gold in exchange for its banknotes. Parities between currencies were determined through their respective values in gold. The volume of paper money in circulation in a country was strictly proportional to the level of reserves, thereby controlling inflation and inspiring confidence.

Britain officially adopted the gold standard in 1816, the parity of a pound sterling being defined as 123.27 grains of gold. Sterling played a key role in the international financial system up to the outbreak of World War I: much of world trade was denominated and financed in sterling; it was the foremost reserve currency; and it was the principal component of the international capital market. Confidence in the strength and stability of the British state and the prestige and expertise of the Bank of England made sterling literally 'as good as gold' and inspired confidence in the whole system.

Other countries adopted the gold standard in the latter decades of the nineteenth century, the US dollar becoming convertible into gold in 1879. Britain and other European countries came off the gold standard in 1914 because of World War I, and the US dollar became the gold standard's standard-bearer instead. The European currencies returned to the gold standard in the 1920s. Sterling became convertible again in 1925, but at an overvalued parity. With the onset of the international depression, Britain was forced to devalue and to drop the gold standard altogether in 1931. When the US abandoned the gold standard in 1933, the environment of international fixed exchange rates effectively came to an end: sterling and the dollar had become floating currencies, although their exchange rates were managed by their central banks.

The 1930s saw the collapse of international trade and international financial flows as countries erected tariff barriers and imposed restrictions on capital flows. The onset of World War II in 1939 exacerbated the disruption of the international economy.

THE BRETTON WOODS SYSTEM, 1944–73

The Bretton Woods system took its name from the resort hotel in New Hampshire, US, that hosted the conference attended by 45 countries in July 1944 at which post-war international financial arrangements were agreed. The objective of the participants was to forge a new international financial framework that would prevent a recurrence of the problems of the 1930s and promote post-war economic growth and prosperity. They were suspicious of the role of the international markets in bringing about the depression of the 1930s and wanted a stable exchange-rate environment. US Treasury secretary Henry Morgenthau captured the intention when he pronounced that the Bretton Woods system would 'drive the usurious money lenders from the temple of international finance.'[1]

The Bretton Woods system was an $N-1$ exchange-rate system, with the US dollar as the pivotal currency. The key features of the Bretton Woods system were:

- pivotal role of the US dollar
- fixed but adjustable exchange rates
- the International Monetary Fund
- the World Bank

Pivotal role of the US dollar

By the end of World War II, the US was overwhelmingly the world's dominant economy and held 70 per cent of world gold reserves. The US dollar was assigned a pivotal role in the new arrangements – the dollar was fixed to gold and the US authorities undertook to sustain the convertibility of dollars into gold. The dollar/gold price was set at $35 per ounce.

Fixed but adjustable exchange rates

The Bretton Woods system was a fixed-rate system, but with mechanisms for flexibility and adjustment. Other currencies were assigned a central parity against the US dollar. Currencies were permitted to fluctuate +/− 1 per cent of the central parity. As a last resort in circumstances of 'fundamental disequilibrium', countries were allowed to revalue (raise) or devalue (lower) their currency relative to the dollar. This flexibility was intended to allow governments to correct persistent balance-of-payments problems through the exchange rate rather than by resort to import controls or domestic deflation.

The International Monetary Fund (IMF)

The IMF was established to oversee the operation of the new international financial system (see Chapter 5). The IMF exists to provide credit facilities to relieve temporary balance-of-payments difficulties and debt problems. These credits come from the quotas placed with the IMF by each participant. The larger the resort to such funds, the more stringent the conditions attached to rectify the underlying payments problem.

The World Bank

At the outset, the role of the International Bank for Reconstruction and Development (IBRD), usually called the World Bank, was the reconstruction of war-torn Europe. Today, in conjunction with its twin institution, the International Development Association (IDA), it assists developing countries by providing long-term financing of projects and programmes (see Chapter 5).

1940s and 1950s: reconstruction to convertibility

At the end of the war, the US was booming while Europe was exhausted and devastated. Only the US could furnish the goods needed to get the European economies going again, but those economies were unable to buy them because of a lack of foreign exchange – the so-called 'dollar shortage'. To remedy this situation, the US government furnished a massive package of credits and grants, known as the Marshall Plan, which in the years 1948–52 provided $14 billion to finance the import from the US of capital goods and raw materials required for reconstruction. As a result, the US had a substantial current account surplus while the countries of Europe ran large deficits. The Marshall Plan funds were administered by the Organisation of European Economic Co-operation (OEEC). Its job done, it became the Organisation for Economic Co-operation and Development (OECD), Canada and the US joining in 1961 and Japan in 1964. This institution's contribution was as a forum for policy research and debate.

The Bretton Woods system of fixed exchange rates became operational in March 1947 – but only partially so, since the European currencies remained unconvertible because of the lack of reserves and the widespread preference for dollars over any of them. An attempt to restore the convertibility of sterling in July 1947 was abandoned after only a few weeks, two-thirds of the UK's reserves having been used up supporting the pound. In 1949, the UK, France and some Scandinavian countries devalued. The IMF accepted that the parities set in 1944 were now too high, and exchange-rate adjustment was deemed better than harsh deflation.

In the early 1950s, the US balance of payments went into deficit, while European countries and Japan began to run surpluses. The increase of dollars in international circulation was welcomed because it facilitated international trade and payments, and it also enabled European central banks to build up their dollar reserves. With replenished reserves and economic prosperity, the European countries were ready for convertibility. In December 1958, the countries of Europe jointly moved to convertibility, lifting restrictions on the use and trading of their currencies.

The universal clamour for dollar credits gave a commanding competitive advantage to US banks in international lending. Moreover, as world trade revived, they were best placed to furnish the financing, much raw material trade now being denominated in dollars. As a result, the 1950s saw a boom in the international banking business of the major US commercial banks.

1960s: US deficits and the Euromarkets boom

The US balance-of-payments deficit developed into a serious problem in the 1960s. The war in Vietnam was an important reason, dollar capital exports to fund the overseas expansion of US multinational corporations another. The deterioration of the US balance-of-payments position prompted the US, together with nine other countries, to establish the General Agreement to Borrow (GAB) in 1962. This was an undertaking to make additional funds available to the IMF to support the dollar against speculative attack. The participants in the GAB continued to meet to discuss the international economy, becoming known as the Group of Ten (see Chapter 5). The Interest Equalisation Tax, introduced into the US in 1964, was intended to restrict European borrowing in the US capital market; in fact, the outflows continued through different channels. Thus yet further controls were imposed, limiting US banks' offshore lending and direct investment overseas by US corporations.

The US controls gave a big boost to the development of the Eurodollar market, especially in London, Luxembourg, Switzerland and a new set of 'offshore' financial centres (see Box 6.1, Chapter 6). American multinationals responded by depositing their offshore earnings in the Euromarkets, and also began to use them to fund their financing requirements. Regulation Q, a US regulation setting ceilings on rates of interest paid on deposits by banks, was a further factor. It provided a significant stimulus to the Eurodollar market depositors receiving higher rates and US banks themselves using the market as a source of funds. US banks established overseas branches to service their multinational clients and to participate in the burgeoning Euromarkets, especially London.

The substantial devaluations of sterling in 1967 and the French franc in 1968, reminded the markets that exchange rates were adjustable and there was money to be made when currencies were overvalued. As the US balance-of-payments deficit grew, it became ever more obvious that the dollar was overvalued. In April 1971, for the first time in the twentieth century, the US trade balance – visible exports less visible imports – lurched into deficit. Holders of dollars rushed to sell, anticipating a devaluation. Demand for Deutschmarks was so great that foreign-exchange trading in Frankfurt was suspended and the German currency was revalued by 7 per cent. But this proved to be just the prelude to a massive speculative attack on the dollar, which forced the abandonment of its convertibility into gold in August 1971.

In a last-ditch attempt to save the Bretton Woods system, the Group of Ten finance ministers, meeting at the Smithsonian Institute, Washington, in December 1971, agreed to raise the price of the dollar against gold from $35 to $38, an 8.6 per cent devaluation against other currencies, and to widen the bands within which other currencies could fluctuate against the dollar from +/– 1 per cent to +/– 2.25 per cent. 'The most significant monetary agreement in the history of the world,' declared US President Richard Nixon. Although, indeed, a landmark in international financial co-operation, the Smithsonian Agreement had little impact on the US payment deficit, which soared to new heights.

The final chapter of the Bretton Woods story opened in June 1972, when the UK, which had deficit problems of its own, floated sterling. In February 1973, another bout of speculation against the dollar forced a further devaluation of 11 per cent, accompanied by the floating of the Swiss franc and the yen. Then in June 1973, the European Economic Community currencies floated. The Bretton Woods system of fixed exchange rates was finished. The international economy entered a new era of variable exchange rates.

Reasons for the downfall of the Bretton Woods system

Several factors played a part in the downfall of the Bretton Woods system, most notably the 'liquidity problem' and the 'adjustment problem', both described further below.

The liquidity problem
Central banks were happy to hold dollars, so long as they were confident that they could be converted into gold at $35 per ounce. The growth of international trade led to an increase in central bank requirements for dollar reserves. This necessitated a US balance-of-payments deficit, which was the case from the early 1950s. But the rate of increase of US gold reserves did not keep pace with the overseas accumulation of dollars. In consequence, the ratio of US gold reserves to overseas dollar liabilities deteriorated, and in the 1960s full convertibility became impossible. The growing inevitability of a US devaluation undermined confidence in the system.

The adjustment problem
Although the Bretton Woods system made provision for parity realignments, in practice they were rare. Countries with balance-of-payments surpluses, notably Germany, Japan and Switzerland, were reluctant to revalue because it would make their exports less competitive. Deficit countries were reluctant to devalue for political reasons, electorates associating devaluation with economic mismanagement, or to adopt the domestic deflationary policies that would redress the deficit because of the electorally unpopular unemployment that would result.

The US was in a uniquely problematic position. The pivotal position of the dollar meant that devaluation would undermine confidence in the whole system. Furthermore, US competitiveness would not be enhanced by a dollar–gold devaluation if other countries maintained their exchange-rate parities against the dollar. So long as US balance-of-payments deficits were modest, the rest of the world was happy to hold dollars. But in practice, control of the US deficit by deflationary economic policies came a poor second to domestic political popularity. And then the Vietnam War sent spending soaring, resulting in widening deficits and increasing inflation.

Given the universal reluctance to adjust either exchange-rate parities or economic policies, the maintenance of fixed exchange rates in the face of persistent balance-of-payments imbalances was a conundrum. In the 1960s, it was solved by surplus countries providing central bank credits to deficit countries. But that just put back the day of reckoning.

FLOATING EXCHANGE RATES, 1973 ONWARDS

Since 1973, the international financial system has featured market-driven floating exchange rates, tempered by central bank intervention and multilateral accords. Although often referred to as a 'system', it is really a 'non-system': 'if a wheel falls off your car,' observes a sceptic, 'it's no use re-christening it a tricycle.'[2] Exchange rates have certainly been more variable than under the Bretton Woods system, average month-by-month volatility of the exchange rates of the seven leading industrial economies being four times greater in the 1990s than in the 1960s;[3] but this has not been entirely due to the abandonment of fixed exchange rates, the variability of other factors such as inflation and current account imbalances also having increased.

Amendments to the IMF's Articles of Agreement to take account of the new floating-rate regime were worked out at its annual conference in Kingston, Jamaica, in January 1976. The official price of gold was abolished and Special Drawing Rights (SDRs) were given an enhanced importance in international reserves (see Box 5.1, Chapter 5). Fund members were given wide discretion about their exchange-rate arrangements, albeit notionally under the 'firm surveillance' of the IMF.

The dollar, the yen and sterling moved with market forces, fluctuations being moderated to some extent by co-ordinated central bank intervention. Many developing countries pegged their exchange rate to the dollar or another international currency. The members of the European Economic Community established arrangements to restrict exchange-rate fluctuations between their currencies, although floating against outside currencies such as the dollar or the yen was permitted. This system, known as 'the snake', was set-up in 1971 (see Chapter 9). In 1979, it was replaced by the European Monetary System.

Oil price rises and petro-dollar recycling

The devaluation of the dollar in the early 1970s inflicted losses on dollar holders and on producers of commodities denominated in dollars, notably oil. At the end of 1973, the Organisation of Petroleum Exporting Countries (OPEC) retaliated by hiking the price of oil, the Arab–Israeli war at that time being an additional reason for the Arab OPEC members to do so. The quadrupling of petroleum prices inflicted massive dislocation upon the international economy, laying to rest any plans for the re-establishment of a system of fixed exchanges.

The oil price increases caused balance-of-payments surpluses for many oil producers, and deficits for oil importers. The OPEC members enjoyed an increase in their current-account surplus from $6.2 billion in 1973 to $66.7 billion in 1974. On the other hand, Japan, which was entirely dependent on imported oil, saw a current-account surplus of $100 million in 1973 turn into a $4.5 billion deficit in 1974. Yet the hardest hit were non-petroleum-exporting less developed countries (LDCs). In aggregate, the LDCs' current account deficits soared from $8.7 billion in 1973 to $51.3 billion in 1975. In response, in mid-1974, the IMF set up an 'oil facility', borrowing funds from oil producers and lending them to LDCs. This marked the beginning of the great 'petro-dollar recycling' boom.

The lion's share of petro-dollar recycling was undertaken by the commercial banks, especially the overseas branches of US banks. The flows were routed through the eurocurrency market, particularly in London, Luxembourg and some offshore financial centres. Petro-dollar recycling obliged the US authorities to suspend official capital controls, allowing US banks to compete freely for petro-dollar deposits and loans. The 1970s thus saw a boom in international banking business through syndicated loans – banks acting in syndicates because the sums involved were too large for sole lenders.

Between 1973 and 1978, LDC debt rose from $130 billion to $336 billion. But these were years of strong economic growth, and debt servicing was not a problem. Then a series of shocks raised the burden to breaking point: in 1979, as a result of the Iranian revolution, oil prices shot up for a second time, more than doubling from $13 to $32 per barrel. Again the recycling machine went into action, LDC debt growing from $336 billion in 1978 to $662 billion in 1982. The countries of Latin America were particularly prolific borrowers.

The first oil shock had fuelled inflation in developed countries both because it increased energy costs and because governments lowered interest rates to mitigate the deflationary impact on growth and employment. Determined to control inflation, the authorities of the OECD countries responded to the second oil shock with stringent monetary policies. In the US interest rates rose from 9.5 per cent in mid-1978 to 16.6 per cent in mid-1981. This hike in interest rates triggered a sharp recession in the developed economies, which then hit LDC export earnings because of depressed demand for their products and services from the developed economies and because of an associated adverse movement in LDC terms of trade – the ratio of a country's export prices to import prices. Moreover, the cost of debt servicing soared because most LDC borrowing was at floating rates. The high US rates caused the dollar to appreciate against LDC currencies, increasing the real value of LDC debt servicing, while loans became harder to come by since the higher rates diverted flows towards the US.

The debt crisis

The impact of these external shocks on LDC debt in the years 1981 and 1982 is shown in Table 1.1. The LDCs' debt problem was exacerbated by the uses to which much of the money had been put. Instead of being invested in productive projects, it had been squandered by governments on current consumption to purchase popularity or on propping up inefficient state enterprises, or it had simply disappeared into the pockets of politicians and officials. The outcome was that, by 1982, many LDCs were burdened with vast debts that they were unable to service (Table 1.2).

Table 1.1: Impact of external shocks on developing country debt in 1981 and 1982

Shock	Increase in debt (per annum)
Terms of trade loss	$40 billion
Oil price rise in 1979 (relative to 1978)	$37 billion
Real interest rate increase (excess over 1961–80 average)	$20 billion
Export volume due to recession	$10 billion

Source: Cline, W. R., *International Debt: Systematic Risk and Policy Response* (Washington D.C., Institute for International Economics, 1984).

The debt crisis began in August 1982 when Mexico, the second-largest LDC debtor, announced a payments moratorium. New loans and a rescheduled timetable for repayments were required. The Mexican moratorium was a shock to the international banks, which realised that other LDCs faced similar problems. American banks in particular were very exposed to LDC debt. Many major US banks had exposures greater than their capital: for instance, Manufacturers Hanover was exposed at 2.6 times capital, Citibank 1.7 times, and Chase Manhattan 1.5 times.[4] How had they got themselves into this perilous position? Inadequate appreciation of the adverse impacts of a rise in US interest rates was one reason. Miscalculation of country risk another. 'Sovereign borrowers do not go bust,' pronounced the chairman of Citibank. True – but it doesn't mean they always pay their debts. The banks themselves were far from blameless, having relaxed their credit criteria in their eagerness to profit from the petro-dollar recycling business. Moreover, the syndicated loan system provided a false sense of security: surely they couldn't all be wrong? Well, yes they could.

Table 1.2: External debt of leading LDCs in 1982

Country	External debt
Brazil	$92.8 billion
Mexico	$86.0 billion
Argentina	$43.6 billion
Venezuela	$32.1 billion

Source: World Bank, World Debt Tables.

Bank exposures to highly indebted countries posed a threat to the Western banking system. Developed country governments and international institutions became involved in the management of the debt crisis (see Box 1.1). Resolution of the debt problem imposed burdens on the borrowers, in the form of austerity and unemployment on bank shareholders, and on taxpayers in the developed world who ultimately paid for their governments' rescue operations through the international financial institutions. Citibank, which had led the charge to lend, began the process of restoring the quality of the international banks' balance sheets, making a $3 billion (30 per cent of its total) provision against possible bad debts in 1987. Other banks followed suit, reporting losses to shareholders.

Box 1.1: Management of the 1980s debt crisis

There were three principal phases in the co-ordinated management of the debt problem in the 1980s. Despite these common phases, each country was handled on a case-by-case basis.

- *Crisis management* The handling of the Mexican crisis of summer 1982 furnished a precedent for other cases. The US government and the Bank for International Settlements provided emergency bridging finance to forestall default. Meanwhile, the IMF took a key role in brokering debt rescheduling and restructuring agreements between banks and borrowers: countries were obliged to implement austerity measures and economic reforms; and banks were required to make further loans. The IMF itself look the lead as a lender. The commercial banks' participation was often reluctant because it meant assuming additional risk. But it was not unprofitable, large fees being earned in the process.

- *Baker Plan, October 1985* The debtor countries soon became disenchanted with the economic hardships inflicted by the IMF-brokered 'adjustment programmes'. In 1985, US treasury secretary James Baker launched a three-year initiative to promote growth in 15 large debtor nations through a mixture of economic liberalisation – privatisation, trade liberalisation, government expenditure cuts – and the injection of new foreign loans, $20 billion coming from the commercial banks and $10 billion from the multinational institutions. The outcome was disappointing, partly because bank lending did not resume on the scale envisaged but also because of economic mismanagement on the part of the LDCs.

- *Brady Plan, February 1989* The Brady Plan extended support for the case-by-case arrangements that had been arrived at between borrowers and banks under the Baker Plan. However, in the interim, Western governments and banks had accepted that debt reduction was part of the solution to the debt problem. Thus the Brady Plan included official support for limited debt reduction. The foremost mechanism was the exchange of outstanding bank debt, at a substantial discount, for bonds backed by a US Treasury guarantee. These new bonds were known as 'Brady bonds'. Mexico gave a lead, negotiating new rescheduling arrangements that converted the bulk of its debt into Brady bonds. Other countries followed suit. By the late 1990s, the credit worthiness of many Latin American borrowers had improved so much that they were able to pay off the Brady bonds with cheaper 'sovereign bond' issues without the US guarantee.

In the 1970s and early 1980s, prior to the Mexican moratorium, the developing countries were net recipients of international capital flows – that is, new loans exceeded interest payments plus repayments of principal. With the onset of the debt crisis, the payments pattern reversed and there were substantial net transfers from developing to developed countries. These were achieved by the devloping countries at the cost of recession, real per capita expenditures declining by almost one-fifth in Latin America in the 1980s.

The Plaza and Louvre Accords

The initiatives to manage the international debt problem in the 1980s were echoed in endeavours at multilateral financial policy co-ordination. The Plaza Accord of September 1985, announced days prior to the Baker Plan, was an agreement amongst the leading industrial nations to take co-ordinated measures to establish greater international currency stability and appropriate exchange rates. In particular, they sought to curb the rise of the dollar, which had appreciated 60 per cent since 1981. The dollar was indeed overvalued, and declined rapidly – so rapidly that the ministers of the Group of Seven (G7) – Canada, France, Germany, Italy, Japan, the United Kingdom and the United States – met to halt the slide.

The Louvre Accord of February 1987 was an agreement that the dollar's depreciation had gone far enough and that exchange rates were now 'broadly consistent with underlying economic fundamentals'. At the time, there were rumours of a secret concordat to keep currencies within agreed ranges of the dollar, a covert return to stable exchange rates. Nothing, however, materialised.

The stock market boom of the 1980s and 1990s

The shift in international financial flows away from the developing world was one of the factors that fuelled the boom on Western stock markets that got underway in 1982. Between August 1982 and October 1987, the Dow Jones Index, Wall Street's yardstick, rose from 780 to 3,600. The global stock market crash of October 1987, when many markets lost a quarter of their value, seemed to be the end of that story. A repetition of the slump that followed the Wall Street crash of 1929 was feared, leading the authorities to relax monetary conditions. In fact, the 1987 crash proved to be but a blip in the upward path of share prices. On Wall Street, the Dow Jones passed 3,600 in 1990 and by 1998 had soared above 8,000, the greatest 'bull run' in US stock market history.

From Communism to capitalism

While capitalism was prospering, Communism was collapsing. The fall of the Berlin Wall in 1989 marked the beginning of the end of the Soviet empire. East Germany was reunified with West Germany, and Hungary, Poland and the Czech Republic moved rapidly towards becoming market economies. The countries of Eastern Europe and their nascent stock markets became magnets for investors seeking higher returns than were available in the expensively valued Western markets.

Russia's transition to democracy and market capitalism was particularly turbulent and faltering. The emergency food and finance package put together by the G7 in August 1991 provided vital relief and was an important gesture of support to Russia's reformers at a critical moment. A stock market and a private banking system were established in Russia, although they were not for the faint-hearted, the former being more like a casino and the latter full of bandits rather than bankers. Nevertheless, after outstanding Tsarist debts were settled, Russia became a welcome borrower in the international capital markets, and Western investment flooded in.

Regional blocs

The early 1990s saw a rising regional orientation on the part of America, Europe and South-East Asia. 'It was at this point that the G7 economies really began to diverge,' says David Mulford, at the time US Treasury under-secretary for international affairs in the Bush administration and subsequently chairman of CS First Boston Europe. 'The US was coming out of recession. The European countries were going in. This was the point at which the tremendous economic and financial costs of German re-unification began to take shape. Europe turned in on itself. Then the Clinton administration came in and they didn't pick up and do anything.'[5]

The formation of the North America Free Trade Area (NAFTA) by the US, Canada and Mexico was a step towards the formalisation of a regional bloc in the Western hemisphere. Countries of Latin America were expected to affiliate. In Asia, Japan focused on building ties with the region's booming 'tiger' economies. The Association of South-East Asian Nations (ASEAN) assisted regional co-ordination.

Regionalism was most advanced in Europe, which was endeavouring to become a single political and economic entity. At the beginning of the 1990s, seven further countries joined the Exchange Rate Mechanism of linked currencies, including the UK (see Chapter 9). But the European economies were moving in different directions and at different speeds. In September 1992, speculative pressure forced the devaluation of sterling, the lira, the punt and the peseta, and the UK left the system all together. Then, in August 1993, the linkages had to be drastically relaxed to relieve speculative pressures on the French franc and the system as a whole. French prime minister Jacques Chirac angrily denounced international currency speculators as, 'the AIDS of the world economy.'[6]

Mexican peso crisis 1994–95

During the 1980s, foreign capital flowed mainly between the industrial countries – mostly to the US. However, from the beginning of the 1990s, flows to the developing world resumed on a substantial scale, as shown in Table 1.3. The foremost recipients were a favoured group of countries in Asia and Latin America, previously 'less developed countries' as already mentioned but now known as 'emerging markets'.

Table 1.3: Global net capital flows, 1975–94

	\$ billion, annual averages					
	1975–82	1983–90	1991	1992	1993	1994
United States	−7.6	96.7	−14.8	25.7	35.3	113.9
Japan	−1.8	−52.7	−90.0	−118.9	−108.0	131.4
Western Europe	21.6	8.6	73.5	45.1	−31.1	−16.5
Developing countries	22.3	37.7	152.9	142.1	151.3	135.7

Source: Turner, Philip *Capital Flows in Latin America: A New Phase*, Bank for International Settlements Economic Papers No. 44 (Basle, May 1995).

Mexico was the biggest recipient. Mexican economic reforms in the early 1990s, plus low interest rates in the US that prompted investors to look overseas, led to a massive inflow of funds into Mexico. Mexican bond and equity prices soared, as did Mexico's current account deficit and public spending ahead of an election. When there was a minor outbreak of political disturbance in the country towards the end of 1994, international investors lost their nerve, fearing another Mexican moratorium. The peso plummeted and Mexican securities were dumped as quickly as a hot *enchilada*. Worried about the money meltdown south of the border, the US cajoled the G7 countries into pledging a record \$40 billion support package for the Mexican government through the IMF. It worked; confidence was restored and the peso recovered.

Fears that the Mexican peso crisis would spread to the rest of Latin America proved unfounded. Across the continent, reform had delivered real improvements in economic performance, and the capital imports of the 1990s had been put to productive uses. Mexico too was fundamentally in sound economic shape – hence the rapid recovery. By 1997, Mexico, Brazil, Argentina, Venezuela and Panama, were sufficiently financially rehabilitated to be able to retire their Brady bonds (see Box 1.1) by substituting new sovereign debt paying lower rates of interest. By so doing, they not only saved money but also cast off the stigma of being 'basket-case borrowers'.

THE EAST ASIAN FINANCIAL CRISIS OF 1997–98

In the 1990s, Asia's tiger economies – Hong Kong, Indonesia, Malaysia, the Philippines, Singapore, South Korea, Taiwan and Thailand – grew rapidly. Between 1990 and 1995, the region generated 60–65 per cent of the growth in world output, a remarkable record. This was achieved by large-scale investment, which expanded at 15–20 per cent per annum and delivered a huge increase in capacity. The funds came from the international banking system and the international financial markets, creating high levels of external debt. Although on the whole the funds were put to productive uses, eventually the accumulated debt burden proved unsustainable.

'1997 was the year the financial markets flexed their muscles,' commented the *Financial Times*.[7] The East Asian financial crisis began in July when Thailand, which had almost exhausted its foreign currency reserves, floated the baht. The Thai currency plummeted, triggering a stock market crash and the collapse of other asset prices. Soon Malaysia, Indonesia and the Philippines were experiencing similar problems. In Hong Kong, the stock market plunged in October 1997, although the currency remained sound, the peg to the dollar being sustained by massive foreign-currency cover and the backing of mainland China. In November 1997 the crisis spread to South Korea, which suffered currency and stock market collapses. Japan was affected too – its stock market fell sharply and there was a rash of failures amongst banks and securities houses (see Chapter 7).

Although debt was at the heart of both the East Asian financial crisis of the 1990s and the LDC debt crisis of the 1980s, they were very different episodes. The Latin American debt problems of the 1980s were exacerbated by a legacy of government profligacy and misallocations of funds. In East Asia, it was the private sector that did the borrowing and incurred the debt problem. Easy credit, liberally provided by both domestic and foreign banks, led to spiralling asset prices. This prompted further borrowing so as to speculate in the booming markets. The outcome was not only heavy indebtedness and overvalued assets, but also serious mismatches between foreign liabilities and domestic assets, and between liquid liabilities and illiquid assets. These problems were exacerbated by structural weaknesses in the banking systems, inconsistent monetary policies, unsustainable exchange rates, and 'crony capitalism' – the encouragement to banks by the political élite to lend to favoured businesses.

Once lenders and investors began to have doubts about the borrowers' ability to pay, confidence evaporated rapidly and credit dried up. Foreign private capital flows went into reverse – a net inflow of $93 billion on 1996 turned into a net outflow of $12 billion in 1997 for Indonesia, Malaysia, the Philippines, South Korea, and Thailand taken together.[8] The stampede to sell currencies and financial assets led to plummeting exchange rates and stock and property market crashes. A lack of credit pushed even intrinsically sound firms into bankruptcy, investment stopped and growth slowed.

An alternative explanation of the collapses was advanced in the region, most vociferously by the Malaysian prime minister Dr Mahathir Mohamad. He accused foreign speculators – 'who should be shot' – of manipulating markets and 'teaming up to impoverish the poor countries.'[9] In particular, he blamed US billionaire financier George Soros for leading the attacks on East Asian currencies. 'All these countries have spent forty years trying to build up their economy,' declared Dr Mahathir, 'and a moron like Soros comes along.'[10] Soros responded by calling Mahathir 'a menace to his own country.'[11] Western opinion was generally on Soros's side, regarding Dr Mahathir's outbursts as attempts to find a scapegoat for politicians' policy failures.

Support packages totalling more than $100 billion were assembled by the International Monetary Fund. Thailand received $4 billion from the IMF, plus $13.2 billion from the World Bank and Asian Development Bank. Indonesia got $10 billion from the IMF and $8 billion from the ADB. South Korea was the recipient of a record $55 billion bail-out, $21 billion coming from the IMF, $14 billion from the World Bank and ADB, and $20 billion being on standby from the G7. But there were strings attached. The IMF adjustment programmes required borrowers to adhere to stringent macro-economic policy measures, instigate reforms to their financial systems, improve protection for corporate shareholders and liberalise trade and capital flows.

The IMF's measures attracted a measure of criticism in the West. 'Why

has the IMF imposed its same old belt-tightening adjustment programmes on Thailand, Indonesia and Korea – programmes that were
quite inappropriate to their present needs?' *Financial Times* editor Richard
Lambert asked IMF managing director Michel Camdessus.[12] 'Here Mr
Camdessus became indignant,' reported the newspaper. 'The new
agreements represented a marked departure from the IMF's traditional
approach. They were not built on a set of austerity measures, but rather
on far-reaching structural reforms to strengthen financial systems,
increase transparency, open markets and restore confidence. It was true
that the agreements had been accompanied by a sharp increase in interest
rates. But this had to be seen in the context of a collapse in confidence. ...
To reverse this process, countries had to make it more attractive to hold
their currencies – and that required temporary increases in interest
rates.'[13]

An intriguing proposal was put forward by the controversial George
Soros. On New Year's Eve 1997, he called for the establishment of an
International Credit Insurance Corporation as a sister institution to the
IMF. Its function would be to guarantee international loans, for a modest
fee. Based on information about all borrowings, the new authority would
set ceilings for its guarantees to particular countries. This would enable
them to raise funds cheaply up to the level of the guarantee, but
additional borrowing would be expensive, and thus they would be
encouraged to limit their indebtedness to prudent amounts. The proposal
was received with sceptical curiosity. 'A recipe for bureaucracy,' was the
verdict of the *Financial Times*.[14]

GLOBAL FINANCIAL MARKETS

The 1980s and 1990s saw the rise of a vast global financial market. This
global market has a variety of dimensions: the foreign-exchange market;
international bank lending; long-term bonds; medium-term securities
(Euronotes); international equities; and derivatives. International management consultants McKinsey estimate that the total stock of financial
assets traded in the global capital market expanded from $5 trillion in
1980 to $35 trillion in 1992. This is a rate of increase two-and-a-half times
faster than the rate of growth of the economies of the OECD countries.[15]
McKinsey forecast that by the year 2000 the market will have grown to
$83 trillion, equivalent to three times the aggregate gross domestic
product of the OECD countries.

Estimates of financing in international markets published by the Bank for International Settlements show a fivefold increase over the years 1982–96, from $1.3 trillion to $6.9 trillion (Table 1.4). The bulk of financing in international markets is still international bank lending, but there has been a gradual increase in the proportion of financing through the issue of securities, which rose from 20 per cent to almost 30 per cent over these years.

Table 1.4: Outstanding net financing in international markets, 1982–95

	Stock at year end, $ billion		
	Net international bank lending	Net Euronote placements	Net international bond financing
1982	1,020		259
1983	1,085		345
1984	1,265		410
1985	1,480		550
1986	1,770		700
1987	2,220		984
1988	2,390	72	1,085
1989	2,640	79	1,252
1990	3,350	111	1,473
1991	3,610	145	1,651
1992	3,660	177	1,687
1993	3,780	256	1,850
1994	4,240	406	2,048
1995	4,645	594	2,210
1996	5,015	834	2,391

Source: Bank for International Settlements, *Annual Reports*, 1983–1997.

The advance of the global financial market is the product of the expansion of international banking, plus several other factors:

- liberalisation of international capital flows
- deregulation of financial markets
- revolution in communications technology
- dynamic financial innovation

A liberalisation of international capital flows
Liberalisation of international capital flows means the removal of controls on cross-border financial movements. The rise of the Eurocurrency market in the late 1950s marked the resumption of cross-border

financial flows, initially in the form of bank lending. A free foreign-exchange market existed from 1958 as a result of the adoption of convertibility by the European economies, but it was not until the demise of the Bretton Woods system of fixed exchange rates in 1973 that it assumed a central role.

Capital controls, imposed to channel domestic savings into domestic investment, were increasingly undermined by the expansion of the Euromarkets in the 1960s. By 1973, the US, Canada, Germany and Switzerland had abolished their restrictions. Pressured by market forces that made the controls ineffective except in relation to encouraging international business to choose less regulated locations, other countries followed suit. The UK scrapped controls in 1979, Japan in 1980; France and Italy threw in the towel in 1990, Spain and Portugal in 1992.

Deregulation of financial markets

The removal of barriers to international cross-border flows has been accompanied by the dismantling of domestic restrictions on financial activities, a process known as deregulation. Notable milestones were: 1 May 1975 – the so-called 'Mayday' – when the New York Stock Exchange abolished fixed commission charges; and October 1986, 'Big Bang', when London did likewise as well as revising the rules on the ownership of securities firms so as to allow the combination of broking, market making, and banking business. Japan has plans for its own 'Big Bang' by 2002 (see Chapter 7).

Revolution in communications technology

Technology, in the form of computers and telecommunications, has transformed the speed of international financial flows and broadened the scope of international investment and trading.

Dynamic financial innovation

Financial innovation has created new products and new markets. 'Securitisation' – that is, the replacement of traditional bank lending by the issuance of tradable securities – has increased the volume and variety of tradable financial assets. It is a phenomenon well advanced in the US and growing elsewhere.

Even more important is the proliferation of 'derivatives', contracts or tradable instruments that bear a contractual relationship to an underlying cash instrument or financial index. Using derivatives, transactions cost perhaps only 10 per cent as much as transactions in the underlying cash markets. In the early 1980s, currency and interest-rate derivatives scarcely existed, but by 1996 the worldwide total stock of financial derivative instruments traded on organised exchanges was $327 trillion.[16]

Governments and global markets

A generation ago, governments had an array of instruments for economic management – interest rates, public expenditure, taxation, credit controls, capital controls, incomes policies, and exchange rates. The effectiveness of these tools has been blunted by liberalisation and deregulation, and by the rise of the global financial markets. The massive expansion of international financial flows over the past two decades has transformed the relationship between governments and the international money markets. In the early 1980s, the aggregate currency reserves of the OECD countries were several times the daily volume of international foreign-currency trading, allowing central banks a degree of influence over exchange rates; today, the mighty market rules – the $640 billion total foreign-currency reserves of the OECD countries is half the global foreign exchange markets' daily turnover of $1.2 trillion. 'The foreign-exchange market is a 1,000-pound gorilla and intervention is a flimsy leash,' comments US economist Jeffrey Frankel. 'When the gorilla has a good idea where it wants to go, there is no point in trying to restrain him. But sometimes the gorilla is willing to be led.[17]

National economic sovereignty has been eroded by the rise of the global financial markets. Governments are constrained in their choice of economic policies and priorities by the necessity of pleasing the financial markets. If the market loses confidence in a country, there can be dire consequences – a currency crisis, higher interest rates, capital flight, a stock market slump, or greater unemployment. 'I used to think that if there was re-incarnation, I wanted to come back as the president or the pope,' remarks James Carville, an adviser to President Clinton. 'But now I want to be the bond market; you can intimidate everybody.[18]

The power of the global markets

The 'brute force' of the global financial markets has been demonstrated repeatedly in recent years – the ERM crises of 1992–93, the Mexican peso crisis of 1995, and the East Asia crises of 1997–98.[19] Have the global financial markets become over-powerful? Every episode of financial turbulence generates denunciations of speculators and calls for governments to curb the power of the markets through closer international policy co-ordination, the re-introduction of capital controls, or the imposition of a turnover tax. Underlying these proposals is the proposition that the financial markets – which are held to be divorced from productive economic activity and indifferent to social issues and long-term considerations – should not be accorded greater influence over policy than democratically elected governments.

In contrast, the record of economic management by post-war administrations leaves plenty to be desired. The external discipline of the global financial markets imposes a salutary rigour on politicians, curbing their scope for irresponsibility and abuse of power. The financial markets are no more than a mechanism for pricing capital and allocating it to the most productive purposes. Markets gather and process information. By punishing public profligacy with higher borrowing rates, they provide a strong incentive for governments to mend their ways. Greater honesty and openness would forestall destabilising adjustments of expectations.

Markets tend to exaggerate bad news (and good) but they rarely invent problems. Sometimes they have to react brutally before politicians will take appropriate but unpopular reforms. Then markets bounce back, giving the impression that the initial reaction was excessive. But without the over-reaction, the beneficial policy changes would not have happened.

The global financial markets received a boost in December 1997 when, after years of haggling, representatives of 102 countries signed a World Trade Organisation agreement on financial services. The signatories pledged to open their banking, insurance and securities sectors to foreign competition (to varying degrees) and to subject financial services to legally binding fair-trade rules and disciplines. The agreement, which comes into force in March 1999, involves an estimated $38,000 billion in international bank lending, $18,000 billion in global securities assets and $2,500 billion in worldwide insurance premiums. Sir Leon Brittan, the European Union's trade commissioner, hailed the deal as 'a triumph for the multilateral system and good for the world economy'.[20]

The global financial markets are not only here to stay but they're also getting bigger and bigger. International financial flows are now unprecedented in scale and scope, and they are growing relentlessly.

In a Nutshell

The international financial system is the framework of agreements, rules, conventions, and institutions within which international markets and firms operate. The evolution of the international financial system in the ⇨

twentieth century has seen three major phases: the gold standard up to the 1930s; the Bretton Woods system in 1944–73; and floating exchange rates since 1973.

The Bretton Woods system was a system of fixed exchange rates between the world's principal currencies. Since 1973, currencies have fluctuated in value against each other, but their variations have been moderated by multilateral co-ordination and regional arrangements such as Europe's Exchange-Rate Mechanism.

The 1970s were a decade of turbulence in the international financial system, featuring high levels of inflation, currency instability and petro-dollar recycling. The 1980s saw the debt crisis in Latin America and elsewhere, but booming financial markets in the West and Asia as well. The 1990s witnessed progress towards the resolution of the 1980s' debt crisis, but also financial problems in Asia that began in Japan in 1990 and East Asia generally in 1997.

The 1980s and 1990s saw the rise of a vast global financial market. International management consultants McKinsey estimate that the total stock of financial assets traded in the global capital markets will grow sixteenfold over these decades, rising from $5 trillion in 1980 to a projected $83 trillion by the year 2000. International financial flows are now unprecedented in scale and scope, and they are growing relentlessly.

FURTHER READING

Gibson, Heather, *International Finance: Exchange Rates and Financial Flows in the International System* (London, Longman 1996)
Giddy, Ian, *Global Financial Markets* (Lexington Mass., D.C. Heath, 1994)
Pilbeam, Keith, *International Finance* (London, Macmillan, 1992)
Valdez, Stephen, *An Introduction to Global Financial Markets* (London, Macmillan, 1997)

NOTES AND REFERENCES

In the list below for this chapter, any reference to an author alone should be taken to be a reference to his/her work in 'Further reading' above.

1 Quoted in *The Economist*, 7 October 1995
2 McMahon, Sir Kit, *The International Monetary System: The Next 25 Years* (Basle, Bank for International Settlements, 1988) quoting Janos Fekete

3 *The Economist*, 7 October 1995

4 Nunnenkamp, P., *The International Debt Crisis of the Third World* (Brighton Wheatsheaf Books, 1986)

5 *Euromoney*, May 1995

6 Survey of the World Economy, *The Economist*, 7 October 1995

7 *Financial Times*, 27 and 28 December 1997

8 *The Economist*, 7 February 1998

9 *Financial Times*, 23 July 1997

10 *Financial Times*, 12 January 1998

11 *Financial Times*, 12 and 13 January 1998

12 *Financial Times*, 9 February 1998

13 *Financial Times*, 9 February 1998

14 *Financial Times*, 2 February 1998

15 Survey of the World Economy, *The Economist*, 7 October 1995

16 *Bank for International Settlements, Annual Report*, 1996–97

17 Survey of the World Economy, *The Economist*, 7 October 1995

18 Survey of the World Economy, *The Economist*, 7 October 1995

19 *Financial Times*, 27 and 28 October 1997

20 *Financial Times*, 15 December 1997

CHAPTER 2
International Financial Markets

INTRODUCTION

This chapter surveys the leading international financial markets, namely: the vast global foreign-exchange market; the international money market, particularly the eurocurrency market; the international bond market; the international equity market; the rapidly growing global derivatives market; and the gold market, the world's oldest financial market.

THE FOREIGN-EXCHANGE MARKET

The global foreign-exchange market is huge. A survey for the Bank for International Settlements in 1995 revealed that global daily turnover was $1,260 billion.[1] By comparison, the record daily value of trading on the New York Stock Exchange, the world's largest stock exchange, is $28 billion.[2]

The foreign-exchange market is where the currencies of different countries are traded for each other. It is where financial claims between countries are settled, which arise from trade – imports and exports – and from international capital flows. Furthermore, there is a large volume of speculative trading through the market, where speculators seek to profit by correctly predicting currency fluctuations resulting from factors such as changes in interest rates or inflation rates.

The foreign-exchange market operates without an institutionalised framework of the stock exchange sort. Buyers and sellers, mostly in bank dealing rooms, trade with each other by telephone or computer. They are supported by up-to-the-moment data furnished by financial information providers such as Reuters or Bloomberg.

Market participants

The principal participants in the foreign-exchange market are central banks, commercial banks, investment banks, importers and exporters, investors, and the international financial institutions. They use the market for a variety of reasons: to hedge their currency exposures; to transfer purchasing power from one country to another; and for overseas investment.

The large international commercial banks are the biggest players in the foreign-exchange market. The multinational oil companies and other commodity companies are also major participants, their products being generally priced in dollars in the wholesale markets but in local currencies at retail level. Exchange rates are important factors in generating or reducing inflationary pressures and balance of payments problems, and so central banks keep a watchful eye on the market. Usually they stay on the sidelines, but occasionally they actively intervene to influence exchange rates up or down. In some circumstances, central bank purchases may be a more effective way of supporting a currency than raising interest rates. However, their capacity for decisive intervention has waned since the 1980s as the rate of growth of the foreign-exchange market has outstripped that of the central banks' reserves: by the late 1990s, aggregate central bank reserves amounted to little more than one day's turnover in the global foreign exchange market.

The growth of the global foreign-exchange market since the demise of the Bretton Woods system has been phenomenal. In the early 1970s, the daily volume of global foreign-exchange trading was perhaps $10–$20 billion per day. By 1983, it had grown to around $60 billion per day, and by 1986 exceeded $250 billion per day. The rapid expansion of the foreign-exchange market prompted the Bank for International Settlements to undertake a survey in 1986, the first attempt to produce precise statistics. The 1986 survey covered only the four leading centres, but subsequent studies in 1989, 1992 and 1995 were comprehensive. Table 2.1 shows the global foreign-exchange market turnover revealed by these last three surveys. Over the period as a whole, the total doubled from $620 billion per day to $1,260 billion per day, a rate of increase of 42 per cent in 1989–92, and 43 per cent in 1992–95.

The expansion resulted from the growth of world trade, huge capital movements, increased cross-border investment, and the greater use of the foreign-exchange markets to reduce businesses' exposure to volatile floating exchange rates.

Table 2.1: Foreign exchange market turnover, 1989–95

	$ billion daily		
	1989	**1992**	**1995**
Spot transactions	350	400	520
Forwards and swaps	240	420	670
Futures and options	30	60	70
Total	620	880	1,260

Source: Bank for International Settlements, *Central Bank Survey of Foreign Exchange and Derivatives Market Activity 1995* (Basle, 1996).

The nature of the foreign-exchange market

Table 2.1 also shows the growth of the component foreign-exchange market segments. There are four forms of foreign-exchange trading: 'spot' transactions, meaning immediate delivery; 'forward' transactions for future delivery; 'swaps', namely simultaneous buy and sell transactions; and 'futures and options' – derivative instruments for currency dealing. Forwards and swaps are the foremost forms of foreign-exchange trading, having grown as a proportion of the market from 38 per cent in 1989 to 53 per cent in 1995.

The US dollar is much the most important currency in the worldwide foreign-exchange market, both because of its importance in international trade and because of its use as a vehicle currency for cross-trading between other currencies. In 1995, the US dollar was involved in 41.5 per cent of all worldwide currency transactions (Table 2.2). (Note that every foreign-exchange transaction involves two currencies, and so the percentages of all transactions in Table 2.2 represent exchanges into and out of currencies.)

The Deutschmark is the second most important currency in the foreign-exchange market, being involved in 18.5 per cent of all transactions (Table 2.2). The US dollar and the Deutschmark are the only currencies that are traded in large volumes against a wide range of other currencies. Together, the US dollar and the Deutschmark account for almost all trading in the Canadian dollar (98 per cent), Australian dollar (97 per cent), Japanese yen (97 per cent), Swiss franc (95 per cent), French franc (95 per cent) and sterling (93 per cent).[3] The Japanese yen is the third most widely traded currency, involved in 12 per cent of all transactions worldwide (Table 2.2). Other currencies are much less traded. The share of sterling, the fourth most traded currency declined from 17 per cent to 5 per cent between 1992 and 1995.

Table 2.2: Currencies traded worldwide:
transactions, April 1995

	Percentage shares
US dollar	41.5
Deutschmark	18.5
Japanese yen	12.0
Pound sterling	5.0
French franc	4.0
Swiss franc	3.5
Other currencies	15.5
All currencies	100.0

Source: Bank for International Settlements, *Central Bank
Survey of Foreign Exchange and Derivatives Market Activity
1995* (Basle, 1996).

Despite the waning use of sterling as a trading and reserve currency, the UK – that is London – is the world's foremost location for foreign-exchange dealing. In 1995, the leading foreign-exchange markets were London ($464 billion per day), New York ($244 billion), Tokyo ($161 billion), Singapore ($105 billion), Hong Kong ($90 billion), Switzerland ($86 billion), Frankfurt ($76 billion) and Paris ($58 billion). London's pre-eminence increased over the years 1989–95, its market share growing from 26 per cent to 30 per cent – almost double New York's 16 per cent market share, three times Tokyo's 10 per cent share and six times greater than Frankfurt or Paris. Table 2.3 sets out the turnover for the leading dealing locations in the BIS survey years.

The foreign-exchange market has close ties with local money markets and the eurocurrency market. The ties with local money markets arise from discrepancies in interest rates. When interest rates are higher in one money market than another, funds will flow to the higher-yielding centres, generating spot foreign-exchange transactions. In order to eliminate exposure to currency risk, foreign investors will sell the currency forward. This is a swap transaction – a simultaneous spot purchase and forward sale of a foreign currency.

Interest rate differentials in the eurocurrency markets also provide opportunities for 'arbitrage' – namely, profit from the difference between the price of assets in different markets – across different eurocurrency sectors. The same banks and major currencies play the leading roles in both the foreign-exchange market and the eurocurrency market. But foreign-exchange trading and eurocurrency trading are not the same thing. In the foreign-exchange market, the stock-in-trade is 'sight deposits', which do not pay interest. 'Time deposits' on the other hand – interest-paying deposit-account balances – are the stock-in-trade of the eurocurrency markets.

Table 2.3: Foreign-exchange market turnover by country, 1989–95 [a]

	1989		1992		1995	
	Amount ($ bn daily)	% share	Amount ($ bn daily)	% share	Amount ($ bn daily)	% share
United Kingdom	184	26	290	27	464	30
United States	115	16	167	16	244	16
Japan	110	15	120	11	161	10
Singapore	55	8	73	7	105	7
Hong Kong	49	7	60	6	90	6
Switzerland	56	8	66	5	86	6
Germany	na	na	55	3	76	5
France	23	3	33	19	58	4
Other countries	126	17	212		288	18
Total 'net gross' turnover [b]	718		1,076		1,572	

Source: Bank for International Settlements, *Central Bank Survey of Foreign Exchange and Derivatives Market Activity 1995* (Basle, 1996).
[a] Reported foreign exchange market turnover adjusted for local double-counting by country.
[b] Percentages may not sum to 100 due to rounding.

THE INTERNATIONAL MONEY MARKET

The international money market comprises:

- 'traditional' international banking
- eurocurrency markets

'Traditional' international banking comprises the use of domestic funds by a domestic bank to make a loan abroad, or branch activities in overseas markets. Traditional international borrowing and lending is subject to the banking and other regulations of the respective national markets. This is a key difference – and disadvantage – compared with eurocurrency financing.

The euromarkets are the international money and capital markets that trade in currencies outside their country of origin. Eurodollars, for instance, are dollar deposits acquired by banks outside the US and used to make dollar loans outside the US. Likewise, euroyen are yen deposits acquired by banks outside Japan and used to make yen loans outside Japan. The prefix 'euro' has nothing to do with Europe and is a source of confusion – 'external' would be a more fitting term to indicate markets and currencies distinct from domestic or national financial systems.

It is an essential feature of the euromarkets that they operate free of the regulation of national authorities. For instance, the markets for dollar-denominated deposits, loans and bonds outside the US are not subject to US banking or securities regulation, such as reserve requirements, interest ceilings or deposit insurance fees. For this reason, operations in the euromarkets enjoy a cost advantage over traditional international banking business.

Developments of the euromarkets

The euromarkets have their origins in the Cold War of the 1950s. The political tensions of the era led communist bloc banks to deposit their US dollars with European banks so that they should not be vulnerable to seizure by the US authorities in a crisis. Another factor that stimulated their development was the British authorities' ban on using sterling to finance trade between non-residents, issued in 1957. This gave British banks an incentive actively to seek dollar deposits, providing London with an early lead in eurocurrency activity that it has sustained ever since.

At the outset, the eurodollar market and eurocurrency market were synonymous entities. As the market expanded and developed, other eurocurrencies, such as the euromark, the euro Swiss franc, the euro French franc, eurosterling, and the euroyen became widespread and 'eurocurrency' came into use as a generic term.

The euromarkets provide a full spectrum of international financial facilities. Funds on offer in the eurocurrency market are for terms ranging from 24 hours to one year. Medium-term loans provided by banks in the eurocredit market reach from one to ten years, the usual span being around five years. The euronote and eurobond markets provide longer term loans (see next section).

The principal participants in the eurocurrency market are commercial banks, central banks, the international financial institutions, and major corporations. The eurocurrency market is principally an interbank market: banks bid for funds and offer funds to each other, transactions being conducted between bank dealing rooms linked by telephones and computer screens. The eurocurrency market is highly competitive and margins are slim. But the market not only keeps funds fully employed; active participation ensures that banks have access to this source of funds when required.

Banks participate in the eurocurrency market to raise deposits, adjust their liquidity positions, and lend. There are two types of eurocurrency deposit instrument: time deposits and certificates of deposit, as follows:

- *Time deposits*: the non-negotiable time deposit constitutes 90 per cent of eurocurrency deposits. These are funds committed for a specified duration at a specified rate of interest. Most time deposits in the eurocurrency market have short maturities of three months or less. Being a wholesale market, demand deposits are unusual.
- *Certificates of deposit (CDs)*: CDs are negotiable claims issued by the bank that receives the deposit. They enable a depositor to place its funds for a fixed term or on a long maturity, thus receiving a higher rate of interest, while being able to sell the CD in the secondary market should it need to raise cash. Issuing banks benefit from the receipt of the funds. The liquidity of the secondary market in CDs makes it attractive to investors, who can buy and sell as they require. Eurodollar CDs were introduced by Citibank in 1966. They constitute about 10 per cent of the eurocurrency market.

Lending in the eurocurrency market takes three forms: syndicated loans; euro-commercial paper; and euro medium-term notes (see Table 2.4). They are described further thus:

Table 2.4: Eurocurrency markets lending, 1996

	$ billion	
Syndicated loans		792
Euronotes		364
– commercial paper	72	
– medium-term notes	292	
Total		1,156

Source: Bank of England Quarterly Bulletin, February 1997.

- *Syndicated loans*: (sometimes called syndicated credits) are loans provided by a group of banks. They comprise 70 per cent of eurocurrency lending. Syndicated lending developed in the 1970s due to the escalating scale of loans demanded by sovereign clients. It was a mean by which banks diversified risk, syndication permitting banks of different sizes and different countries to participate in international loans. Syndicated loans usually have maturities of between three and eight years.
- *Euro-commercial paper (ECP)*: commercial paper is bearer-form, general-obligation notes issued by companies, banks or governments for short-term borrowing. Euro-commercial paper is commercial paper issued outside the country of the currency. The cost of funds to borrowers is less than bank loans or syndicated loans. ECP is issued by major corporations and governments in large denominations. The market began in London in 1985.
- *Euro medium-term notes (MTNs)*: these are similar to euro-commercial paper but their issue is underwritten by investment banks meaning that the issuer is guaranteed the proceeds, but pays a fee for the privilege. MTN maturities range from nine months to 30 years, although 2–3-year maturities are most common. MTNs constitute 25 per cent of total eurocurrency lending (see Table 2.4). They are popular with investors as well as issuers, since the terms of issue can be tailored to investors' needs in relation to maturity, currency and other features. Issuers appreciate their flexibility, ease of issue and liquidity. They take bearer form and many are listed on the Luxembourg stock exchange.

The eurocurrency market has grown phenomenally since its origins in the late 1950s. In 1964, net international bank lending was $12 billion; a decade later it was $221 billion. By 1981, in the wake of two oil-price hikes and the boom in petro-dollar recycling, it had increased sixfold to $1,155 billion. During the 1980s and 1990s it has grown fourfold to $5,015 billion in 1996 (see Table 2.5).

The pattern of net flows of international bank lending via euronotes and eurobonds over the years 1976 to 1996 are shown in Table 2.6. Despite considerable year-to-year variations due to market conditions, there has been a steady increase in the importance of medium-term euronote financing relative to both international bank lending and international bonds. Annual net financing through the issue of international bonds has been somewhat less volatile than net international bank lending, averaging around 30 per cent of net international financing in the 1990s.

Table 2.5: Eurocurrency market, 1980–96

Year	Market turnover ($bn)	Year	Market turnover ($bn)
1980	755	1989	3,530
1981	1,155	1990	3,350
1982	1,285	1991	3,610
1983	1,382	1992	3,660
1984	1,430	1993	3,780
1985	1,678	1994	4,240
1986	2,076	1995	4,645
1987	2,584	1996	5,015
1988	3,200		

Source: Bank for International Settlements, *Annual Reports* (various years).

Table 2.6: Annual net financing in international markets, 1976–96

Year	Net international bank lending ($ bn)	Net euronote placements ($ bn)	Net international bond financing ($ bn)	Total net international financing minus double counting ($ bn)
1976	70		30	97
1977	75		31	102
1978	90		29	113
1979	125		28	145
1980	160		28	180
1981	165		32	190
1982	95		59	145
1983	85		58	130
1984	90	5	81	145
1985	105	10	123	180
1986	205	13	158	295
1987	320	23	108	400
1988	260	20	139	350
1989	290	8	175	415
1990	430	33	131	515
1991	185	35	170	355
1992	165	40	111	245
1993	200	72	125	275
1994	190	140	146	415
1995	330	192	119	530
1996	405	265	275	745

Source: Bank for International Settlements, *Annual Report*, various years between 1991 and 1997.

THE INTERNATIONAL BOND MARKET

The international bond market has two component parts: foreign bonds and eurobonds, as follows:

- *Foreign bonds* are long-term securities issued on a single national market on behalf of a foreign borrower. Traditionally, the issues have been underwritten by a group of banks primarily, but not exclusively, located in the country of issue. 'Underwriting' means that the banks guarantee to buy or find buyers for the issue in return for a fee. The bonds are denominated in the currency of the country where they are issued.
- *Eurobonds* are bonds underwritten by an international syndicate of banks and distributed internationally in countries other than the country of the currency in which the bond is denominated. Thus the issue is not subject to national restrictions.

The development of Eurobonds

Eurobonds marked a new stage in the development of the euromarkets. The first eurobond was issued in London in 1963 for the Italian highways utility Autostrada. In the same year, the US introduced the Interest Equalisation Tax, which was intended to discourage foreigners from raising capital in the US – and had exactly that effect. It provided a major boost to the fledgling eurobond market, which never looked back. The volume of eurobond issues soon dwarfed offerings of traditional foreign bonds.

Table 2.7: International bond issues, 1982–96

	Issue value ($ bn)		Issue value ($ bn)
1982	78	1990	241
1983	76	1991	317
1984	107	1992	334
1985	168	1993	446
1986	226	1994	362
1987	177	1995	356
1988	226	1996	575
1989	263		

Source: Bank for International Settlements, *Annual Reports* (various years).

The growth of international bond issues in the 1980s and 1990s is shown in Table 2.7. In 1982, international bond issues – both foreign bonds and eurobonds – totalled $78 billion; by 1996 they were $575 billion. In the mid-1990s, around four-fifths were straight fixed-rate issues. Floating-rate notes (FRNs), namely bonds with variable interest rates, and equity-linked bonds comprised the bulk of the remainder. The US dollar was much the most important currency of denomination, followed by the yen and the Deutschmark.

The bond market became internationally integrated in the 1980s, when cross-border trading took off. The outstanding stock of international bonds plus euronotes grew tenfold, from $259 billion in 1982 to $2.8 trillion in 1996. The largest single component of the international bond market remains US Treasury debt, which saw a massive increase in international transactions: in the years 1983–93, aggregate cross-border sales and purchases of US Treasury bonds increased from $30 billion to $500 billion.[4]

London is the foremost location both for new issues of eurobonds, and for eurobond secondary trading. The market is largely unregulated: eurobonds are bearer securities, meaning that possession is taken to be evidence of ownership, and this makes them popular with investors who wish to remain anonymous for tax reasons.

eurobond maturities are typically in the 5–15-year range, considerably shorter than the 20–30 years common to foreign bonds. This is a deliberate device for appeal to the wealthy private investors who are an important market for eurobonds, since shorter maturities mean relatively greater price stability. Eurobond yields generally follow rates in the domestic capital market of the currency in which they are denominated. New eurobond issues proceed in the following way: the issuer appoints a 'lead manager', either an investment bank with which it has close relations or the bank that offers the best terms, which organises syndicates of banks to underwrite and market the securities. The syndicates comprise banks from a number of countries, the more cosmopolitan the larger the number of markets covered. But issuing in a variety of currencies also increases the risks of being affected by adverse currency developments, notably interest rate rises or currency depreciation. To compensate for the more varied risks assumed by the issuers, eurobond underwriting fees are substantially greater than those for foreign bond issues.

Eurobond secondary market
An active secondary market – a market for trading issued securities – is a

vital consideration for potential purchasers of new issues. Secondary trading in eurobonds is conducted between banks by telephone and computer – there is no trading floor or organised exchange. London is the foremost such centre for eurobond trading, although Luxembourg is important too. There are two clearing systems for eurobond trades that facilitate transfers between sellers and buyers: Euroclear in Brussels and Cedel in Luxembourg. These institutions provide financing as well as settlement services, providing funding to market makers secured against the value of their bond portfolios.

The market makers are the key players in the eurobond secondary market. Being always ready to buy and sell, they guarantee the market's liquidity. However, the costs of fulfilling this role are considerable and from time to time the market-making operations require cross-subsidies from profits from eurobond issuing and trading.

The globalisation of investment banking and competition for mandates to issue bonds led to a new phenomenon: global bond issues. Global bond issues are offered simultaneously in every major market. Naturally, this involves a formidable amount of negotiation and preparation to clear regulatory hurdles and to put in place effective marketing arrangements; nevertheless, global bond issues have attractions for both issuers and investors:

- the large number of potential purchasers enables the raising of huge amounts of capital at reasonable rates
- the large, widely-distributed issues have high international secondary-market liquidity
- the widespread recognition of the borrower enhances its ease of future fund-raising
- there is mutual value in the establishment of a global benchmark

The World Bank, which has a voracious appetite for capital, pioneered the issue of global bonds in the early 1990s. It was in a unique position to do so, being an international agency and having an AAA credit rating. Besides raising funds at the cheapest rates on behalf of developing countries, its issues established useful new international financial reference points.

THE INTERNATIONAL EQUITY MARKET

Trading domestic equities is the traditional business of stock exchanges. Trading *international* equities – equities issued on other stock exchanges –

is a relatively recent phenomenon. It is another dimension of the evolution of global markets, but is much less developed than the international bond market. It has grown along with the increasingly international outlook of investors and issuers.

Trading in international equities was pioneered by the London Stock Exchange through SEAQ International, the exchange's electronic quotation system for non-UK equities, introduced in the 1980s. Share prices are quoted in the home currency of each country sector, and transactions are settled through the local settlement system. The London exchange built up a formidable business, and in 1993 the value of international equities trading overtook domestic business.[5] By 1996, international equities turnover in London was $865 billion, almost two-thirds of the worldwide total of $1,350 billion.[6]

London's lead in international equities trading is vigorously contested by the major European bourses. There is also a new challenger, EASDAQ (European Association of Securities Dealers Automated Quotation), a computer-based European over-the-counter equities market based on NASDAQ in the US. It was launched in 1996, as 'one pan-European stock market across 12 European countries, with one regulatory structure, one rule book and one seamless trading and settlement system'.[7]

Listing shares on overseas exchanges offers international firms the opportunity of raising funds in different capital markets, as well as having their shares locally traded. Shares of major multinational corporations such as General Electric, Exxon, Toyota Motor Corporation, IBM or Nestlé are listed in London, New York, Tokyo, Paris and other centres as well as on their home exchanges. In the US and some other countries, listings of foreign equities are made through the device of 'depository receipts' – claims on foreign shares. Multiple listings make it easier for domestic investors to buy foreign shares, particularly trustees who are prohibited from investing in securities that are not locally quoted. However, multiple listing is expensive since it necessitates meeting the listing requirements of each exchange, which involves preparing accounts and filings to meet local specifications.

The international integration of equity markets has been restrained by international differences in accounting practices and unfamiliarity with foreign corporations. Restrictions on the level of holding of foreign equities by pension funds has also played a part. Yet the pattern is shifting as the restrictions are relaxed: over the years 1980–93, US pension funds increased their holdings of foreign securities from 0.7 per cent to 6 per cent, while British pension funds raised their overseas holdings from 10 per cent to 20 per cent.

'Euroequities' are international equities issued on stock exchanges outside the country in which the company is based and denominated in a foreign currency. They are distributed internationally through multinational banking syndicates. Conceptually they are akin to eurobonds, but in practice they tend to find their way back to their domestic market. There is no distinct secondary market for euroequities, being traded over the counter on the issuing company's domestic stock exchange. Exchange rate fluctuations can be disruptive to trading in multicurrency equities.

DERIVATIVES

The financial derivatives market is the newest and most dynamic of the international financial markets. The development of the global financial derivatives market in the 1990s is shown in Table 2.8. Total amounts outstanding at year end rose fourfold in six years, from $7.9 trillion in 1991 to a staggering $34.1 trillion in 1996.[8]

Table 2.8: Markets for selected derivative instruments, 1991–96

	Estimated amounts outstanding at year-end ($ bn)					
	1991	1992	1993	1994	1995	1996
Exchange-traded instruments	3,519	4,634	7,771	8,863	9,188	9,885
– Interest rate futures	2,157	2,913	4,959	5,778	5,863	5,931
– Interest rate options[a]	1,073	1,385	2,362	2,624	2,742	3,278
– Currency futures	18	27	35	40	38	50
– Currency options	63	71	76	56	43	47
– Stock market index futures	76	80	110	127	172	199
– Stock market index options	133	159	230	238	329	380
Over-the-counter instruments	4,449	5,346	8,475	11,303	17,713	24,292
– Interest rate swaps	3,065	3,851	6,177	8,861	12,811	
– Currency swaps[b]	807	860	900	915	1,197	
– Other swap-related derivatives[c]	577	634	1,398	1,573	3,705	
Total	7,968	9,980	16,246	20,166	26,901	34,177

Source: Bank for International Settlements, *Annual Report*, 1996–97.
[a] Calls and puts.
[b] Adjusted for reporting of both currencies.
[c] Caps, collars, floors and swaptions.

'Derivatives' is a generic term for a range of financial instruments derived from various financial products. There are three important instrument types:

- futures
- options
- swaps

and three principal product types:

- interest rate
- currency
- stock market index

Futures
Financial futures are contracts which commit both parties to a transaction in a financial product on a future date at a pre-arranged price. They are negotiable instruments that can be traded in futures markets. Contracts can be used to hedge reducing exposure to risk in order to curb losses, or to speculate, increasing exposure to risk but in the expectation of making profits.

Options
Financial options are contracts giving the holder the right to buy or sell a financial product at an agreed price within a specified time period. There is no obligation to execute the transaction. The option holder is able to profit from favourable price movements, only risking the premium paid if prices move adversely. Options are negotiable instruments traded in derivatives markets.

A 'call' option confers the right to buy at a pre-agreed price. Calls are used to reduce the risk that the price of an asset will rise by the time it comes to be purchased at some point in the future. Calls are also used to speculate that prices will rise. A 'put' option confers the right to sell at a pre-agreed price. Puts are used to reduce the risk to asset holders that the price will fall. Puts are also used to speculate on a price fall.

Swaps
Swaps are transactions in which two parties undertake to exchange streams of payments. Swaps are used to change an existing market exposure on account of a loan, security, currency, or interest rate to a different exposure. Investors use swaps to achieve a range of investment

objectives, such as boosting current income (yield pickup swap), portfolio diversification or concentration (substitution swap or sector swap), obtaining better price performance in the event of a movement of interest rates (rate anticipation swap), or tax minimisation. Central banks employ swap arrangements to obtain foreign exchange for intervention in the foreign-exchange market through reciprocal short-term credit agreements.

Interest rate derivatives
Interest rate futures and options are forms of financial derivatives in which the contract is in respect of the interest rate on the underlying asset. Interest rate swaps involve two parties exchanging streams of payments, where the transaction allows a borrower with a relatively poor credit-rating to benefit from the lower interest rate available to a better credit-rated borrower – the latter charging a fee for this service.

Currency derivatives
Currency futures and options are forms of financial derivatives in which the contract is in respect of the exchange rate of a currency. Currency swaps involve the exchange of two streams of identical interest rates, but in different currencies.

Stock market index derivatives
Stock market index futures and options are forms of financial derivatives in which the contract is in respect of the movement of stock market indices, such as the Dow Jones, *FTSE* or Nikkei indices. Stock market index contracts are used by investors for protection against losses on their shareholdings, or by speculators to gamble on stock market movements.

Derivatives trading
The users of the financial derivatives market include banks, bond dealers, corporate treasurers, equity market makers, institutional investors, private investors, syndicate managers, and traders. They employ derivatives for three purposes: hedging, speculating and arbitrage, thus:

- *Hedging* is protecting a market position aginst adverse movements in the future, and is a means of reducing exposure to risk, and potential losses.
- *Speculating* is gambling on future price movements to make money, being a means of increasing exposure to risk but also potential

profits ('trading' is the genteel term).

- *Arbitrage* is (as defined earlier in this chapter) profiting from price discrepancies between derivatives markets and their underlying markets.

Derivatives are traded in two different ways: over the counter (OTC), or on organised specialist exchanges such as the Chicago Mercantile Exchange, the London International Financial Futures Exchange (Liffe), and Frankfurt's Deutsche Terminbörse. OTC transactions are conducted directly with a bank or trader. The advantages of exchange trading are liquidity, competitive prices, and protection against default.

However, bespoke OTC products may be better suited to a client's requirements. In fact, the volume of OTC instruments has grown twice as fast as exchange-traded instruments in the 1990s, especially since 1994. Interest rate swaps are much the largest instrument in the OTC market. Interest rate futures and options are the leading exchange-traded instruments.

GOLD

Throughout the history of civilised mankind, gold has been used as a medium of exchange – money – and as a store of value. It is also used by certain industries, notably electronics, dentistry and aerospace, and for jewellery on account of its malleability, durability and lustre. Furthermore, gold is a speculative instrument, being held as a hedge against inflation and political instability. In times of diplomatic or economic crisis, demand for gold soars since it is believed to be safer than paper money.

Gold can be purchased physically in the form of coins, bullion (gold bars) or jewellery. Investment also takes the form of gold futures and options contracts, gold mining stocks, gold certificates, and mutual funds. The leading gold producers are South Africa and Russia. South African Krugerrands are much-prized for hoarding.

The principal bullion markets are London, New York, Hong Kong and Singapore. By long-standing arrangement, the central banks deal with each other at an official fixed price that is determined twice a day at London merchant bankers N.M. Rothschild. Other participants deal in the open market at prices determined by demand and supply. US citizens have been legally permitted to hold bullion since 1974. The same year saw the launch of gold futures contracts on several commodities exchanges. The leading gold futures markets are Chicago, London, Hong Kong, Tokyo, Singapore, Sydney and Winnipeg.

In a Nutshell

In 1995, the global foreign-exchange market had a turnover of $1,260 billion per day. Short-term bank lending in the eurocurrency markets totalled $1,156 billion in 1996. Long-term international bond issues totalled $575 billion in 1996. Global turnover of international equities trading was $1,350 billion in 1996. The global volume of financial derivatives outstanding in 1996 was $34.4 trillion. Not only are the international financial markets huge, but they get bigger year by year.

FURTHER READING

Bank for International Settlements, *Annual Reports*

Eng, Maximo V.; Lees, Francis A. and Mauer, Laurence J., *Global Finance* (New York, HarperCollins, 1995)

Johnson, R. B., *The Economics of the Euro-Market: History, Theory, Policy* (London, Macmillan, 1983)

Tucker, Alan, Madura, Jeff and Chang Thomas, *International Financial Markets* (New York, West, 1991)

Walmsley, Julian, *International Money and Foreign Exchange Markets: An Introduction* (Chichester, John Wiley, 1996)

NOTES AND REFERENCES

In the list below for this chapter, any reference to an author alone should be taken to be a reference to his/her work in 'Further reading' above.

1 Bank for International Settlements, *Central Bank Survey of the Foreign Exchange and Derivatives Market*, 1995

2 *Fact Book for the Year 1996* (New York, NYSE, 1997)

3 Bank for International Settlements, *Central Bank Survey of the Foreign Exchange and Derivatives Market*, 1995

4 Bank for International Settlements, *Annual Report*, 1996

5 Bank of England, 'Foreign Equity Turnover in London', *Quarterly Bulletin*, February 1997

6 *Fact Book for the Year 1996* (New York, NYSE, 1997) £519 bn converted at $1.65 = £1

7 First anniversary advertisement, *Financial Times*, 27 November 1997

8 Bank for International Settlements, *Annual Report*, 1996–97

CHAPTER 3

International Commercial Banking

INTRODUCTION

Banks are the principal players in the international financial markets. Since the 1960s, international banking has grown rapidly in scale and scope, developing a diverse range of services and activities. Recent years have seen a wave of mergers amongst the international banks, driven by competition, globalisation, technology and deregulation, producing more and more powerful players.

BANKING AND BANKS

The essence of commercial banking is taking deposits and making loans. However, commercial banks also offer a variety of other financial services, such as foreign exchange, insurance, and credit cards. Commercial banks operate at both retail and wholesale levels. Retail banking is servicing the general public and small businesses, traditionally through a branch network; it involves a large volume of low-value transactions. Wholesale banking comprises dealings with fellow banks (both commercial banks and investment banks), central banks, and other financial institutions, especially in the interbank market – the money market in which banks lend and borrow amongst themselves; wholesale banking involves a relatively small number of high-value transactions. International commercial banking is mostly wholesale banking.

The range of activities conducted by commercial banks varies from country to country. In the US and UK, commercial banks that take deposits and make loans have traditionally been separate entities from investment banks and merchant banks, whose business is securities underwriting and related activities (see Chapter 4). In the US the separation is a legal requirement imposed by the Glass–Steagfall Act, but in Britain it has been merely customary.

Universal banks, as developed in Germany and Switzerland, conduct deposit taking and lending, plus securities underwriting, as well as a range of other activities such as insurance, investment management and corporate and advisory services. Other countries' banking systems combine elements of both models. Increasingly, universal banking is becoming the international norm. In the UK, the 'Big Bang' deregulation of the securities industry in 1986 was accompanied by the development of investment banking activities by the commercial banks and was followed by the virtual disappearance of the specialist merchant banking sector (see Chapter 4). Even in the US, the Glass–Steagall legislation has been eroded and its repeal is anticipated. The European Union's banking legislation reflects an assumption that universal banking is the relevant form.

INTERNATIONAL BANKING

International banking has two dimensions: international bank service activity; and multinational banking.

'International bank service activity' means servicing the international requirements of clients such as importers, exporters, or foreign travellers at home and abroad. To such ends, most banks maintain 'correspondent' relationships with a set of banks overseas. As correspondents, the banks act as each other's local agent. They make and receive payments between each other, maintaining mutual deposit balances to do so. If a close relationship develops, they may provide other services such as swapping client credit ratings, and even refer business to one another. The correspondent relationship is the most rudimentary level of international banking. As the international economy has become more integrated, banks have established their own presence in overseas markets.

Multinational banking takes a variety of forms:

- *Subsidiary* An overseas subsidiary is a legal entity separate from the parent bank. It may be wholly owned by the parent, or there may also be local shareholders. It may be established from new, or by acquisition of an existing bank. Subsidiaries are authorised to undertake the full range of banking activities.
- *Branch* An overseas branch is a wholly owned offshoot of the

parent bank, though under local regulatory jurisdiction. The liability of the parent for operating losses allows branches to be licensed to conduct a full spectrum of banking activities. The development of an international branch system allows international banks to service their multinational corporation clients on the ground. An international network also allows banks to become more sophisticated participants in international financial markets, shifting their dealing book from time zone to time zone to take advantage of market developments and reduce the risk of being caught wrongly positioned.

- *Agency*   An agency is similar to a branch as regards the responsibilities of the parent bank. However, agencies are not able to accept local deposits. The agency approach is adopted when host governments will not allow foreign banks to open branches. It may also be used when lending is the principal activity of the local operation and the pattern of loans is such that a deposit-taking branch would fall foul of regulatory rules – for instance when there is a large loan exposure to a few clients.
- *Representative office*   Representative offices serve as points of contact with local banks and clients but do not take deposits or make loans. They are established where host governments will not permit foreign banks to establish branches or subsidiaries, or as a preliminary to the formation of a fuller form of representation such as a subsidiary or branch.
- *Consortium bank*   Such a bank is jointly owned by several banks and undertakes international banking activities not conducted by the shareholder banks. Many were formed in the 1970s to participate in the booming eurocurrency markets, especially in London. They were wound up when the shareholder banks began to undertake eurocurrency business on their own account.
- *Edge Act corporation*   This is a special US vehicle for the conduct of international banking. Edge Act corporations are federally chartered entities incorporated under the Edge Act 1919, and they undertake foreign exchange, trade finance and international money-market services. They provide a means by which US and foreign banks operating in the US can circumvent US restrictions on interstate banking.
- *International banking facility (IBF)*   This is an accounting device that allows US banks to compete for international deposits and lending business in offshore dollars. IBFs permit offshore dollar deposits to be taken without infringing US reserve requirements or interest-rate

restrictions. They were introduced in 1981 in order to enable New York and other US financial centres to compete for eurocurrency business (see Chapter 7).

THE DEVELOPMENT OF INTERNATIONAL BANKING

International banking has a long history. In the middle ages, the famous Medici Bank of Florence operated across Europe with eight offices and a staff of 57. Today, Citibank operates across the world with 3,500 offices in more than 90 countries and almost 90,000 employees.

International banking grew rapidly in the 1960s. US banks led the charge to establish overseas operations in order to service their domestic corporate clients, which were rapidly expanding their multinational activities. An additional motive was to participate in the booming eurocurrency market, notably in London and offshore financial centres (see Chapter 6). In 1960, eight US banks had 124 overseas branches, with assets totalling $12 billion. A decade later, 79 US banks had 532 overseas branches, with assets of $145 billion. Between 1963 and the end of the decade, the volume of 'international banking assets' – international banks' foreign currency assets, a measure of international eurocurrency banking activity compiled by the Bank for International Settlements – grew from $12 billion to $70 billion, an annual average rate of growth of 29 per cent (see Table 3.1).

Table 3.1: International banking assets, 1963–96[a]

Year	Assets ($ bn)	Year	Assets ($ bn)	Year	Assets ($ bn)
1963	12	1975	289	1987	4,155
1964	14	1976	341	1988	4,509
1965	18	1977	419	1989	5,139
1966	26	1978	549	1990	6,253
1967	31	1979	834	1991	6,240
1968	45	1980	1,010	1992	6,196
1969	70	1981	1,196	1993	6,516
1970	92	1982	1,513	1994	7,110
1971	114	1983	1,573	1995	8,072
1972	149	1984	2,153	1996	8,299
1973	215	1985	2,511		
1974	247	1986	3,219		

Source: Bank for International Settlements, *Annual Reports* (various years).
[a] 'Foreign currency assets of reporting banks'.

The 1970s and early 1980s saw further rapid growth in multinational branching and eurocurrency banking activity, driven by the huge demands for borrowing by oil importing countries and the rise of the syndicated loan market. The international expansion of US banks continued, and by 1980 there were 159 US banks with 787 overseas branches and $311 billion in assets. European and Japanese banks, and banks from other countries (notably Canada and Australia), also established overseas operations so as to participate in the profitable business of petro-dollar recycling. Many of them set up in the US, especially New York: the number of foreign banks operating in New York increased from 73 in 1971 to 323 in 1985. Over the years 1970–82, the volume of international banks' foreign assets grew from $92 billion to $1,513 billion, a rate of increase averaging 22 per cent per year.

The onset of the international debt crisis in 1982, when Mexico and other large sovereign borrowers experienced payments problems, triggered a slowing in the pace of growth of international banks' foreign-currency assets and multinational branching. Western banks became wary of lending to developing countries and devised innovative off-balance-sheet ways of servicing their customers' financial requirements. Nonetheless, from 1983 to the end of the decade, the foreign-currency assets of international banks grew from $1,573 billion to $6,253 billion, an annual average rate of growth of 15 per cent.

The deceleration in the rate of growth of multinational branches was more marked, largely because of retrenchment in international representation on the part of some US banks. The number of overseas branches of US banks declined, falling from 864 in 1985 to 703 in 1992. Another factor contributing to the slowdown from the mid-1980s was that the major international banks had already established a presence in the principal international financial centres. Nevertheless, there was still some new multinational branch activity as banks from rapidly developing economies, such as the 'tiger' economies of South-East Asia, pushed overseas.

The recession in the industrialised countries in the early 1990s brought a halt to the increase in international banks' foreign-currency assets in 1991 and 1992, although growth resumed thereafter. Between 1990 and 1996, international banking assets grew from $6.2 trillion to $8.2 trillion, an annual average growth rate of 7 per cent. The relatively slow rate of growth of international banking assets in the mid-1990s reflected the increasing use of the issuance of securities as a substitute for bank financing – a development known as 'securitisation.' In fact, securitisation and other innovations were just different ways of doing business for the international commercial banks. The Bank for International Settlements' Annual Report of 1996–97 observed:

> In spite of the growth of securitisation worldwide, commercial banks have generally been able to retain their dominant position at the core of the financial system by more active asset and liability management, by offering new off-balance-sheet services and by acquiring securities houses and investment funds. For their part, investment banks have been making inroads into areas hitherto dominated by commercial banks, such as syndicated lending and credit-risk assessment. These trends have heightened the convergence between commercial and investment banks, with both groups also facing competition on their own ground from other market participants.

ACTIVITIES OF INTERNATIONAL COMMERCIAL BANKS

Traditional international commercial banking activities are:

- *trade finance*: the financing of import and export transactions in the time-honoured form of 'bills of exchange' – an IOU between the parties that is guaranteed by a bank, an endorsement of payment that transforms it into a negotiable instrument – or by other means
- *currency trading*: trading foreign exchange (see Chapter 2)
- *foreign lending*: the provision of loans to overseas clients

The 1960s and 1970s saw the development of new euromarket activities:

- *eurocurrency trading*: dealing activities in eurocurrencies
- *syndicated lending*: participations in lending in eurocurrencies by groups of banks (see Chapter 2)
- *eurobonds*: underwriting eurobond issues on behalf of corporations and governments, and eurobond trading (see Chapter 2)

The 1980s and 1990s have seen a variety of financial innovations, driven largely by securitisation and globalisation:

- *Derivatives and innovative financing*: devising and trading new products including 'note issuance facilities' (NIFs) – a form of medium-term eurocredit guaranteed by a bank – and financial

futures, options and swaps
- *global money-market operations*: round-the-clock money-market dealing in instruments such as US Treasury securities, likely to be performed by passing the trading book from branch to branch, or sometimes by operation of a 24-hour centralised trading desk
- *global custody*: cross-border securities settlement and administration services for fund managers and other large investors (an estimated $40,000 billion in assets being under custody worldwide)[1]
- *global private banking*: the provision of bespoke banking and investment services to wealthy individuals; the target market being a global pool of wealth estimated at $17,000 billion[2]

THE WORLD'S TOP BANKS

In the 1960s, US banks topped the league tables of the world's largest banks, and Canadian and British banks were the other leaders. In the 1970s, they were joined by a set of French, German and Japanese banks, whose growth rates outstripped many of their Anglo-Saxon counterparts. The 1980s and early 1990s saw the domination of the upper echelons of the banking league tables by Japanese banks. But the mid-1990s saw a rapid retreat down the charts by many Japanese banks as the problems of the Japanese economy and the Japanese financial system took their toll.

The world's top twenty banks in 1997 ranked by 'tier-one capital' – equity capital plus disclosed reserves – are shown in Table 3.2 (left-hand columns). It is derived from the survey of the world's top 1,000 banks published in *The Banker* each July. The top twenty based on tier-one capital comprise seven Japanese banks, four from the US, three British banks, two French banks, and one each from China, Germany, Holland and Switzerland. The ratings range from HSBC Holdings, with a tier-one capital of $25.7 billion, to National Westminster Bank, with $11.9 billion.

The Banker also publishes an annual league table of the world's most international banks, ranked by the proportion of assets based overseas.[3] The top twenty most international banks are shown in Table 3.2 (right-hand columns) and comprise four French banks, three UK banks, three from the US, three Swiss banks, two Austrian banks and one each from Australia, Canada, Germany, Holland and Ireland. The range runs from Standard Chartered, with 74.3 per cent of assets based overseas, to CIBC at 44.0 per cent.

Table 3.2: International bank league table

	Tier-one capital		Business overseas	
Rank	Bank	($ bn)	Bank	(0 %)
1	HSBC Holdings	25.7	Standard Chartered	74.3
2	Bank of Tokyo-Mitsubishi	24.3	Credit Suisse	74.2
3	Crédit Agricole Indosuez	22.2	UBS	71.0
4	Chase Manhattan Corp	21.1	Crédit Agricole Indosuez	70.3
5	Citicorp	20.1	SBC	64.6
6	Deutsche Bank	18.5	HSBC Holdings	62.8
7	BankAmerica Corp	17.1	Citicorp	59.6
8	ABN AMRO Bank	16.1	Paribas	55.6
9	Sumitomo Bank	15.9	Credit Lyonnais	52.5
10	UBS	15.7	Creditanstalt-Bankverein	52.3
11	Fuji Bank	15.7	Erste Bank	50.9
12	Dai-Ichi Kangyo Bank	15.1	JP Morgan	50.9
13	Sanwa Bank	15.1	Bankers Trust	49.5
14	Sakura Bank	14.7	ABN AMRO Bank	49.3
15	Bank of China	13.7	Allied Irish Banks	48.8
16	NationsBank	12.6	National Westminster Bank	47.3
17	Barclays Bank	12.6	Société Générale	46.8
18	Industrial Bank of Japan	12.3	National Australia Bank	46.7
19	Groupe Caisse d'Epargne	12.3	Deutsche Bank	46.5
20	National Westminster Bank	11.9	CICB	44.0

Sources: Tier-one Capital, The Banker, July 1997. Business Overseas, The Banker, February 1998.

Six banks appear in both league tables, having leading positions both in terms of size of tier-one capital and the proportion of business overseas. They are ABN Amro, Citicorp, Credit Agricole Indosuez, HSBC Holdings, National Westminster, and UBS.

CAPITAL ADEQUACY

The level of bank capital relative to the level of lending plays an important role in safeguarding bank solvency and the protection of depositors. For many years, individual countries have had legislation stipulating prudential levels of bank capital. But the growth of multi-national bank branches has undermined national capital-adequacy ratios as safeguards, since there was a tendency for overseas branches to operate at higher levels of loan activity than their parent banks. A number of prominent bank failures drew attention to the regulatory problems posed by the growth of international banking operations: the collapse of Lebanon's Intra Bank in 1967; of Germany's Bankhaus Herstatt in 1974 because of foreign-exchange losses; of the Franklin National Bank of New York in 1974, again through massive foreign-exchange losses; and of Italy's Banco Ambrosiano in 1982.

Growing appreciation of the problem of capital adequacy in the era of multinational banking led to the Basle Concordats of 1975 and 1983, named after the location of the Bank for International Settlements, which played a leading role in negotiating them. The senior financial authorities agreed that in the event of a solvency crisis affecting an international bank, the central bank of the country in which it was headquartered would act as lender of last resort. These arrangements were replaced by a new and more comprehensive international risk-based capital-adequacy agreement named the Basle Accord, which was agreed in 1988. The Basle Accord establishes common criteria for the definition of bank capital and for the calculation of the level of a bank's asset risk; it also provides a schedule of minimum capital-to-risk-asset ratios.

The urgent need for a more comprehensive and rigorous system of international banking regulation was demonstrated by the collapse of the Bank of Credit and Commerce International (BCCI) in 1991 (see Chapter 10). Registered in Luxembourg, headquartered in London, and active in offshore financial centres around the world, BCCI was structured so as to make it impossible for any national regulatory authority to see the full picture. Its collapse and the immediate revelation of massive fraud made the full implementation of the Basle Accord in 1992 a very timely move.

CHALLENGES AND KEY TRENDS

The commercial banking industry is experiencing a range of forces for change: growing competition; new products; dynamic technology; and deregulation. In combination, these forces are generating powerful pressures for mergers and takeovers amongst commercial banks.

Competition
Competition in commercial banking is increasing around the world. In industrialised countries, banking is becoming more and more a commodity product. Profit margins are under pressure because of intense competition amongst banks, both domestic and foreign, and from non-banks. Retailers, for instance, have begun offering banking services to their consumer clientele.

In emerging markets, the provision of financial services by international banks has offered attractive growth prospects and good returns. But there too, competition is growing both from international banks and from indigenous banks often invigorated by recent privatisation.

Technology
Technology is rapidly transforming the products that banks can offer and also their means of delivery. Traditional bank branches, with their heavy fixed costs, are becoming increasingly obsolete as new delivery mechanisms became popular, such as telephone banking and computer banking.

Deregulation
Deregulation is changing the scope for horizontal and vertical integration amongst banks and other financial institutions, creating new financial hybrids and opening the way for new entrants.

Mergers and takeovers
The pressures bearing down on the commercial banks provide powerful motives for mergers and takeovers. Amalgamations can provide scope for cost cutting and the achievement of economies of scale; they may also relieve, to some extent, competitive pressures. Moreover, by the achievement of greater mass, a bank itself becomes less vulnerable to a takeover by a rival.

The 1990s have seen a wave of bank amalgamations around the world. In the US, there have been a host of mega-mergers, including the $10 billion acquisition of Chase Manhattan Bank by Chemical Bank, and the $60 billion merger pact between NationsBank and BankAmerica, creating America's biggest bank. In Japan, the combination of the Bank of Tokyo and Mitsubishi Bank formed the world's biggest bank. Many other countries are also witnessing increasing concentration in their banking sectors.

In Europe, a merger wave is underway amongst banks in many countries: in Switzerland, the merger between Swiss Bank Corporation and Union Bank of Switzerland created the world's second-largest commercial bank, with assets of almost $600 billion; in Belgium there was the $33.6 billion acquisition of Générale de Banque by Belgo–Dutch banking and insurance group Fortis; and in the UK, there has been the $15.3 billion acquisition of the Trustee Savings Bank by Lloyds Bank.

A special factor driving consolidation amongst European banks is the European single currency. It is triggering a new wave of cross-border bank mergers, that is producing a new European banking landscape.

In a Nutshell

There are two types of bank, commercial banks and investment banks, though increasingly the distinction has become blurred and the hybrid universal bank is becoming the norm. The essence of commercial banking is taking deposits and making loans. International banks operate mainly in the wholesale financial markets. Since the 1960s, their activities have expanded rapidly in scale and scope. Growing concern about the stability of the international banking system has led to multilateral initiatives to establish rigorous and universal prudential standards known as the Basle Accord. Across the world, competition between banks, and from non-banks, technology and deregulation are driving mergers between banks. The outcome is bigger and bigger banks, initially within national systems but eventually on a cross-border basis.

FURTHER READING

Eng, Maximo V., Lees, Francis A., and Mauer, Laurence J., *Global Finance* (New York, HarperCollins, 1995)

Gibson, Heather D., *International Finance: Exchange Rates and Financial Flows in the International System* (London, Longman, 1996)

Heffernan, Shelagh, *Modern Banking in Theory and Practice* (Chichester, John Wiley, 1997)

NOTES AND REFERENCES

In the list below for this chapter, any reference to an author alone should be taken to be a reference to his/her work in 'Further reading' above.

1 *Financial Times*, 11 July 1997

2 *Financial Times*, 28 November 1997

3 *The Banker*, February 1998

CHAPTER 4
Global Investment Banking

INTRODUCTION

Investment banking comprises four core functions:

- *raising capital*: underwriting, structuring and selling equities and debt for corporations, governments and institutions
- *trading*: making markets in securities for investors who want to buy and sell, and trading on a bank's own account
- *corporate finance*: advising companies and governments on a wide variety of financial matters
- *asset management*: professional management of funds for institutional investors and in-house mutual funds and unit trusts

Investment banks conduct these functions in different ways. The business activities and organisational structures of leading investment banks, as they describe them, are shown in Box 4.1.

Securities underwriting, securities trading, corporate finance and asset management are the principal business activities of the international investment banks, but not the only ones. Other notable revenue-earning activities include trading foreign exchange, commodities and derivatives, management buy-outs and venture capital, money management, and specialist forms of banking. Some of these activities overlap with those of commercial banks, whose basic business is taking deposits and making loans.

There is growing overlap between investment banks and commercial banks, and the traditional distinctions between them are becoming more and more blurred.

INVESTMENT BANKING BUSINESS

Equity underwriting

Investment banks assist companies with the raising of new capital by underwriting the issue of equities (shares). The process is similar for privatisations when the vendor of the shares is a government. Underwriting guarantees that the issuer or seller of the shares receives the proceeds of the sale, irrespective of whether the securities are bought by retail investors or are left in the hands of the underwriter wholesalers. The underwriters are rewarded by fees, commissions and discounts that derive from their work in winning the business, organising the issue and marketing the securities. The investment bank that secures the mandate from the issuer or seller usually plays the role of lead manager to the issue – it takes the leading part in the management of the issue and the organisation of syndicates of investment bank that purchase and market the securities.

Debt underwriting

Debt, in the form of long-term bonds, medium-term notes or short-term paper, is issued by corporations, governments and other creditworthy institutions. The issuing process is similar in principle to the equity new issues outlined above, although there are numerous differences of detail. The market for new issues – known as 'initial primary offerings' (IPOs) – of debt and equities is called the 'primary market'. The market in issued securities – the bulk of stock market business – is known as the 'secondary market'.

Market making and trading

Investment banks deal in a range of financial products – equities, debt, foreign exchange, commodities, and derivatives. Market making means acting as a broker–dealer who is prepared to buy and sell specific securities at all times and thus make a market in them. Trading is conducted both as agent for clients and as principal on the investment bank's own account. Trading is an important aspect of an investment bank's money management services – treasury operations – and a significant source of revenues. But as some have learned to their cost, it is also potentially hazardous – see Table 4.1.

Table 4.1: Investment bank trading losses

Bank	Date	Loss $ bn	Reason
Barings	Feb 1995	1.40	Derivatives
Daiwa Bank	Oct 1995	1.10	Bond trading
Morgan Grenfell	Sep 1996	0.71[a]	Unauthorised investments
Kidder Peabody	Apr 1994	0.35	Bond trading
Salomon	1995	0.28	Accounting errors
Chase Manhattan	Oct 1997	0.16	Bond trading
NatWest	Mar 1997	0.12[a]	Mispricing
Salomon	Aug 1997	0.10	Share trading

Source: The Economist, 13 December 1997.
[a] provision

Mergers and acquisitions, restructuring, and privatisation

Investment banks act as advisers to corporations that want to buy corporations; alternatively, they advise firms being acquired. Both services generate hefty fees. Merger and acquisition (M&A) activity takes three forms:

- *mergers* – agreed combinations of corporate equals
- *acquisitions* – one corporation absorbs another with consent
- *take-overs* – one corporation acquires another without consent through a hostile take-over bid

Most M&A activity comprises agreed combinations of companies, whether by merger or acquisition. Occasionally, agreed amalgamations make the headlines if the companies involved are large or high-profile, but most transactions proceed without fanfare. Contentious hostile take-over bids for major companies are a different matter, attracting enormous media attention and arousing strong emotions. They also yield fat fees for the investment bank advisers on all sides; in fact, sometimes companies are put 'in play' by entrepreneurial investment banks just so as to generate business revenue.

The 1980s saw a wave of high-profile take-overs in the US and Britain, some of them (notably Guinness's purchase of Distillers and the activities of Ivan Boesky on Wall Street) becoming public scandals – see Chapter 10. The 1990s saw a waning of hostile bids for several reasons: better market understanding of the value of companies left less margin for predators; a crackdown on merger accounting meant that the considerable cost of hostile take-overs was revealed to shareholders; and restrictions on the scope for raiding the target company's accumulated pension fund surplus. Thus the gain no longer outweighed the pain. 'There are very few entrepreneurs who appear to have the appetite for the bruising business of a hostile merger and acquisition,' observes Brian Keelan, managing director of corporate finance at Warburg Dillon Read. 'Corporate executives can add value elsewhere without exposing themselves to the difficulties of a hostile bid.'[1] But Lord Hanson, doyen of bid battles, believes their day will come again. 'What goes round comes round,' he says. 'Hostile bids are alive but asleep and I have no doubt whatsoever that the situation will change.'[2]

Restructuring involves advising firms on reforms featuring major organisational changes and transfers of ownership. Restructuring work takes many forms, including management buy-outs, spin-offs, divestitures, share repurchases, asset sales, and strategic reviews.

Privatisation work involves advising governments on privatisation strategy and underwriting the sale of the equities to the public. Investment banks also act as advisers to the industry or entity that is being privatised. Since the start of privatisation in Britain in the 1980s, privatisation has grown into a worldwide money-spinner for investment banks.

Asset management

Most investment banks undertake asset management. The relatively steady revenues generated by asset management are prized as a stabiliser to the volatile earnings from underwriting, M & A and trading. The purchasers of the asset management services provided by the investment banks are institutional investors (notably pension funds and insurance companies) and investment funds (mutual funds, unit trusts and investment trusts), which can be either in-house or independent. The fund manager charges a fee for running the fund, plus costs such as broker's commissions. There is fierce competition for asset management mandates, and performance is closely and incessantly monitored.

Specialist banking services

UK and Continental European investment banks furnish various specialist banking services for corporate and institutional clients. Traditionally, they specialised in trade finance through the provision of bills of exchange – short-term marketable credits guaranteed by the bank – to importers and exporters. Since the 1980s, investment banks have focused on banking advisory services rather than lending itself, counselling clients on appropriate forms of trade and other finance.

'Project finance' involves advising and arranging complex syndicated loans and other forms of finance for infrastructure projects such as airports, bridges or power stations. 'Structured finance' involves devising and implementing sophisticated financial arrangements such as securitisation – substituting bank loans for marketable debt in the form of securities – and private placements – raising finance by matchmaking investors and borrowers.

The UK government's Private Finance Initiative (PFI), launched in the early 1990s, is a new source of work for the investment banks. The purpose of the PFI is to raise private-sector funds for public-sector capital projects such as schools, hospitals, museums or the Channel Tunnel Rail Link. The investment banks provide expertise in structuring the mix of private and public funding and arrange the private contribution. PFI work is a rapidly growing activity, with enormous international potential.

Other activities

Being entrepreneurial organisations, investment banks develop new activities as and when they perceive profitable opportunities. Such initiatives are often developed by separate subsidiaries, which may well be sold if an attractive offer comes along. Insurance broking, like assurance, leasing, property development and real estate agency are some of the businesses that investment banks have become involved in in recent years. Their bullion dealing and commodity trading activities derive from traditional ties to various commodity markets.

Investment banks' involvement in management buy-outs (MBOs) and venture capital can be either as the manager of a fund, or as an investor. MBOs involve the acquisition of a company – usually a specialist subsidiary of a large company – by its management, advised by an investment bank and financed by a venture-capital fund. Another application of venture-capital funds is to back fledgling private companies that are too small or too new to win conventional finance. In exchange for providing finance, the venture capital fund takes a stake in the firm, hoping to realise a large capital gain when it is floated on the stock market at a later date.

THE DEVELOPMENT OF INVESTMENT BANKS

International investment banks derive from several origins, as follows:

- US investment banks and brokerage houses
- British 'merchant banks'
- Continental European universal banks
- Japanese securities houses

These are discussed in turn below.

US investment banks and brokerage houses

At the turn of the century, JP Morgan and Kuhn Loeb & Co., plus their respective networks of banking and broking associates, dominated US securities underwriting; they also provided banking services for corporate clients. The United States Glass–Steagall Act of 1933 imposed a legal separation between commercial banking and investment banking: commercial banks – banks that take deposits and make loans – were barred from the securities business; investment banks – banks that undertake securities underwriting – were prohibited from taking deposits. JP Morgan decided to focus on specialist corporate commercial banking, the partners who wanted to perform securities underwriting forming a separate firm, Morgan Stanley. Kuhn Loeb plumped for underwriting and closed down its banking business.

Morgan Stanley, Kuhn Loeb, Lehman Brothers and Dillon Read were the foremost Wall Street investment banks of the 1940s and 1950s. The 1960s saw challenges to their pre-eminence in the securities underwriting business from some leading brokerage houses – stock exchange firms that act as broker–dealers – and from other investment banks. Merrill Lynch became a major force in underwriting by developing an unrivalled ability to distribute new issues to retail investors. Salomon Brothers, Goldman Sachs and upstart Donaldson, Lufkin & Jenrette, founded in 1959 won their reputations by servicing institutional investors. At the same time, the investment banks were building up their securities trading operations and the distinction between investment banks and some of the big brokerage houses was becoming fuzzy.

The abolition of the New York Stock Exchange's 183-year-old system of fixed brokerage commission rates on 1 May 1975 was a landmark in the evolution of US investment banking. Commission levels plummeted, triggering a wave of amalgamations amongst brokers. The outcome was the emergence of a handful of large leading firms and a set of smaller 'boutique' houses. The venerable Kuhn Loeb disappeared in the process, being absorbed into Lehman Brothers. The Wall Street investment banks played an active and lucrative part in the hostile takeovers amongst US corporations that were a feature of the 1980s. 'Merger mania' was fuelled by the novel 'junk bond' financing pioneered by Drexel Burnham Lambert. Unfortunately, the firm became mixed up in the illegal activities of Ivan Boesky and Michael Milken and went into liquidation (see Chapter 10).

The 1980s and 1990s saw a drive by the Wall Street investment banks to expand their international operations. London's 'Big Bang' process of 1983–86 provided an opportunity to boost their presence there, either by buying British brokers, as Lehman Brothers and Merril Lynch did, or by hirings. In addition, Merrill Lynch, Morgan Stanley and Goldman Sachs were among the first wave of foreign firms to become members of the Tokyo Stock Exchange when membership was opened to foreigners in February 1986. By the late 1990s, most of the firms listed in Table 4.2 had established a presence in every financial centre of any importance as well as in a number of emerging markets.

Table 4.2: Leading US investment banks

Bank	Shareholders' funds 1996 $bn	Revenues 1996 $bn	Employees 1996
Morgan Stanley Dean Witter	10.5	12.0	45,000
Salomon Smith Barney	9.0	10.5	8,500[a]
Merrill Lynch	6.9	13.1	54,000
Goldman Sachs	5.3	6.1	10,000
Lehman Brothers	3.9	3.4	8,000
Bear Stearns	3.6	3.5	8,000
PaineWebber	1.7	3.7	16,000
Donaldson, Lufkin & Jenrette	1.6	3.5	5,000
JP Morgan[b]	11.4	6.9	15,500
BT Alex. Brown[b]	4.4	4.2	15,000[c]

Sources: annual reports and information from firms; *Financial Times*, 25 September 1997.
[a] Salomon Brothers only before acquisition by Smith Barney.
[b] Commercial bank with large investment banking business.
[c] Brokers Trust only.

The 1990s saw further consolidation among Wall Street investment banks and more amalgamations with brokerage houses. Not only were the combined firms larger, but they also conducted a more comprehensive and complementary range of activities spanning retail broking, corporate finance, trading, asset management, and fund-raising in the wholesale financial markets. Notable combinations were Dean Witter Discover's purchase of Morgan Stanley and Travelers Group's acquisition of Salomon Brothers to form Salomon Smith Barney, both in 1997.

There emerged a two-tier hierarchy among the leading US investment banks: the so-called 'bulge-bracket' firms – Goldman Sachs, Merrill Lynch, Morgan Stanley Dean Witter, and Salomon Smith Barney; and the others. The bulge-bracket firms have extensive worldwide networks, strong US capital markets and corporate finance operations, and (with the exception of Goldman Sachs) large US securities retail capacities. They share the ambition of being not just the leaders on Wall Street but in the investment banking market of the entire globe. And they have been increasingly successful. Between them, they lead-managed 40 per cent of the $107 billion of international equity issues in 1997.[3]

Although the US's Glass–Steagall legislation of 1933 remains unrepealed despite frequent calls for reform, the 1990s saw a considerable slackening of its constraints. Commercial banks JP Morgan and BT Alex. Brown have built up substantial investment-banking operations, especially outside the US, and in some activities they rank alongside the bulge-bracket investment banks. The 1998 merger of international commercial bank Citicorp and Travelers Group, owner of Salomon Smith Barney, created America's first universal bank. By giving its consent, the Federal Reserve Board signalled the end of the Glass-Steagall constraints. Citigroup, with assets of $698 billion, became the largest US bank and the world's biggest financial services group – a global financial supermarket offering a comprehensive range of products through a wide variety of distribution channels. Citicorp chairman, John Reed, called it 'the model of the financial services company of the future'.[4] Chase Manhattan made no secret of its ambition to follow suit, a teaming with Merrill Lynch being touted by industry observers. A new round of mega-mergers had begun.

British merchant banks

The traditional British term 'merchant bank' – now little used – reflects the historical origins of London-based investment banks as merchants engaged in international trade. At some point, often in the eighteenth or nineteenth century, they came to specialise in the finance of trade, providing facilities via bills of exchange for other merchants. In the nineteenth and early twentieth centuries, international trade was mostly denominated in sterling and the market for international trade finance was focused on London, the world's leading international financial centre. That is why many of the British merchant banks, such as Barings,

Hambros, Kleinworts, Rothschilds, and Schroders, were established there by enterprising foreign merchants.

The expansion of the international economy in the nineteenth century required an enormous transfer of capital from European savers to borrowers in the Americas, Asia and elsewhere. The London merchant banks, with their unrivalled international commercial ties, were ideally placed to act as intermediaries. For a fee, they sponsored and managed the introduction of international bonds, – mostly for governments and railways companies – to the London capital market. Two further activities were developed in the early twentieth century, asset management and corporate finance, the latter comprising M&A advisory work plus fund-raising for British companies.

The 1960s and early 1970s were a heyday for the British merchant banks, which benefited from buoyant international trade and capital flows and a boom in corporate mergers and restructuring at home. But the secondary-banking crisis of 1974–75 caused the failure of some minor firms and clipped the wings of others. Competition from bigger and more dynamic US investment banks, and also from British and foreign commercial banks, led to amalgamations amongst the British merchant banks. Although they retained leading positions in UK corporate finance and asset management, they failed – with the exception of Warburgs – to develop a significant position in eurobond issuing or the eurocurrency markets, the very international businesses that were booming in their own backyard during these years.

The key developments of the 1980s were, first, the addition of securities business to the portfolio of merchant bank activities and, secondly, the establishment of offices in overseas financial centres. The merchant banks responded to the deregulation of the London Stock Exchange in 1983–86 by becoming brokers and market makers, thereby boosting their trading activities. The opening of offices in overseas financial centres was prompted by opportunities to sell their expertise and by the increasing globalisation of financial markets. At the same time, competition intensified in their home market as many of the Wall Street investment banks, leading European banks, and the 'Big Four' Japanese securities houses built up their operations in London.

In the late-1980s, the top tier of the British merchant-banking sector comprised eight leading independent firms plus the subsidiaries of UK clearing banks Barclays and NatWest. The independents – Barings, Flemings, Hambros, Kleinwort Benson, Morgan Grenfell, Rothschilds, Schroders and Warburgs – were prestigious houses that were active across the range of merchant bank businesses, but much smaller in capital than their Wall Street counterparts. The commercial bank subsidiaries Barclays de Zoete Wedd (BZW) and County NatWest (later NatWest Markets) had the backing of their parents' big balance sheets and thus in principle the resources to take on the Wall Street houses. There was also a second rank of firms, such as Charterhouse, Hill Samuel, Lazards and Samuel Montagu.

The 1990s saw a boom in international investment banking in London – in 1995 international wholesale financial transactions there generated revenues of £15 billion and employed 150,000.[5] Nevertheless, these years also saw the acquisition of five of the top-tier independents by foreign banks and the end of the aspirations of the leading UK commercial banks to compete in international investment banking. The process began in 1989 when Morgan Grenfell was purchased by Deutsche Bank. Barings was acquired by Dutch banking and insurance conglomerate ING in March 1995; Warburgs was bought by Swiss Bank Corporation in May 1995; Kleinwort Benson succumbed to an offer from Dresdner Bank the following month. Hambros was broken up in December 1997, its corporate finance arm being sold to Société Générale of France and its corporate lending activities to Générale de Banque of Belgium.

A crisis in the conduct of business was a common trigger to many of these sales. Morgan Grenfell fell under a cloud because of its involvement in the Guinness take-over scandal and Hambros suffered similarly because of its sponsorship of a controversial take-over bid for the Co-operative Wholesale Society. Barings went bust thanks to 'rogue' trader Nick Leeson (see Chapter 10). Warburgs was undermined by a series of strategic miscalculations. Kleinwort Benson, on the other hand, simply sold out while the going was good, concluding that it was too small to prosper in the fast-consolidating global investment banking industry. Leading securities house Smith New Court did likewise, being bought by Merrill Lynch in 1995.

The sell-off of such British financial institutions also embraced asset management. In October 1997, the ambitious Zurich Group of Switzerland announced the acquisition of the asset management and insurance arms of BAT industries, including Allied Dunbar, Eagle Star and Threadneedle Asset Management. The following month, Merrill Lynch purchased leading fund management firm Mercury Asset Management (MAM) for $5.1 billion. MAM had been unable to implement its global expansion strategy, in particular failing to develop a substantial business in the US, and so the management sold out instead.

In Autumn 1997, both Barclay and NatWest announced that they were abandoning the ambition of competing with the bulge-bracket US firms in the global investment banking market place. NatWest 'restructured' its NatWest Markets investment banking arm, selling its equities business to BT Alex. Brown and its derivatives unit to Deutsche Morgan Grenfell. NatWest Markets' debt business and investment management operation were integrated into the rest of the group. Barclays sold its equities and M&A businesses to Credit Suisse First Boston. The refocused BZW was renamed Barclays Capital.

These moves stunned observers since both banks had recently spent much money and effort building up their investment banking operations. Moreover, they flew in the face of conventional wisdom that investment banking could only be conducted successfully on an integrated basis. But the banks argued that the global industry was rapidly consolidating and that without a major presence in the US – necessitating the costly and risky acquisition of a Wall Street house – there was no way they could compete as global players. 'A year is a long time in this business,' mused Martin Taylor, Barclays' chief executive, announcing the decision to break up BZW.[6]

Does it matter to London's leading position as a location for the conduct of international investment banking that the players are mostly non-British? Not at all, argue many. 'It does not really matter where ultimate ownership of a City institution lies,' says leading City figure Stanislas Yassukovich. 'We should look on it as a compliment not as a problem. Wimbledon is still the world's greatest tennis event, yet when did we last have an English player in the top ten seeds?'[7] But others are less sanguine. George Mallinckrodt, president of Schroders, the leading independent investment bank, comments 'there has to be a balance between domestically owned banks and foreign-owned banks.'[8]

The decision of the foreign proprietors of a number of major London-based asset managers to relocate management control overseas was a disturbing development. In 1997, Dresdner Bank announced the creation of an integrated international asset management subsidiary called Dresdner RCM Global Investors, based in California. United Bank of Switzerland announced the transfer of control of big City-of-London-based pension fund manager PDFM to Brinson, its Chicago-based operation. The UK investment banking industry has, in reality, become but a shadow of its former self.

Continental European universal banks
'Universal banking' – meaning commercial banking *plus* investment banking – is the long-standing domestic banking pattern in Continental Europe. French bank Paribas was the pioneer in international investment

banking among the Continental European banks. In 1973, it forged an alliance with London merchant bank Warburgs through a mutual share exchange. The following year they jointly established a presence on Wall Street with the purchase of US investment bank AG Becker. But the alliance with Warburg did not last, chiefly because of different management styles and rivalries, and it was unwound in 1982. The loss-making AG Becker was sold to Merrill Lynch in 1984. In the meantime, Credit Suisse had also taken the partnership route into international investment banking. In 1978, it established CS First Boston, a joint venture with First Boston Corporation, which became an outstanding success. Credit Suisse subsequently acquired full ownership, and the name was changed to Credit Suisse First Boston.

Table 4.3: Leading European investment banks

Bank	Shareholders' funds 1996 $bn	Revenues 1996 $bn	Employees 1996
Warburg Dillon Read		$3.5[a]	14,000[b]
Credit Suisse First Boston	$7.2	$5.3	10,000
Banque Paribas	$4.5	$2.6	9,000
Deutsche Morgan Grenfell	$0.8	$1.0	7,000
Flemings	$1.2	$0.7	7,000
Schroders	$1.5	$1.6	5,000
Dresdner Kleinwort Benson	$0.7	$0.8	3,000
ING Barings			3,000
HSBC Investment Banking (1995)	$1.3		2,500
ABN-Amro Investment Banking			n/a

Sources: annual reports and information from firms.
[a] SBC Warburg only, before acquisition of Dillon Read and merger with Union Bank of Switzerland.
[b] Combined Warburg Dillon Read and Union Bank of Switzerland investment banking staff.
n/a: not available.

The leading European investment banks are listed in Table 4.3. Although the major Continental European banks already had a branch or office in London, several took advantage of the shake-up in the UK securities industry in 1983–86 to purchase a broker or jobber – Union Bank of Switzerland, Credit Suisse, Bank Centrade, Banque Bruxelles Lambert, BAII of Luxembourg, Credit Commercial de France, Paribas and Gironzentrale to name the prime movers. Deregulation of the Continental bourses in the late 1980s and early 1990s, imitating London's Big Bang, allowed European banks to expand their securities activities across the Continent. Furthermore, the opening-up of the Tokyo Stock Exchange to foreign members in 1986 was accompanied by an influx of European banks: by the end of the year, securities entities had been established in Tokyo by Banque Indosuez, Deutsche Bank, Union Bank Swiss, Swiss Bank Corporation, Dresdner Bank, Société Générale, DG Bank, Westdeutsche Landesbank, Commerzbank, ABN-Amro, Paribas, NatWest, Midland Bank, Hongkong and Shanghai Bank, Jardine Fleming and SG Warburg.

The acquisition of London merchant banks by Deutsche Bank, ING, Dresdner Bank, Swiss Bank Corporation, Société Générale and Générale de Banque is discussed above. In May 1996, Dutch bank ABN-Amro forged a link with Rothschilds to undertake equity capital markets business – underwriting and distributing equities in Europe and Asia. Other Continental banks grew their investment-banking activities in London organically, notably Westdeutsche Landesbank, Crédit Lyonnais and Paribas. And not only in London: by the late 1990s, Paribas had built up a substantial international investment-banking business operating in 60 countries.

But most European banks with global aspirations have a gaping hole in their international investment-banking networks, namely Wall Street. There are three exceptions: Credit Suisse, UBS (the merged Union Bank of Switzerland and Swiss Banking Corporation), and Schroders. The strongest is Credit Suisse, whose subsidiary Credit Suisse First Boston, with 10,000 employees and operations in 30 countries, is not only a first-division Wall Street house, but a rival to the US bulge-bracket firms in international business. A few months prior to the merger with UBS, SBC established a significant foothold on Wall Street in 1997 with the purchase of Dillon Read, which was combined with its non-US investment banking interests to form Warburg Dillon Read. Schroder Wertheim, the UK firm's US subsidiary has some useful niche positions and a staff of 1,500.

Japanese securities houses

In Japan, as in the US, there is a legal separation between commercial banking and investment banking. The legislative basis is Article 65, the Japanese counterpart of the Glass–Steagall Act, which was introduced in Japan by the US administration of occupation immediately after World War II. By 1996, the investment banking industry in Japan comprised 230 domestic securities firms, plus about 50 foreign securities companies.[9] For decades, the business was dominated by the 'Big Four' securities firms – Nomura, Daiwa, Nikko and Yamaichi – which have extensive branch networks throughout Japan. Since the 1980s, they have also had overseas offices and a significant presence in London and New York.

Secondary-market stockbroking is the principal domestic activity of the Japanese securities houses. Securities trading is a significant source of revenue, and financial-derivatives trading has grown since the mid-1980s. Underwriting the bond issues of the Japanese government is a long-standing obligation. Since the 1980s, Japanese corporations have made extensive use of the euromarkets for debt financing. Although the Big Four have traditionally dominated corporate underwriting, they have faced lively competition from US and European investment banks, which have won market share in the 1990s. Corporate advisory work is a growing activity. The overseas offshoots have developed forms of specialist banking for corporate clients. However, they have been challenged in euro-yen issues for non-Japanese borrowers by branches of the big Japanese commercial banks.

The 1980s were a prosperous decade for the Japanese securities houses, especially the Big Four. Growing use of the capital market by corporate borrowers instead of bank borrowing boosted revenues from underwriting and distribution. And secondary trading was highly profitable, thanks to a booming stock market and fixed commissions – over the years 1983 to 1987, commission revenues quadrupled.[10]

The 1990s were a very different story. The continual slide in Japanese share prices from 1990 – by 1995 they had lost 60 per cent of their value – created difficult trading conditions. Brokerage commissions were depressed and the value of shares held was eroded. From July 1995, prices staged a faltering recovery, but the rises were reversed by a sharp downturn in autumn 1997. For several banks and securities houses, it was the last straw (see Chapter 7): Sanyo Securities, Japan's seventh-largest securities house, was one of the casualities; Yamaichi Securities, one of the Big Four and which celebrated its centenary that year, was another.

Yamaichi's tribulations began in spring 1997, when it was revealed that the firm had been making illegal *sokaiya* protection payments to gangsters (see Chapter 10). In August 1997, Yamaichi's chairman, its president and nine executives resigned *en masse* and some were arrested by the police. Three days later, a senior manager was stabbed to death in a Tokyo street, apparently confirming the alleged links with organised crime. Then in November 1997 it was revealed that the firm had been unprofitable for most of the 1990s and had amassed losses totalling $2 billion hidden from the regulators in dummy companies in the Cayman Islands. 'This unexpected situation in our company's 100th anniversary year is heartbreaking. We don't know how to beg the pardon of our customers, shareholders and related people,'[11] sobbed the tearful Yamaichi president, Shohei Nozawa, announcing the company's collapse with the loss of 9,500 jobs and debts of $24 billion.

So then it was the 'Big *Three*' – Nomura, Daiwa, and Nikko. But they too were embroiled in the *sokaiya* scandal and were discredited and disrupted by resignations and some arrests of leading executives. Having struggled for years to make money in Tokyo, foreign investment banks were suddenly inundated with orders. In October 1997, Merrill Lynch and Morgan Stanley did more business on the Tokyo Stock Exchange than any Japanese house – even Nomura – and this was a notable milestone.[12]

GLOBAL INVESTMENT BANKS

Investment banking is a global business. The international reach of leading investment banks is shown in Box 4.2. The leaders are the US bulge-bracket firms, but there are plenty of other banks jostling to join their ranks. Further consolidation amongst US and European banks, perhaps also embracing Japanese firms, is inevitable.

The requirements for 'bulge-bracket' status are:

- a global presence, including a substantial US operation
- a large capital base to back capital market transactions and trading positions
- provision of the full range of investment banking services
- top-calibre personnel
- cutting-edge information technology

The struggle amongst the international investment banks is based on the proposition that a handful of successful firms with scale, expertise and global reach will prosper by selling their investment banking services to global corporations and the world's savers. It is thus anticipated that demand for the services provided by the top-tier international investment banks will boom: international corporate advisory services are even now in heavy demand as firms become more international, especially in Europe as a result of the single currency; emerging countries need investment banks to help them secure foreign capital; in the developed world, the growth of savings will generate greater demand for asset-management services; and the shift from bank borrowing to the issue of tradable debt will favour investment banks over commercial banks.

But many of these favourable factors have been operating during much of the 1980s and 1990s, yet in these decades the margins achieved by the international investment banks have been shrinking and the industry's return on capital has declined steadily overall. Intense rivalry between the players is one reason, but there are other factors at work too. The investment banks' role as intermediaries has been eroded as high-quality real-time financial data has become widely available thanks to communications technology. Customers have become more powerful and more demanding, both as regards services required and fees paid. Competition from commercial banks encroaching onto the investment banks' traditional turf has squeezed earnings and sent salary costs soaring as the new entrants bid for scarce skills.

The investment banks have responded to the profits squeeze by becoming bigger, in order to achieve greater market clout and economies of scale, and by taking greater risks. The quest to improve returns has led firms to conduct underwriting and trading activities in riskier, but potentially more profitable, forms, such as bought deals and block trades, although the collapse of Peregrine Investment Holdings, Hong Kong's biggest investment bank, in January 1998 was another stark reminder of the perils of the underwriting business. Investment banks are also betting more of their own money in the markets through proprietary trading – the use of a sliver of the firm's capital plus a slug of borrowings against it to play the markets. This leverage can turn small price movements into big gains – or big losses.

As investment banking has become riskier, the requirement for capital has become greater. Since 1980, the equity capital of the top nine US firms has grown by more than 1,000 per cent. Larger firms are better able to cross-subsidise essential but loss-making aspects of their activities. And the greater the scale of capital, the greater the barrier to entry, limiting competition. If the situation stabilises with the global investment business in the hands of an oligopoly of mega-firms, it may prove possible to curtail costs and extract higher fees, thus reversing the decline in the return on capital. But given the number of banks with aspirations to bulge-bracket size and status, that day appears a long way off.

In a Nutshell

Investment banking comprises four core functions:

- *raising capital*: underwriting, structuring and selling equities and debt for corporations, governments and institutions
- *trading*: making markets in securities for investors who want to buy and sell, and trading on a bank's own account
- *corporate finance*: advising companies and governments on a wide variety of financial matters
- *asset management*: professional management of funds for institutional investors and in-house mutual funds and unit trusts

Individual firms also conduct a variety of ancillary activities.

International investment banking is dominated by four US firms – Goldman Sachs, Merrill Lynch, Morgan Stanley Dean Witter, and Salomon Smith Barney – the so called 'bulge-bracket' firms. These firms all have strong US capital markets and corporate finance operations, large capacities for retail broking in US securities, and extensive international networks. Various commercial banks might claim or aspire to bulge-bracket status, including BT Alex. Brown, Chase Manhattan and Morgan Stanley of the US, and European banks ABN-Amro, Credit Suisse, Deutsche Bank, Dresdner Bank, ING, Paribas and UBS.

Competition in investment banking is fierce, and profit margins are always under pressure. Endeavouring to raise rates of return significantly, investment banks have assumed greater risks and have merged to achieve larger capital bases, greater market clout, and to provide a comprehensive range of services. There will be further consolidation, but with so many banks aspiring to sell investment banking services to global corporations and the world's savers, competition will continue to be fierce.

FURTHER READING

Alletzhauser, Al, *The House of Nomura* (London, Bloomsbury, 1990)

Chernow, Ron, *The House of Morgan* (New York, Atlantic Monthly Press, 1990)

Clay, C. J. J. and Wheble, B. S., *Modern Merchant Banking* (Cambridge, Woodhead, 1983)

Hayes, Samuel, and Hubbard, Philip, *Investment Banking* (Boston Mass., Havard Business School Press, 1990)

Letwin, Oliver, *Privatising the World* (London, Cassell, 1988)

Roberts, Richard, *Schroders: Merchants & Bankers* (London, Macmillan, 1992)

Sobel, Robert, *Salomon Brothers* (New York, Salomon Brothers, 1986)

NOTES AND REFERENCES

In the list below for this chapter, any reference to an author alone should be taken to be a reference to his/her work in 'Further reading' above.

1 *Sunday Telegraph*, 7 September 1997

2 *Sunday Telegraph*, 7 September 1997

3 *Financial Times*, 22 December 1997

4 Watch out for the Egos; *The Economist*, 11 April 1998

5 *Sunday Times*, 2 July 1995

6 *Financial Times*, 4 and 5 October 1997

7 *Sunday Times*, 2 July 1995

8 *Sunday Times*, 2 July 1995

9 Japan Securities Research Institute, *Securities Markets of Japan 1996*, (Tokyo, J.S.R.I, 1996)

10 Hayes and Hubbard, p. 171

11 *Financial Times*, 25 November 1997

12 *Sunday Times*, 23 November 1997

Box 4.1: What Do Investment Banks Do?

Business activities and structural organisation

Compagnie Financière de Paribas
- Corporate banking
- Capital markets
- Asset management
- Advisory services

Source: Banque Paribas, *A Wholesale Bank with Global Perspectives*, (Paris, Banque Paribas, 1995)

Credit Suisse First Boston
- Corporate and investment banking – debt, equity and convertible   ⇨

underwriting/mergers and acqusitions/acqusition finance/corporate sales
and divestitures/corporate lending and syndicated finance/leveraged
finance/leveraged buy-outs/generic and structured trade finance/joint
ventures/takeover defence/corporate restructurings/correspondent
banking/privatization/private placements/asset finance/project finance/
leasing
- Fixed income – government and corporate fixed income securities/global
  foreign exchange/emerging markets/new issues underwriting/asset
  backed securities/leveraged finance/mortgage securities/real estate
  finance/money markets/bank notes/precious metals/fixed income
  research
- Equities – research/sales/trading/underwriting/equity finance – prime
  brokerage/convertible warrants/derivatives/proprietary trading
- Credit Suisse Financial Markets – interest rate products/equity products/
  foreign exchange products/commodity products/asset trading and credit
  derivatives

Source: Credit Suisse First Boston Annual Review, 1996

Daiwa Securities
- Securities brokerage
- Trading
- Underwriting
- Strategic advice
- Product development
- Structured finance

Source: Daiwa Securities Report and Accounts, 1997

Deutsche Morgan Grenfell
- Global markets
- Equities
- Investment banking
- Institutional asset management
- Emerging markets
- Structured finance

Source: Deutsche Bank Annual Report, 1996

Dresdner Kleinwort Benson
- Global corporate finance – new issues business, mergers and acquisitions,
  and financial advisory
- Global equities – trading and distribution of shares; research ⇨

- Global finance – project and structured finance
- Global markets – new issues, trading and distribution of fixed-interest securities, foreign exchange and precious metals, derivatives, market risk management

Source: Dresdner Bank Annual Report, 1996

Flemings
- Asset management
- Investment banking
- Securities
- Banking

Robert Fleming Holdings Limited Annual Report, 1996

Goldman Sachs
- Investment banking
- Fixed interest
- Equities
- Currency
- Asset management

Goldman Sachs Annual Review, 1996

HSBC Investment Banking
- Advice and financing
- Equity securities
- Asset management
- Private banking
- Trustee services

The HSBC Group: A World of Financial Services, 1997

ING Barings
- Equity broking, trading, sales and research
- Debt and derivatives, trading and sales
- Banking and structured finance
- Corporate finance – developed markets
- Corporate finance – emerging markets
- Operations and central management

ING Barings Annual Review, 1995/6

JP Morgan
- Finance & advisory – advisory/debt and equity underwriting/credit
- Market making – fixed income/equities/foreign exchange/commodities ⇨

- Asset management and servicing – asset management/private client services/futures and options brokerage/euroclear system
- Equity investments – equity investment portfolio management for Morgan's own account
- Proprietary investing and trading – market risk positioning for Morgan's own account/capital and liquidity management

JP Morgan Annual Review, 1996

Morgan Stanley

- Investment banking – mergers, acquisitions and restructuring/equity underwriting/debt underwriting/real estate finance
- Sales and trading – equities/fixed income/foreign exchange/commodities/structured products/research
- Asset management and administration – institutional asset management/retail asset management/private client services/private equity/global custody

Morgan Stanley Annual Report, 1996

Nomura Securities

- Securities brokerage
- Trading
- Investment banking
- Commercial banking

The Nomura Securities Co. Annual Report, 1996

Rothschilds

- Banking and treasury
- Corporate finance

NM Rothschild Limited Annual Report, 1996

Schroders

- Investment banking – corporate finance and equity capital markets/project finance
- Financial markets and structured products
- Banking and leasing
- Investment management
- Management buy-outs and venture capital

Schroders plc Annual Report, 1995

SBC Warburg

- Foreign Exchange

- Interest Rate Products
- Equities
- Corporate Finance

Swiss Bank Corporation Annual Report, 1996

Box 4.2: Global Reach of International Investment Banks

BT Alex. Brown
80 offices in 50 countries

Credit Suisse First Boston
55 offices in 34 countries
Source: Annual Report, 1996

Daiwa Securities
158 offices in 27 countries
Source: Annual Report, 1997

Deutsche Morgan Grenfell
40 offices
Source: Annual Report, 1996

Dresdner Bank Group
1,600 offices in 70 countries
Source: Annual Report, 1996

Flemings
67 offices in 40 countries
Source: Annual Report, 1996

Goldman Sachs
34 offices in 20 countries
Source: Annual Report, 1996

HSBC Holdings
5,500 offices in 79 countries
Source: Annual Report, 1997

ING Barings
33 countries
Source: Annual Report, 1995/6

⇨

JP Morgan
33 countries
Source: *Annual Report,* 1996

Lehman Brothers
34 offices in 22 countries
Source: *Annual Report,* 1996

Merrill Lynch
45 countries
Source: *FactBook,* 1996

Morgan Stanley Dean Witter
419 offices in 22 countries
Source: Telephone conversation

Nomura Securities
27 countries
Source: *Annual Report,* 1996

PaineWebber
298 offices in 9 countries
Source: *Annual Report,* 1996

Paribas
220 offices in 60 countries
Source: *Banque Paribas. A Wholesale Bank with Global Perspectives* (Paris, Banque Paribas, 1995)

Schroders
44 offices in 33 countries
Source: *Annual Report,* 1995

CHAPTER 5

International Financial Institutions

INTRODUCTION

This chapter surveys the principal public institutions of international finance. These bodies provide the framework within which international financial markets and firms operate. The rapid expansion in the scale of international financial markets in recent years has diminished the significance of international financial institutions. Ironically, the rise of the markets is a result of the success of the international financial institutions in promoting an open international trading system, freedom of capital movements, and worldwide economic development.

THE INTERNATIONAL MONETARY FUND AND WORLD BANK

The International Monetary Fund (IMF) and the World Bank (see below) were the outcome of the international conference of 44 nations held at Bretton Woods in July 1944 to plan the post-war monetary system. Despite their common origin, the IMF and World Bank are independent institutions with different objectives, summarised in Table 5.1.

International Monetary Fund

The IMF, which commenced operations in March 1947, is the foremost international financial institution, fulfilling some of the functions of a global central bank. It was established as the institutional framework for the promotion of world trade and economic growth, through order, stability and co-operation in international monetary affairs. Charged with stabilising and sustaining the system of fixed exchange rates established at Bretton Woods, it was provided with the authority and means to assist nations with temporary balance-of-payments deficits. With a well defined mandate and a carefully balanced structure of members' contributions, borrowing rights and voting power, plus sustained political support, the IMF became an authoritative and effective institution that made an important contribution to the prosperity of the 1950s and 1960s.

Table 5.1: Spot the difference: the IMF and the World Bank

	IMF	World Bank
Purpose	Monetary institution.	Development institution.
Activities	Stabilisation of the international monetary system. Finance of temporary balance of payments deficits.	Promotion of economic growth and development in developing countries.
Source of funds	Official reserves and countries' currencies. Special Drawing Rights (SDRs).	Capital quotas. Issues in the international bond market.
Eligible borrowers	All members.	Developing countries.
Outlook	Short-term.	Long-term.
Credit horizon	3–5-year loans (maximum 10 years).	15–20-year loans (maximum 50 years).
Staff	2,300	9,500

The IMF's funds are provided by quota subscriptions from member countries paid in gold, currency and Special Drawing Rights (SDRs). Quotas are determined by a formula taking account of a range of economic and financial variables, revised every five years. In 1962, the resources available to the IMF were substantially increased when the Group of Ten countries (see below) signed the General Agreement to Borrow, by which a $6,500 million credit was made available to the IMF should it be required. This credit facility has been repeatedly raised. Further funding was provided by the introduction in 1970 of a new form of international money, Special Drawings Rights (see Box 5.1).

Box 5.1 – Special Drawing Rights (SDRs)

SDRs are a form of international money created by the IMF for international transactions amongst central banks. They are composed of a weighted average of the five leading international currencies – the dollar, yen, German mark, French franc and UK pound sterling. They are allocated to members in proportion to their IMF quota subscriptions. Through the IMF, a member can exchange its SDRs with other members for hard currency (usually US dollars), which can be used to meet international obligations.

SDRs were invented as a co-ordinated response to the problem of the international financial system's reliance on the US dollar, the gaping US payments deficits of the late 1960s undermining confidence that the dollar would continue to hold its value. The first allocation of SDRs was in January 1970, subsequent years seeing further issues.

The IMF's financial transactions are denominated in SDRs, and SDR-denominated deposits are now accepted by commercial banks. Nonetheless, this IMF-issued international currency has failed to fulfil the aspirations of its creators that it would become a major reserve asset of the international financial system.

The demise of the Bretton Woods system introduced adjustment through flexible exchange rates, eroding the importance of the IMF as a provider of funds to tide countries over balance-of-payments problems. But when serious currency problems arose, such as the sterling crisis of autumn 1976, even the industrialised countries turned to the IMF for assistance.

The 1970s saw large scale external borrowings by developing countries from international banks. By 1982, the accumulated debt of developing countries totalled $600 billion. Increases in US interest rates from 1979, and the appreciation of the dollar, put pressure on the ability of the developing countries to service their debts.

The IMF played a vital role in coping with the Mexican debt moratorium of August 1982 that marked the beginning of the 'debt crisis' (see Chapter 1). The Fund not only provided assistance from its own resources, but co-ordinated and cajoled contributions from international banks and creditors. The IMF took on the role of key intermediary between all the parties. A balance was struck between 'rescheduling' – the extension of existing loans and the supply of new funds – and 'adjustment' – the adoption of more stringent economic policies by borrowers – on a case-by-case basis. The Brady Plan of 1989 (see Box 4.1, Chapter 4) added a new dimension, allowing the IMF to set aside 25 per cent of the resources provided by a funded programme for debt reduction.

Debt reduction and debt forgiveness are particularly relevant in the cases of the very poorest countries. Since the 1980s, the IMF has been confronted with the problem of repayment arrears. Some countries have been suspended from eligibility to use the Fund's resources until the arrears are cleared. But for the world's poorest dozen countries, such as Guyana, Mozambique, Nicaragua and Uganda, even if 90 per cent of outstanding debt was cancelled the remainder would still be unserviceable. Solutions to these problems that do not undermine the Fund's basic principles and practices are being pursued.

The break-up of the Soviet Union led to an influx of new members. The IMF has provided crucial assistance to countries undergoing the transition from centrally planned to market-based economies. It has provided both financial facilities and technical support for the development of sound economic management, a dynamic financial sector, and the privatisation of state enterprises. A new systemic transformation facility (STF) was established in 1993 to provide support on flexible terms for such countries. In 1995, Russia and the Ukraine also obtained large stand-by credits from the IMF.

Mexico became engulfed in a new financial crisis in late 1994, the peso dropping by 50 per cent. It was feared that Mexico's problems would cause a loss of confidence in emerging markets, undermining the progress made in resolving the debt crisis. The IMF acted swiftly, putting together a record $40 billion support package plus an adjustment programme. It worked. Confidence was restored and Mexico became rehabilitated in the financial markets.

Naturally, the IMF was heavily involved in the endeavours to resolve the East Asian financial crisis that began in summer 1997. Rescue packages were put together for Thailand and Indonesia, and a record $57 billion bail-out was provided for South Korea. Yet the Fund came in for considerable criticism, mostly for the terms attached to the packages. The IMF's customary requirements of fiscal and monetary austerity were criticised as inappropriate and even damaging in circumstances where government profilgacy or inflation was not the problem. And the insistence on the liberalisation of access by foreigners to local financial markets and institutions was seen in the region as promoting the interests of Western, particularly US, international banks.

In the West, some commentators pondered whether, by rushing to the rescue, the IMF in fact encouraged lax conduct on the part of private lenders and regional governments, relieving them from facing up to the consequences of their imprudence or incompetence – the so-called 'moral hazard' problem. 'The true cost of the Mexican bail-out is today's Asia crisis,' commented *The Economist* in January 1998.[1]

The IMF remains an important forum for discussion amongst the industrial countries, but it has minimal influence over their policy decisions. Its mandate to exercise 'firm surveillance' over members is mostly meaningless – it has no influence over the US deficits or German interest rates. It also has little moderating influence on the swollen international financial markets. The vast expansion in the scale of international financial flows in the 1980s and 1990s, floating exchange rates, liberalised and integrated capital markets, and the inability of the industrial countries to formulate co-ordinated policies have together put the international financial markets beyond the IMF's exhortations, let alone its discipline. Prevention is better than cure, but there is no point in blaming the doctor if the patient does his own thing and medical help is only called in when matters are already out of hand.

World Bank

The International Bank for Reconstruction and Development (IBRD) – generally known as the World Bank – was established at the Bretton Woods Conference in July 1944 and began operations in June 1946. Its head office is in Washington, across the street from the IMF. By early 1998, the World Bank had nearly 180 members and a staff of 9,500.

The World Bank is funded by capital subscriptions from members, proportional to their share of world trade. A fifth of each quota is subscribed in gold and in the member's currency, the other four-fifths being uncalled but available to back World Bank guarantees of private loans to developing countries. Further funds are raised in the international capital market by bond issues.

The original purpose of the World Bank was to promote economic reconstruction in war-torn Europe. It has subsequently become an important source of long-term investment funds and technical and economic advice for developing countries.

It makes loans to governments or to projects under government guarantee. In 1956, it established an affiliate, the International Finance Corporation (IFC), to promote private capital flows to developing countries. The IFC invests directly in private companies, or provides loans or guarantees to private investors. It borrows directly from the

IBRD, and re-lends to private parties without government guarantee. Another important affiliate is the International Development Association (IDA), established in 1960. It specialises in loans to the world's most needy countries at low or zero interest rates for terms as long as 50 years. It provides funding principally for infrastructure projects, such as roads or energy supplies, that do not make short-term commericial returns but are vital for development.

Since 1995, the president of the World Bank, by tradition an American, has been former investment banker James Wolfensohn. Quizzed about his vision of the World Bank's role, Wolfensohn replied, to the surprise of some conventionally minded bankers, that it should be judged by 'smiles on the faces of children' in poor countries. He declared that his goal was to make the World Bank the 'premier global development institution' of the twenty-first century.[2] However, in terms of total financial flows to developing countries, the role of the World Bank has relatively diminished in the 1990s. In 1996, net financial flows into developing countries totalled $247 billion, up tenfold since 1986, but only $27 billion – 11 per cent – came from the multilateral development banks.[3] But the private flows are focused on a few countries in South-East Asia and Latin America. Elsewhere, the World Bank and regional development banks still play an important part.

BANK FOR INTERNATIONAL SETTLEMENTS

The Bank for International Settlements (BIS) – the central bankers' central bank – is the longest-standing international financial institution. Established in 1930, its original purpose was to co-ordinate payments of German war reparations among the European central banks. After World War II, the operational functions of an international central bank were vested in the IMF.

However, the BIS has continued to have a significant role through its monthly meetings of central bank governors from the major industrial countries at its headquarters in Basle, Switzerland. The purpose of these meetings is to achieve mutual understanding and the international co-ordination of monetary policy, in order to ensure orderly conditions in the international financial markets. The BIS also acts as trustee or agent for international financial settlements, when requested by the parties concerned.

The BIS is a public company owned by the central banks of various European countries, Australia, Canada, Japan and South Africa, and some US commercial banks. It is managed by a 17-strong Board of Directors drawn from Belgium, Germany, France, Italy, the Netherlands, Sweden, Switzerland and the UK, and since 1994 also from Canada, Japan and the US.

The principal departments are the Banking Department, and the Monetary and Economic Department. The Banking Department assists central banks in managing and investing their foreign exchange reserves. Currently around 100 central banks keep deposits with the BIS, amounting to some 10 per cent of world foreign exchange reserves. The Monetary and Economic Department collects and publishes data on international banking and financial markets and produces research reports on trends and potential problems. The wide-ranging review of international economic and financial developments presented in the annual report of the BIS each year is highly regarded.

The vast expansion of international lending in the 1970s increased the vulnerability of the international financial system to bank failures. The Basle Committee on Banking Supervision was established by the 'Group of Ten' in 1974 to monitor and harmonise national banking standards. The Basle Concordat of 1975, strengthened in 1983, specified responsibility by the BIS for the supervision of banks' foreign branches and subsidiaries. In 1988, minimum capital adequacy standards for banks were agreed. This not only bolstered confidence in the international banking system, but it also set common competitive conditions for international banks – a level playing field. The BIS capital-adequacy requirements have become standard in all significant international financial centres. In 1995, new prudential standards were introduced to constrain the market risks of derivatives trading.

Being in origin a European institution, the BIS has developed a particularly close relationship with the EU central banks. Prior to the establishment of the European Monetary Institute (see the section below on the European Central Bank), the BIS provided premises and assistance for the secretariat of the Committee of Governors of the central banks of the EC. In 1986, it undertook to act as the clearing house for interbank transactions in European currency units (ecus) that had been conducted by commercial banks.

The BIS acts as a bank for the central banks, accepting deposits and furnishing short-term loans to central banks short of liquidity. The discretion with which it provides such facilities assists their effectiveness in moderating currency speculation. Notable examples were the support arranged for the Bank of England in 1966, 1967 and 1977 and the Banque de France in 1968.

The BIS played a significant role in assisting the IMF to manage the international debt crisis from 1982. Under the auspices of the BIS, the central banks of creditor countries arranged additional credit facilities for the IMF, boosting its resources to meet the growing demands for assistance from developing countries. Additionally, the BIS sometimes puts up short-term bridging finance for developing countries, pending approval of loans from the IMF or World Bank.

CENTRAL BANKS

The role of the central bank varies somewhat from country to country, but the major institutions perform all or most of the following functions:

- *Government's bank* The central bank manages the government's short-term and long-term funding requirements through the issue of bills and bonds. It looks after public receipts and the accounts of government departments.
- *Bankers' bank* The central bank acts as 'lender of last resort' to the country's banks, engendering confidence in the banking system. Should a commercial bank find itself short of funds, it can turn for assistance to the central bank. Since the central bank sets the terms of such accommodation, the role provides important influence over interest rates and the money supply.

  The central bank acts as banker to the commercial banks, accepting deposits from them and making loans to them and to the money market. Commercial banks are usually required to keep a minimum level of funds in their accounts at the central bank, the level of such non-operational deposits being a device for controlling bank behaviour and monetary conditions.
- *Agent or architect of monetary policy* Central banks advise governments on monetary policy, that is, the quantity of money in the economy, the rate of interest and the exchange rate. They implement the government's policy in these matters, and supervise the commercial banking system to meet them. They also manipulate the markets in government bills and bonds to fulfil objectives of monetary policy.

  When countries operate exchange controls – restrictions on the free transfer of money in and out of a country – these measures are conducted by the central bank, as is intervention in the foreign exchange markets to influence the value of currencies. Intervention is more effective if conducted in concert with other central banks, and central bank officials keep in close touch with each other through the Bank for International Settlements, other international financial institutions and informal contracts.

Germany, New Zealand, the UK and the US, have 'independent' central banks that have some degree of devolved responsibility for monetary policy (see Table 5.2). They are charged with delivering stable prices and sometimes other economic objectives, it being believed that governments are too easily tempted to pursue inflationary policies for short-term political ends. A distinction is commonly drawn between 'instrument independence' – when a central bank is given a target but has the freedom to decide how to meet it – and 'goal independence' – when it sets the target too. The Bank of England has the former; the German Bundesbank has the latter.

- *Note issuer* Central banks control the issue of notes and coin.
- *Supervisor and regulator of the financial system* Central banks often, though not invariably, have regulatory responsibility for the banking system, and sometimes for other aspects of the financial system. Requiring regular submissions from the banks, they are able to monitor developments and take action to safeguard the soundness of the banking system.

  Central banks usually act as the licensing authority for commercial banks. To retain their licence, banks must meet stipulated standards of capital adequacy and liquidity, which are policed by the central bank or other banking authority.
- *International role* The central bank conducts transfers of gold and currency with other central banks and international financial institutions. Central banks are members of the Bank for International Settlements, the central bankers' club.

Openness and accountability are desirable features of central bank operations. Openness means that the process by which decisions are made is publicly transparent. Thus the Bank of England and the US Federal Reserve publish the minutes of their deliberations, albeit with a time delay. Accountability means that the non-elected central bankers are ultimately accountable to democratic institutions, legitimising their authority.

Table 5.2: Four forms of central bank independence

Deutsche Bundesbank	Reserve Bank of New Zealand	Bank of England	Federal Reserve System (USA)
Framework			
Statutory independence (sets target and rates).	Sets rates to achieve target. Penalties for failure.	Operational independence (sets rates but not target).	Fully independent but accountable to Congress.
Objectives/target			
'Internal and external price stability' (usually 0–2% inflation/ firm D-mark).	Price stability (0–2% inflation).	Price stability (inflation of 2.5% or less). Supports government growth/jobs policy.	Price stability and maximum employment.
Government powers			
Cannot override without changing law.	Can override in emergency.	Can override in emergency.	Cannot override without change in Fed's terms of reference.
Supervises banks?			
No	Yes	No	Yes
Board/Council			
17 members: 8 from central bank directorate, 9 from the *Lander*.	7–10 members, but mainly to monitor the governor.	9 members 5 from Bank, 4 outsiders.	7-member board/ 12-member Federal Open Market Committee.
Meeting			
Fortnightly; members vote; no minutes.	Governor decides daily; no minutes.	Monthly; one member one vote; minutes published after six weeks.	8 times annually; minutes published.
Head			
Hans Tietmeyer 8-year renewable term.	Donald Brash 5-year rolling term.	Eddie George 5-year renewable term.	Alan Greenspan 4-year renewable term.

Source: *Sunday Times*, 11 May 1997.

The Bank of England

The Bank of England pioneered many of the functions of modern central banking. From its outset in 1694, it acted as the government's bank, raising money to meet its requirements. In the nineteenth century, it acquired a monopoly over the note issue, assumed the role of lender of last resort to the banking system, developed the supervision of the money markets and the regulation of banks, and acted as guardian of the gold standard, the bedrock of the international financial system. The Bank was closely associated with the policy of restoring the pound to the gold standard after World War I, and its prestige suffered when sterling was forced off the gold standard in 1931.

Nationalised in 1946, the Bank at that time became formally subservient to the Treasury, though in practice retaining considerable autonomous authority. From the 1940s to the 1990s, its principal responsibilities were: advising the government on monetary policy and putting its decisions into practice; the provision of funds to government by means of advances and the issue of Treasury bills and bonds; and the administration of UK exchange controls until their abolition in 1979. It also acted as the City's spokesman to government, and vice versa. It communicated with a broad audience through the publication of an annual report and the highly regarded *Quarterly Bulletin*, and through the public pronouncements of the governor and other key officials.

The Bank was also responsible for the supervision and support of the banking system. On occasion, it took action to rescue troubled institutions, notable episodes being the Barings crisis of 1890 and the secondary-banking crisis of 1974–75. However, when Barings went bust for a second time in February 1995, because of the massive losses sustained by a derivatives trader, the Bank of England judged that there was no threat to the financial system as a whole and did not step in to save the firm. The Bank's handling of two other episodes, the failure of Johnson Matthey Bankers in 1984 and the collapse of the Bank of Credit and Commerce International in 1991, attracted considerable criticism. Eventually in May 1997, the Bank's responsibilities for the regulation of the banking system were transferred to a new regulatory body, the Financial Services Authority (see Chapter 6).

The removal of the Bank's responsibility for bank supervision was part of a broader redefinition of its role by the new Labour Party administration in the UK from May 1997. Even more significant was the bestowal of operational independence – the power to set UK interest rates with responsibility to deliver price stability, defined as inflation of 2.5 per cent or less. A new nine-member Monetary Policy Committee was established to determine interest rates, composed of both Bank officials and outsiders. Modelled closely on the US Federal Reserve Open Market Committee, it meets monthly for two-day working sessions. The minutes of its deliberations are published six weeks later. 'It's great for the Bank's economists – their lives have suddenly become more meaningful,' comments a former Bank official. 'They are working their socks off, not least because they are worried about getting it wrong.'[4]

Yet another change was the transfer of the Bank's traditional responsibility for managing the government's debt to the Treasury. But the Bank retains a dealing capability for other customers and to manage short-term interest rates. It also controls part of the UK foreign exchange reserves, which it can use in support of its monetary policy objectives. To run the new system, the post of deputy-governor was split into two. One deputy-governor has responsibility for financial stability, in other words monitoring the health of the financial system and judging when it is threatened by problems in particular institutions; the other has responsibility for monetary policy.

The US Federal Reserve System (Fed)

The US system of central banking, established in 1913, comprises a policy-making body, the Federal Reserve Board in Washington, and a set of operational entities – 12 regional banks, 25 branches and 11 offices. The Federal Reserve acts as the federal government's agent in tax collection and runs the national debt. Federal Reserve Notes form the US currency.

The regional federal reserve banks act as central banks for their regions, providing a range of functions including lender of last resort, which is of particular importance given the fragmented US banking system (three-quarters of the country's 14,000 banks being unitary institutions). Commercial banks are required to hold reserves in the regional reserve banks, which also provide clearing facilities. The Federal Reserve Bank of New York is much the most important of the regional banks.

The Federal Reserve Board in Washington comprises a chairman, appointed for four years by the US President with Senate approval, and seven governors appointed for fourteen years. US monetary policy is determined by the Federal Open Market Committee, composed of the seven members of the Board plus five regional reserve-bank presidents on a rotating basis. The Fed has a high degree of independence, both defining the monetary target and setting interest rates, although its remit is not only price stability but also maximum employment. Its power is counterbalanced by the checks of transparency and accountability. The minutes of the monthly meetings are published, as is the data used in policy making. The Fed is accountable to Congress, the chairman making regular appearances before congressional committees, where he is quizzed by politicians. And Congress has oversight of the Fed's budget and regulatory activities.

Alan Greenspan, Fed chairman since 1987, has achieved a legendary status for his sagacity and capable management of the US economy. His pronouncements moved markets, notably his celebrated remark in December 1996 that equity prices were overvalued due to 'irrational exuberance'. 'He has a remarkable grasp of the detail of the economy,' says a former member of the Fed's Board of Governors, 'that enables him to spot dangers almost the moment before they appear.'[5] 'A national treasure,' eulogises an awe-struck US senator.[6]

Germany's Deutsche Bundesbank

The German central bank is based in Frankfurt-am-Main. Established originally in 1875, it assumed its present form as the pivotal institution of a system of regional central banks (*Lander*) in 1957. Responsibility for German monetary policy is vested in the Bundesbank Council (*Zentralbankrat*), a 17-strong body comprising eight representatives of the *Lander* and nine politicians or academics. The diversity of the membership contributes to the autonomy of the Bundesbank. The powerful president is appointed by the government for a term of eight years, as are the members of the *Zentralbankrat*.

The German system confers strong independence, but puts little emphasis on openness and accountability. The central bank publishes little information that really explains its actions. It is not directly accountable even to the German government or parliament. Yet it is highly regarded at home and abroad for its competence and Germany's low inflation record.

Germany's monetary arrangements reflect the historical experience of two periods of hyperinflation this century and the subordination of the Reichsbank – the predecessor of the Bundebank – to the Nazis during the 1930s. The Bundesbank's constitution explicitly defines the maintenance of stable prices as its primary task. Operating with a high degree of independence from the German government, it determines the principal elements of German monetary policy. Key interest rates are set at the fortnightly meetings of the *Zentralbankrat*.

But even in Germany, the central bank is not always able to resist political pressures. In 1990, during the process of German reunification, a dispute arose when the government proposed monetary union with East Germany on unrealistic terms. When the German Chancellor Helmut Kohl went ahead despite the bank's objections, the highly regarded Bundesbank president Karl Otto Pöhl took early retirement. Another row blew up in May 1997, when the German finance minister announced that the country's gold reserves were to be revalued, generating a windfall gain for the government of perhaps as much as DM60 billion.[7] Painlessly, without having to cut spending or raise taxes, Germany would as a result be able to meet the Maastricht criterion for EMU entry limiting public deficits to no more than 3 per cent of gross domestic product. The central bank condemned the scheme as 'an intervention in the Bundesbank's autonomous right to draw up and present accounts, and thus its independence.'[8] German public opinion was outraged by the attack on the country's most respected institution, and the politicians' creative accounting. Eventually a compromise was achieved whereby the minister withdrew the proposal, but revaluation at a later date was conceded.

The Bank of Japan

The Bank of Japan, established in 1885, acts as lender of last resort, the government's fiscal agent, and oversees the operation of the main market interest rates. It also has a supervisory role in the securities industry, but the commercial banks are regulated by the Ministry of Finance's banking bureau. Moreover, the Bank's authority over monetary policy is limited, since it is the Japan Ministry of Finance that initiates changes in interest rates and the ministry's approval is required for alterations in the reserve ratios set for the commercial banks.

The Bank of Japan is run by a seven-man governing body, comprising the governor, four representatives from the private banking sector, and two from government: the Ministry of Finance and the Economic Planning Agency. Independence is not a characteristic, the bank acting in conformity with government instructions. Indeed, for many years it obligingly lowered interest rates ahead of elections, thereby manipulating the 'feel-good factor' to the electoral benefit of the politicians from the ruling Liberal Democratic Party.

Banque de France

From its foundation in 1800, the Banque de France was an instrument of the state, its nationalisation in 1946 merely formalising the relationship. The governor of the bank is appointed for five years, but unlike most independent central bank governors, he has no guaranteed security of tenure.

The bank announces interest rate changes, but only with the agreement of the finance minister of France. Since 1984, the function of regulating the banking system has been the responsibility of the *Commission Banquaire*, a body independent of the central bank but chaired by the governor. This body formulates policy, the Banque de France implements it.

The Maastricht Treaty of 1992 requires participants in monetary union to bestow full independence on their central banks. In 1994, the formulation and implementation of monetary policy became the responsibility of the Banque de France's Monetary Policy Council, which is forbidden from seeking or receiving instructions from the government.

European Central Bank

Economic and Monetary Union in Europe necessitates the creation of a new institution to supervise the single currency, the euro (see Chapter 9). The first step was the creation of the European Monetary Institute (EMI) in January 1994, a forerunner institution. It was located in Frankfurt to reassure German voters who would ultimately be required to forsake the Deutschmark. From its offices in the Eurotower building, the EMI undertook the task of planning the introduction of the European single currency over the years 1999–2002.

The European Central Bank (ECB) came into existence in its fully-fledged form during 1998. Based on the Bundesbank, independence is its hallmark. Not only does it define its own inflation target and set interest rates to meet its objective, but it is also uniquely insulated from political influence. First, it has no obligation to publish any meaningful account of its deliberations or justification of its actions. Second, its mandate, enshrined in the Maastricht Treaty, is almost impossible to challenge or change. Third, it has little real accountability, either to elected governments, via the Council of Ministers, or to the European Parliament. It is plain that the ECB will take a tough line against inflation, whatever Europe's politicians may want.

The ECB's key bodies are the Executive Board and the Governing Council. The Executive Board comprises the president, vice-president and six members, all appointed for eight-year terms. The first president is Wim Duisenberg, a former head of Holland's central bank and Dutch finance minister. The Governing Council is composed of the members of the Executive Board and the central bank governors of all participating countries. Monetary policy decisions are taken by simple majority.

With the start of European monetary union, the ECB has the sole right to authorise the issue of banknotes within the EU, but it shares the process of issue with the national central banks. Member states may issue national coins, subject to ECB approval.

REGIONAL DEVELOPMENT BANKS

Inspired by the example of the World Bank, a number of regional development banks have been established to focus on the promotion of development projects in particular parts of the world. This was in response to local political demands for institutions with stronger regional roots, both in personnel and expertise. Their organisational and financial structures are modelled on the World Bank. Initially, membership tended to be restricted to countries of the region, but later non-indigenous subscribers to capital became welcome too.

The bulk of the subscribed capital has not been called-up, but by virtue of being committed can be used to back fund-raising by bond issues in the Western capital markets, which are the principal sources of the funds deployed by these institutions.

European Investment Bank (EIB)

The Luxembourg-based EIB is the EU's regional development bank. It has a staff of 800.

In the 1950s, Continental politicians decided to establish their own development bank because they regarded the World Bank as an American-dominated agent of the US State Department. The EIB was an integral part of the 1958 Treaty of Rome that established the European Union, the bank's purpose being to promote economic development especially in the more backward areas of the continent of Europe. The stature of the EIB echoes the articles of agreement of the World Bank, and its position relative to the EU is analogous to that of the World Bank and the United Nations.

The EIB's mandate is to provide loans and loan guarantees for projects in the less developed regions of the EU (plus some ex-French colonies in Africa) to promote European economic integration and development. It is the world's largest multilateral lender, enjoying the highest credit rating available and allowing it to provide finance on advantageous terms. Usually, the EIB provides matching funds that finance around a quarter of the capital cost of projects. Funds are granted on a medium-term basis of seven to twelve years. Overall, the EIB is involved in backing some 4 per cent of Europe's gross capital investment, although in the poorer regions the proportion is as high as 12 per cent. Since the early 1990s, the EIB has been at the centre of the EU's efforts to reduce unemployment.

Inter-American Development Bank (IDB)

The Washington-based IDB was established in 1959 on the initiative of the Organisation of American States. Initially it focused on public infrastructure projects, especially roadbuilding and hydro-electric plants, but in the 1980s and 1990s it has shifted towards supporting private projects, particularly in agriculture and export-oriented undertakings. With a capital of $100 billion, it is a larger provider of capital to the countries of Latin America than the World Bank. In the early 1990s, there was a question mark over the IDB's future for two reasons: first, a long-standing dispute between the US, the principal shareholder, and the Latin American borrowers; and second, the abundance of private investment into the region. But when the private capital flows dried up because of the Mexican crisis of 1995, the whole hemisphere was reminded of the continuing usefulness of the IDB. Staff numbers at the bank are currently around 1,500.

African Development Bank (AfDB)

The AfDB – also known by its French acronym BAD (Banque Afrique de Développement) – was established in 1963. Headquartered in Abidjan in francophone Ivory Coast, it has a staff of about 1,000.

The AfDB, which has a capital of $23 billion (a quarter of that of the IDB) has had a troubled history. By 1995 it was close to collapse. 'Morale is as low as I have ever known it to be,' commented an insider. 'The bank has lost direction, it is demoralised, and the entire lending machinery has come to a grinding halt.'[9] The bank survived that crisis, but the challenges it faces are formidable.

Asian Development Bank (ADB)

The ADB was established in 1966, with its headquarters in Manila, capital of the Philippines. Today the bank has a capital of $47 billion and a staff of 1,700. Its sphere of activity is the emerging countries of the Asia–Pacific region, currently 38 nations including China, which joined in 1986.

The largest shareholders in the bank are Japan and the US, though Australia and New Zealand are also important contributors to capital. Lending activity focuses on energy projects, transportation, agriculture and industry, with Asian governments being the biggest borrowers.

Indonesia has been the largest recipient of funds, taking one-third of all loans. An associated institution, the Asian Development Fund (ADF) grants loans on concessional terms to the poorest countries, such as Bangladesh, Nepal and Sri Lanka.

Recent years have seen calls for greater support for the private sector. There has also been friction between the US and Japan, and complaints that Japanese firms win a disproportionate number of the projects financed by the ADB. The ADB has deliberately fostered the development and integration of Asian capital markets, beginning in 1991 when it placed a $300 million issue simultaneously in Hong Kong, Singapore and Taiwan. More recently, it has been promoting the development of a clearing system between the Asian securities markets to establish an integrated regional secondary market with depth and liquidity.

European Bank for Reconstruction and Development (EBRD)

The London-based EBRD was established in 1991 to assist the economic development of the emerging democracies of Central and Eastern Europe following the collapse of Communism. It operates in 25 countries and has a staff of 750.

The ERBD got off to a controversial start under its publicity-seeking, free-spending first president, Jacques Attali. Attali quit in summer 1993, having incurred the wrath of the bank's international backers for lavish expenditure on its headquarters – including a swathe of Carrara marble that earned it the nickname 'the glistening bank' – while its lending activities fell far short of expectations. He was succeeded by Jacques de Larosière, a dour and distinguished career central banker, formerly managing director of the IMF and governor of the Banque de France. 'When Attali went, the shareholders wanted someone who would come in and clean out the Augean stables,' comments an insider. 'De Larosière . . . found out what was annoying them, and made sure that whatever was getting up their noses stopped.'[10] Under de Larosière, costs were cut back and the EBRD's lending grew rapidly, almost doubling between 1994 and 1995. The shareholders demonstrated their satisfaction by agreeing soon after to double the capital to $16 billion.

The EBRD acts with partners, such as banks, multinational corporations or local companies, putting up on average only one-third of a project's capital. It lends on commercial terms, and has sometimes been criticised for excessive caution. 'We are a bank and we have to behave as a bank,' counters de Larosière.[11] 'We have a profit and loss account. We are judged by the markets. We have to borrow on the markets. We also have to look at the years where we will have to put up provisions for risks. So the bank has to be run like a bank.'

Despite the new discipline, controversy didn't go away. The bank was criticised for allegedly favouring French companies and promoting French interests. Particularly controversial was an $800 million advance to build a nuclear power plant at Mochovce in Slovakia, its largest loan at the time, to a French contractor. It has also been reproached for secrecy and a remote management style. 'Many of the bank's difficulties stem from the schizophrenia of a public-sector institution trying to behave like a private investment bank,' comments *Euromoney*.[12] De Larosière stresses the EBRD's path-breaking work in assisting the former Communist countries. 'There is a vision,' he says. 'It is one of the most important challenges for the West to help that part of the world transform its basic habits and integrate into the world trade system.'[13]

ORGANISATION FOR ECONOMIC CO-OPERATION AND DEVELOPMENT (OECD)

The Paris-based OECD has been described as 'the world's most influential think-tank'.[14] The 2000-strong staff produce a range of highly regarded publications: special studies on topical international economic and financial issues; respected reviews of the economic outlook of member countries; regular statistical series that, along with those produced by the BIS and the IMF, provide the bedrock numbers for international financial analysis. The purpose of these thoughts and reports is to assist members to develop policies so as to deliver the economic dream scenario – growth, high employment, and financial stability. The OECD is also useful as a discussion forum for the industrial countries, especially regarding international monetary issues and assistance for developing countries.

The OECD has its origins in an earlier body, the Organisation for European Economic Co-operation (OEEC), established in Paris in 1947 to promote European reconstruction and to administer the distribution of US 'Marshall Aid' in the years 1948–52. In the 1950s, it focused on assisting the process of dismantling restrictions on inter-European trade and payments, and the movement of labour and capital. The OEEC became the OECD in 1961, when Canada and the US joined as full members. The new organisation assumed a worldwide perspective, adopting the economic development of less developed countries and the promotion of global multilateral trade as objectives. 'Globalisation is extending economic interdependence,' comments OECD secretary general Donald Johnston, adding that 'this will bring peace and stability.'[15]

The 1990s have seen a rush of new applicants to join the OECD. At the beginning of the decade there were 23 members – 17 Western European industrial countries plus Australia, Canada, Japan, New Zealand, Turkey and the US. Mexico, in 1993, became the first newly industrialised country to join, and the Czech Republic, in 1995, the first former Communist state. Four other new member have since been admitted and applications are on the table from Russia, Slovakia, Estonia and Argentina. 'Some fear,' comments the *Financial Times*, 'that this expansion is making decision-making more difficult within the organisation and is diluting what the OECD stands for.'[16]

THE GROUP OF SEVEN AND OTHER DISCUSSION FORUMS

In the 1950s and 1960s, which was the era of fixed exchange rates, the international financial institutions – especially the IMF and the OECD – were the forums for the discussion of international financial and monetary issues. The BIS fulfilled this function for the central banks, becoming increasingly important in the 1960s when the US joined the Basle meetings.

As more and more countries became members of these international institutions, those with similar interests began to convene in smaller and more informal groups. In contrast to the Bretton Woods institutions and their spin-offs, these groups have usually operated without a permanent secretariat and are convened as required. The most important of these forums are the Group of Ten, the Group of Twenty-Four, and the Group of Seven.

The Group of Ten (G10)

The G10 had its origins in 1962 in a meeting convened by the US to increase the funds available to the IMF by the General Agreement on Borrowing (GAB). The nine signatories to the GAB undertook to provide a minimum of $100 million, a hurdle high enough to elimiante all but the major industrial countries as intended. This grouping became the G10 in 1964 when Japan became a member. Switzerland became the eleventh member in 1983, but the name was left unchanged.

The G10 was an important forum for ministerial meetings in the 1960s, but from the 1970s it was increasingly bypassed in favour of still smaller groups of the most important industrial countries. Yet the G10 remains a significant grouping for meetings of officials, notably the monthly consultations amongst G10 central bank governors at Basle.

The Group of Twenty-Four (G24)

In 1964, the developing countries established their own grouping, the Group of Seventy-Seven (G77). The G24, a sub-group of the G77 specialising in financial matters, was set-up in 1972 to counterbalance the influence of the G10 amongst international institutions. The G24 is composed of eight representatives each from Africa, Asia and Latin America. In the 1970s the G24 was a significant pressure group, but in the 1980s and 1990s its influence has been minimal.

Also known as the Group of Twenty-Four is the committee established in 1989 to co-ordinate assistance from the industrial nations to the countries of Central and Eastern Europe as they move to market economies. Chaired by the European Commission, it comprises members of the OECD, with representatives of the World Bank, IMF and EBRD in attendance.

The Group of Seven (G7)

The G7, the most important of the discussion forums, had its origins at a meeting of the finance ministers and central bank governors of France, Germany, Japan, the UK, and the US in 1967. The purpose was to formulate co-ordinated measures to shore up the Bretton Woods system, but to no avail. The meetings shifted to head-of-state level in 1975 when the five, plus Italy, met to discuss financial and economic issues at Rambouillet, France. The following year, Canada was invited too, and the gathering became the G7. Since 1977, the president of the European Commission has also attended. With Russia in attendance it is called the Group of Eight – G8.

The G7 took over from the G10 as the leading financial and economic grouping in the 1970s. In 1986, the G7 was put on a semi-formal basis, a development described by US treasury secretary James Baker as 'the biggest thing since the switch to floating exchange rates.' The following year saw the Louvre Accord, in which the G7 members undertook to curb the rise of the dollar.

Since then, the finance ministers of the G7 have held regular meetings to discuss international financial issues, and the G7 has become the leading forum for the co-ordination of policy. Statements issued after their get-togethers indicate their joint view of appropriate exchange-rate relationships and responses to developments. The decisions of the G7 have crucial influence on the IMF, despite its much larger membership.

Naturally, this arouses suspicion and resentment on the part of excluded countries and the international financial institutions; but the G7 is nevertheless an entrenched political reality. The challenge is to develop effective co-ordination with the broad-based international institutions, especially the IMF, that possess the means of implementing its proposals while carrying other countries along too.

In a Nutshell

The international financial institutions provide the framework within which international financial markets and firms operate. First and foremost are the International Monetary Fund and the World Bank. The IMF is a monetary institution, whose purpose is the stabilisation of the international financial system. The World Bank is a development institution, focusing on the promotion of economic development in developing countries. A variety of regional development banks provide services similar to the World Bank for their regions: the European Investment Bank; the Inter-American Development Bank; the African Development Bank; the Asian Development Bank; and the European Bank for Reconstruction and Development.

Central banks act as the government's banker and as the 'lender of last resort' to the banking system. 'Independent' central banks have autonomous powers to set interest rates to achieve price stability. The central banks of the US and Germany have been independent from political direction for many years. More recently, Britain, France and other European Union countries have bestowed independence on their central banks. The European Central Bank is a highly independent institution.

Since the 1960s, countries with similar levels of development have held non-institutionalised meetings to discuss mutual interests and to influence international economic policy. The most important of these groupings are the Group of Seven and the Group of Ten amongst the industrialised countries, and the Group of Twenty-Four amongst the developing countries.

FURTHER READING

Bakker, A. F. P., *International Financial Institutions* (London, Longman, 1996)

Broughton, James M., and Sarwar Lateef, K., (eds), *Fifty Years after Bretton Woods: The Future of the IMF and World Bank* (Washington D.C., I.M.F., 1995)

Dean, Marjorie, and Pringle, Robert, *The Central Banks* (London, Hamish Hamilton, 1994)

Marsh, David, *The Bundesbank: The Bank that Rules Europe* (London Heinemann, 1992)

Richardson, Richard W., and Haralz, Jonas H., *Moving to the Market: The World Bank in Transition* (New York, 1994)

Roberts, Richard, and Kynaston, David, (eds), *The Bank of England: Money, Power and Influence 1694–1994* (Oxford OUP, 1995)

NOTES AND REFERENCES

In the list below for this chapter, any reference to an author alone should be taken to be a reference to his/her work in 'Further reading' above.

1 *The Economist*, 10 January 1998
2 'Time to roll out a new model', *The Economist*, 1 March 1997
3 *Financial Times*, 4 October 1996
4 *Financial Times*, 4 August 1997
5 *Financial Times*, 11 August 1997
6 *Financial Times*, 11 August 1997
7 EMU Guide in *Financial Times*, 28 May 1997
8 *Euromoney*, August 1997
9 'Time to scrap the AfDB?', *Euromoney*, May 1995
10 'De Larosière's new Banque de France', *Euromoney*, April 1996
11 *Financial Times*, 29 December 1995
12 'De Larosière's new Banque de France', *Euromoney*, April 1996
13 *Financial Times*, 29 December 1995
14 *Financial Times*, 21 February 1997
15 *Financial Times*, 21 February 1997
16 *Financial Times*, 21 February 1997

CHAPTER 6

London – A Global Financial Centre

INTRODUCTION

International financial centres are cities that specialise in the provision of international financial services. Their function is to intermediate international financial flows. This is undertaken by the financial markets and the financial firms located in them. The set of financial institutions present in a financial centre determines the range of financial activities conducted there.

Why do financial firms cluster in financial centres? The reason is the powerful pull factors that affect the financial services industry, which result in a concentration of international financial service providers in a pecking order of centres: global centres; regional centres; and offshore centres. There is also a fourth type of financial centre, a domestic financial centre, serving a local client base, although today almost every financial services firm has some sort of international connection. Although, in theory, modern communications allow financial firms to operate from anywhere, there is as yet no evidence that international financial centres are an endangered species.

The four types of centre are differentiated thus:

- *global financial centres* provide a wide range of services, especially wholesale financial markets, to a worldwide clientele. There are three global financial centres: London, New York and Tokyo. Each is the biggest centre in its time zone
- *regional international financial centres* supply financial services to a region (e.g. Europe or Asia) and intermediate the financial flows from the global centres, other regional centres and domestic centres. The principal regional financial centres are: in Europe – Amsterdam,

Frankfurt, Luxembourg, Milan, Madrid, Paris and Zurich; in Asia–Pacific – Hong Kong, Singapore and Sydney, with Manila, Seoul, Shanghai and Taipei growing rapidly; in North America – Chicago, Boston, Los Angeles and Toronto. Bahrain, Rio and Johannesburg are also significant regional financial centres

- *offshore financial centres* are financial entrepôts that intermediate international flows having little connection with the financial system of the country in which the financial centre is located. Usually the term applies to places such as the Cayman Islands, the Bahamas, the Netherlands Antilles and the Channel Islands. But the definition also embraces much of the international financial activity conducted in Luxembourg and Switzerland, and even London in relation to the euromarkets; occasionally, reference is made to offshore business in such contexts. See Box 6.1 for a fuller description

- *domestic financial centres* serve national or provincial financial requirements, focusing on retail services and bilateral trade between the centre's own economy and other economies

THE ECONOMICS OF INTERNATIONAL FINANCIAL CENTRES

Why do financial firms and markets concentrate in financial centres? The 'powerful pull factors' mentioned in the previous section are primarily twofold: 'external economies of scale' and 'economies of agglomeration'.

External economies of scale accrue to firms when a positive relationship exists between efficiency and the size of the industry in which they operate – an industry in the current context being a financial centre. There are many reasons why a larger financial centre provides a more advantageous operating environment than a smaller centre. The quality of financial markets – that is, their liquidity and efficiency – is strongly correlated with the scale of operations. These are highly desirable features, meaning lower dealing costs and diminished likelihood of market failure.

Furthermore, the larger number and greater range of activities of other financial firms produces a more innovative environment, which may generate new business opportunities and demand from other practitioners. It may also stimulate competition, perhaps promoting efficiency and probably engendering keener pricing, which will persuade clients to place their business with firms based in a larger financial centre rather than a smaller one.

Economies of agglomeration accrue to financial firms from the presence of concentrations of complementary activities in financial centres. The ready availability of the services of, for instance, commercial lawyers, accountants, specialist printers, information technology experts and public relations consultants enhances the competitiveness of financial firms and the attractiveness of location in a particular centre. The bigger the centre, the more extensive and more varied the concentration of complementary activities.

The logical outcome of the effects of the dynamics of external economies of scale and economies of agglomeration is that all activity should concentrate in a single financial centre. But centralisation also generates *diseconomies* of scale, such as crowding and congestion. It may also raise costs, through competitive bidding for scarce resources such as prime locations or skilled personnel. For retail financial services, centralisation may even increase information costs because of the distance from clients. Smaller domestic centres, where local firms are easily in touch with clients, can enjoy a competitive advantage in retail financial services. Moreover, in the real world, political factors and regulatory barriers and incentives exist that distort the unfettered operation of the centralising economic forces. So regional and domestic centres continue to exist.

Above all else, the crucial factor for success for financial firms is *information*. The quantity and quality of information is vital for the competitiveness of financial firms and, other things being equal, new firms will locate in financial centres with superior information flows, while centres with inferior information flows will lose financial firms, either through failure due to uncompetitiveness or through firms' migration to other centres. Superior access to up-to-date and high-quality information has traditionally been the most significant external economy provided by location in a financial centre.

ESSENTIALS FOR SUCCESSFUL INTERNATIONAL FINANCIAL CENTRES

There is a variety of political, economic and financial requisites for a city to function as a major international financial centre. Ten essentials are:

- *peace and political stability*: war is the greatest catastrophe that can befall an international financial centre (see Box 7.1, Chapter 7)
- *rule of law*: a sound legal system based on the independence and

integrity of the judiciary, commanding international respect and confidence

- *good communications*: efficient and effective information flows and communications between markets and market participants
- *a skilled labour force*: a substantial supply of high-quality specialist skilled labour
- *financial markets*: a broad range of liquid, efficient and resilient markets
- *financial instruments*: a sophisticated set of financial instruments (for instance, a variety of bonds and shares) with which to conduct business
- *prudential supervision*: a regulatory system that generates confidence and stability
- *complementary services*: a developed range of legal, accounting, information, computing and other complementary services
- *a market economy*: freedom for firms and individuals to save, invest, work and consume
- *an urban infrastructure*: a sound urban infrastructure, especially transportation for moving people and paper

There is a further set of factors favourable to promoting the prosperity of international financial centres, though they are not universal features. Ten favourable factors are:

- no discrimination against foreign firms in favour of domestic firms
- low taxation
- regulatory light-handedness
- a currency used for international transactions
- the headquarters of large multinational corporations
- convenient time-zone overlaps for trading
- a political and administrative capital city
- a cosmopolitan culture
- the location of a central bank
- a widespread command of the English language

LONDON AS A GLOBAL FINANCIAL CENTRE

Introduction
London, where the financial services industry is often referred to as 'the City' – the name of the traditional banking district – has been a leading

international financial centre for several centuries. Today it is the world's foremost international financial centre, as well as being the focus for the UK banking and securities business. London's scale of activity and world rank amongst international financial centres by a variety of yardsticks is shown in Table 6.1. In international banking it ranks first, both in cross-border lending and the presence of foreign banks. It is also the leading location for foreign-exchange trading. London ranks second as a centre for derivatives trading (behind Chicago). It is second to Tokyo as a location for fund management. Both New York and Tokyo have larger stock market capitalisations, reflecting the scale of their domestic economies, but London is much the most important centre for trading international equities – shares of non-UK companies listed in London as well as on their domestic market.

Table 6.1: London as an international financial centre: some indicators

	Volume/number	World rank
International banking		
Cross-border bank lending[a]		
(UK 1996)	$1459 billion	1
Foreign banks present[b]		
(London 1995) branch, subsidiary, rep. office etc.	536	1
Capital market		
Equity market capitalisation[c]		
(UK 1995)	$1407 billion	3
International equities turnover[d]		
(UK 1996)	$860 billion	1
Asset management		
Institutional equity holdings[e]		
(London 1995)	$1016 billion	2
Money markets		
Foreign exchange turnover[f]		
(UK 1995) net daily turnover	$465 billion	1
Derivatives contracts[g]		
(LIFFE 1997) average monthly volume	17 million	2

Sources:
[a] IMF, *International Financial Statistics* (Washington D.C., August 1997).
[b] Jao, Y.C., *Hong Kong as an International Financial Centre* (Hong Kong, City University of Hong Kong Press, 1997).
[c] *Emerging Stock Markets Factbook 1996* (Washington D.C., International Finance Corporation, 1996)
[d] *London Stock Exchange Fact File* (London, London Stock Exchange, 1997).
[e] British Invisibles, *UK Financial Trends & World Invisible Trade 1997* (London, 1997).
[f] Bank for International Settlements, *Triennial Survey of Foreign Exchange* (Basle, BIS, 1995).
[g] Liffe, *World Volumes* (London, August 1997).

Some 310,000 people work in finance and insurance in London, fewer than the 443,000 in New York or the 512,000 in Tokyo, but a higher proportion are engaged in international activities. On the broader occupational definition, namely 'finance and other business services', the total of those employed is 617,000, only a few less than the total population of Frankfurt.[1] The physical place known as 'the City' – roughly the square mile around the Bank of England – has in the last few years been unable to accommodate the demand for space for the industry. As a result, a new financial node has grown up at Canary Wharf, a massive modern development in a derelict dockland zone nearby. In addition, other banks have relocated to the West End of London, cheaper rentals being the major incentive.

Not only is the City of London (in the financial sense) an important employer, but it also makes a major contribution to the UK's prosperity through its contribution to the balance of payments. In 1996, the net overseas earnings of the UK financial sector totalled £22.7 billion ($37 billion), almost double the £11.9 billion recorded in 1990. The largest contributors were banks (£7.1 billion), insurance institutions (£6.1 billion), pension funds (£2.3 billion) and securities dealers (£2.2 billion).[2] 'Further growth in [the City's] overseas earnings reflects the consolidation and strengthening of London's leading position in many financial markets,' comments Duncan McKenzie of British Invisibles, a body responsible for promoting the development of the UK financial sevices sector. 'Financial services are increasingly important to both the UK and world economy – and the UK is well positioned to build on its present strengths.'[3]

The development of London as an international financial centre
Having surrendered its leading international role to New York after World War II, the City staged a remarkable recovery in the 1960s and 1970s by establishing itself as the focus of the euromarkets. But by the early 1980s, there was concern in the City and in government that London's position was being undermined by an increasingly archaic set of institutional arrangements for the securities industry. Following the example of New York, which had deregulated securities trading in 1975, a process known as 'Big Bang' was begun in 1983. This involved dismantling restrictions on the ownership of Stock Exchange firms by banks, and the introduction of price competition by the abolition of fixed commissions in securities trading. By the end of the operation in October 1986, the City had been transformed. Gone were the plethora of independent British brokers and market makers trading on a tiny capital base. The City was now the stalking ground of the large integrated

international banks and investment houses, and London was strategically positioned to benefit from the trend towards the concentration of international financial services into the hands of a set of worldwide players operating principally out of the global financial centres.

The 1980s and 1990s saw the rapid expansion of City activities – international business especially but domestic business too. Over the decade 1985–94, the UK equity market's captitalisation rose more than threefold despite the crash of October 1987, the bond market grew by two-and-a-half times, and the money market doubled in size (see Table 6.2).

Table 6.2: UK securities market value, 1985/94

	1985 £ bn	1994 £ bn	% inc. 1985/94
Equity market	245	775	316
Bond market	232	581	250
Money market	91	187	205

Source: Bank of Japan, *Comparative Economic and Financial Statistics: Japan and Other Major Countries*, 1996.

The principal activities conducted in London as an international financial centre are:

- international banking
- investment banking
- international bonds
- equities
- foreign exchange
- futures and options
- asset management
- bullion
- insurance
- marine services

The UK's share of some of these international financial markets is shown in Table 6.3.

Table 6.3: International financial markets, 1996

	% share of world market				
	UK	US	Japan	France	Germany
Cross-border lending	17	8	14	7	7
Foreign equities turnover	60	35	1	1	2
Foreign exchange dealing	30	16	10	4	5
Derivatives turnover, exchange traded	16	36	10	5	4
Derivatives turnover, over-the-counter	27	20	12	10	5
Insurance premium income, marine	25	9	14	6	9
Insurance premium income, aviation	35	24	3	15	4
International bonds, primary market	60				
International bonds, secondary market	75				

Source: British Invisibles, *UK Financial Trends and World Invisible Trade, 1997.*

International banking

London is the leading international banking centre, consistently under-taking about one-sixth of total world foreign bank lending during the 1990s (Table 6.3). Estimates suggest that annual revenues of London-based banks from international lending totalled £1.6 billion in the mid-1990s.[4]

London's revival as an international banking centre began in the late 1950s, when it became the focus of the burgeoning eurodollar market. The eurodollar market's location in London was no accident: it was adroitly encouraged by the Bank of England, and some leading London bankers, such as Sir George Bolton of the Bank of London and South America, who were quick to spot the market's potential. US bankers also made innovative contributions. It was the US banks that pioneered the introduction of the eurodollar certificates of deposit in 1965, a crucial money-market development. For the US banks, the absence of reserve requirements and a sympathetic regulatory system made the City 'a very warm place for doing business,' as the chairman of Chase Manhattan put it.[5]

Foreign banks flocked to London to participate in the rapidly growing euromarkets. In the 1960s, the number of foreign banks with branches or representative offices in London doubled, rising from 77 to 163. The influx continued in the 1970s and early 1980s, fuelled by the massive deposits placed by the oil-producing countries following the oil price rises of 1974 and 1979; by 1984, some 470 foreign banks were represented in London, more than in any other international financial centre. They became major City employers, staff numbers rising from 9000 in the mid-1960s to 54,000 in 1986.[6]

After a dip in the late 1980s and early 1990s when, in the aftermath of the international stock market crash of 1987 and the problems of the Japanese financial sector, departures outnumbered new arrivals, the increase resumed in the mid-1990s. The 1997 total (of branches, subsidiaries and representative offices) was a record 561.[7] Russian banks were a substantial contingent of the new arrivals. Migrations from other centres, for instance the transfer of the overseas headquarters of US bank Prudential Basche International from Luxembourg to London, were regarded as significant votes of confidence in the City as Europe's leading money hub. In 1997, staff employed by overseas banks in London totalled 72,000.[8]

The influx of foreign banks into London in the 1960s and 1970s was led by US banks, which dominated eurodollar business. In 1959, seven US banks had a presence in London, with combined deposits of less than $1 billion;[9] by 1975, the number had grown to 55, with deposits of $70 billion, and in the mid-1980s more than 70 US banks were active in London. The number declined slightly in the 1990s, due to amalgamations and the withdrawal from international business of some US regional banks. Nevertheless, the US banks collectively employed 17,000 staff in London in 1997, the largest employers being Citibank with 5,000, JP Morgan with 3,000, and Chase Manhattan with 2,000.[10]

Some Continental European banks have had London branches since the nineteenth century. The 1970s saw a rapid increase in their number, trebling from 50 to 150 over the decade. Expansion continued in the 1980s at a slower rate but accelerated again in the 1990s; in 1997, 249 European banks had a presence in London, more than from any other continent. A growing number of Continental banks have expanded their investment banking operations in London, especially their asset management, corporate finance, fixed income and derivatives activities. The Continental banks with the largest presence in London are Deutsche Bank, with 5,000 staff, Credit Suisse and UBS with around 4,000 each, Dresdner Kleinwort Benson, 2,500, Paribas, 1,500, and ING Barings and Société Générale, some 1,500 each.[11]

The City is the premier location for the European bases of Asian and other non-EU financial institutions. Japanese banks set the pattern, London becoming the largest centre for their international business outside Japan itself in the 1980s. In 1975, 13 per cent of Japanese banks' international assets were booked in London; by 1990, this had doubled to

26 per cent, constituting 36 per cent of all international lending out of the City.[12] However, the problems besetting Japanese banks from the early 1990s prompted some of them to retrench on their international ambitions by closing their London branches or cutting staff. At the end of 1997, Japanese banks nevertheless employed in total some 5,000 London staff, the largest being the Bank of Tokyo-Mitsubishi, 800, Industrial Bank of Japan, 600, and Sumitomo Bank, 300. The 1990s saw new arrivals from the booming Asian tiger economies, especially Korea.

Investment banking

London is Europe's premier investment banking centre. Traditionally, investment banking services were provided by a formidable set of independent merchant banks, notably Barings, Hambros, Kleinworts, Morgan Grenfell, Rothschilds, Schroders and Warburgs (see Chapter 4). In 1989, following an unfortunate involvement in the Guinness scandal (see Chapter 10), Morgan Grenfell was bought by Deutsche Bank. Subsequently, Barings was acquired by Dutch bank ING, Kleinworts by Dresdner Bank and Warburgs by Swiss Bank Corporation, eager for a foothold in London's investment banking business.

Deutsche Bank's decision in 1995 to conduct all of its investment banking operations through its London subsidiary, renamed Deutsche Morgan Grenfell, was a highly significant step. 'This landmark decision,' explained the bank, 'was driven by the globalization of business and the changing demands of clients.'[13] In Frankurt, the decision was greeted with surprise and dismay. 'Here it is seen as a betrayal,' says an executive at a rival German bank in Frankfurt. 'We recognise London is the financial centre for Europe, but Deutsche Bank turned it into a blatant snub.'[14] Where Deutsche Bank led, others followed, with a growing number of EU banks transferring their international banking operations to the City. Announcing that UBS was moving the management of its European regional operations from Zurich to London, chief executive Mathis Cabiallavetta said, 'Basically, London is the predominant financial centre. We are not going to try to fight against market forces.'[15]

For US and Japanese investment banks and securities houses, London is almost invariably the location of their foremost European operations. In October 1997, Nikko Securities announced that it was reorganising its operations to give London rather than Tokyo responsibility for international operations, the first Japanese securities house to do so, and that it was planning to appoint two non-Japanese to the board. 'We have come to the conclusion that with globalization we cannot manage our operations just by Japanese people,' says Nikko president Masashi Kaneto. 'We want to learn from international investment bankers.'[16]

The London offices of the international investment banks provide a range of international corporate advisory services: mergers and acquisitions; privatisations; restructurings; and the raising of capital. These services generate substantial fees: in 1995, a good year, the top-10 London-based investment banking entities were retained in cross-border merger and acquisitions deals worth $215 billion.[17] Many of these deals were intermediated through London and involved European firms repositioning themselves in the European single market. But London-based investment banks also acted as the principal gateway for US corporations and other non-European companies to make acquisitions in the EU, and vice versa.

International bonds

Since the early 1960s, London has been the centre of the eurobond market. This came about largely because of the relatively restrictive regulatory and fiscal conditions in other centres, but also because of the enterprise of London banks – the first ever eurobond, an issue for Autostrade, the Italian motorway authority, was pioneered by London investment bank SG Warburg in 1963.

Structuring eurobond issues requires complex financial engineering, in which the London operations of the international investment banks have developed leading expertise. Market developments of recent years that have spurred activity in London include the growth of eurodollar bonds with attached equity warrants and the swaps market, in which London is second only to New York. Three-fifths of world eurobond primary market activity – that is, raising funds for borrowers by the issue of new bonds – takes place in London, especially eurobonds denominated in US dollars, yen, Canadian dollars and Australian dollars.

London is even more important as the place for trading eurobonds, three-quarters of secondary market activity being located there (see Table 6.3). Much the biggest tranche of the secondary market comprises US dollar eurobonds, of which around three-quarters of turnover occurs in London. Trading in euro-yen bonds is also concentrated in London.

Secondary market trading in bonds issued in other centres in domestic currencies is also a significant activity. Perhaps 5–10 per cent of turnover in the huge US government bond market takes place in London. London has also captured a significant share of trading in German bonds to avoid German turnover tax, particularly German government bonds (Bunds) and Deutschmark corporate bonds. London is also the dominant market for dealing in Deutschmark floating-rate notes. Most of the major German banks have set up capital markets units in London to trade Deutschmark fixed interest securities.

Equities

Equity business focuses on the London Stock Exchange, the world's third-largest exchange by equity capitalisation. The leading London market makers include ABN Amro Hoare Govett, Bankers Trust, Credit Suisse First Boston, Dresdner Kleinwort Benson, HSBC James Capel, Merrill Lynch, SBC Warburg, and UBS.

The London Stock Exchange lists both domestic equities – the shares of UK companies – and international equities – the shares of foreign companies with listings on their domestic market and perhaps other foreign exchanges. London is much the most important exchange for international equities trading, with 60 per cent of global international equities turnover.[18] In 1996, 533 foreign companies had a London listing, compared with 305 in New York, the next centre. Turnover in international equities that were traded on SEAQ International (Stock Exchange Automated Quotations International) in 1996 totalled £520 billion, substantially more than the £370 billion in domestic equities.[19]

The 'Big Bang' changes in 1986 saw a shift from floor trading – face-to-face transactions between brokers and market makers on the Stock Exchange floor – to the screen-based SEAQ system. The SEAQ screens provided price information, but trading was still done between dealers by telephone. In October 1997, a new automated screen-based dealing system, called SETS, was introduced whereby trades in the FTSE 100 companies were able to be placed directly on a computer and matched together. Some hailed the change as 'Big Bang Two' because the resulting profits squeeze promised a further consolidation amongst the players. 'Anyone without clients – and lots of them – is dead,' declared a senior trader on the eve of the change. 'Some firms will try to buy clients by throwing a lot of capital around over the next year or so. For the smaller players, life can only get tougher.'[20]

Foreign exchange

Foreign exchange dealing is an activity in which London has a global pre-eminence, generating in the mid-1990s some $2 billion in revenues for London banking operations, roughly equivalent to revenues for international bank lending.[21] Worldwide, the 1980s and 1990s saw a vast expansion of foreign-exchange turnover, driven by the continuing growth of international trade and by huge international movements of funds, themselves fuelled by the dismantling of exchange controls and increasing cross-border investments. In London, daily foreign exchange turnover grew from $90 billion in 1986 to $464 billion in 1995, the latter being equivalent to more than $100 *trillion* per annum – an 'absurdly extravagant figure,' commented an awe-struck *Financial Times*.[22]

During the 1990s, London increased its lead year by year as the world's biggest centre for foreign-exchange trading: in 1989 its share of global foreign exchange dealings was 25 per cent; in 1992, it was 27 per cent; and in 1995, it was 30 per cent. London's success in foreign exchange is an example of the powerful effect of the economies of scale in wholesale international financial markets. 'There's critical mass here,' explains an executive director of the Bank of England, '[with] the presence of so many foreign institutions and the fact that there are lots of types of market in London.'[23] London's other critical advantage is the time zone. A London-based trader at Chemical Bank observes that, 'London can deal with other centres all day. From 5 pm our time the US is only dealing with itself. It boils down to time. It has nothing to do with lower costs or greater expertise.'[24]

Futures and options

The London International Financial Futures Exchange (Liffe) is Europe's leading futures and options exchange and one of the City's success stories of the 1990s (see Box 6.2). In 1996, turnover on Liffe was 167 million contracts, that is £159.5 billion per day, up 27 per cent on the previous year. It is estimated that the business focused on Liffe generates 25,000 jobs in the City. Moreover, it contributes £870 million to the UK's invisible earnings. Its success has given an important boost to London's standing as an international financial centre.

For decades, futures trading has been dominated by the Chicago markets (see Chapter 2). Liffe's rapid growth in the 1990s has taken the volume of business to within a whisker of the Chicago Board Options Exchange and has narrowed the gap with the Chicago Mercantile Exchange and the Chicago Board of Trade (Table 6.4). A substantial gulf remains between Liffe and its principal European rivals, Frankfurt DTB and Paris's Matif, which trade at less than half the volume of contracts. But in September 1997, the German, Swiss and French futures exchanges announced an alliance: 'At last, Liffe has a genuine competitor,' comments Etienne Deniau of Fimat, the derivatives brokerage arm of Société Générale.[25]

Table 6.4: Turnover at derivatives exchanges, 1996

Exchange	Total traded contracts 1996 (millions)
Chicago – CBOT	222
Chicago – CME	198
Chicago – CBOE	173
London – Liffe	167
Frankfurt – DTB	77
Paris – Matif	68
Tokyo – Tiffe	29

Source: Deutsche Börse, *Fact Book 1996*.

'The race for the euro has begun,' says Jörg Franke, general manager of Germany's DTB.[26] Liffe's goal is to become the world centre for euro derivatives trading. To that end, it launched euro-denominated contracts late in 1996, but so did Matif and the DTB. The second strand of Liffe's strategy, however, is to forge links with exchanges in other time zones, particularly Japan's Tiffe (Tokyo International Financial Futures Exchange) and Chicago's CBOT and CME, that will allow market users to trade continuously in the world's three main currencies of the US dollar, the yen and the euro.

Liffe's traditional trading system was 'open-outcry', namely face-to-face transactions between traders on the dealing floor. The DTB, on the other hand, adopted an electronic screen-based trading system, which proved to be cheaper for clients and allowed the installation of screens in other financial centres, including London. As a result, the DTB gained market share of the ten-year German government bund futures contract, overtaking Liffe in trading this benchmark product and by 1998 had won four-fifths of the market. Liffe's dominant position in trading European short-term interest rate contracts was also threatened by the same cost factor. Rattled, but demonstrating 'the existence of a survival instinct,' Liffe announced a general shift to screen-based trading.[27] At the same time, Liffe revealed plans to list futures contracts on a new pan-European stock market index, the 'Eurotop 100'.

London also houses Europe's leading commodity futures exchanges – the London Metal Exchange (LME), trading base metals contracts, and the International Petroleum Exchange (IPE), trading energy products. The LME is the world's foremost metals market, with about 5 per cent of world turnover in metals futures and a strong position in physical metals too – it has 380 warehouses in 42 locations worldwide. Its growth in the 1990s has been phenomenal, turnover increasing sevenfold in the years 1990–96.[29] The decision in 1997 by Metallgesellschaft, the major German industrial and trading group, to transfer its physical metal trading to London and New York, was a blow to Frankfurt but a vote of confidence in the LME. The IPE has 20 per cent of world trade in energy products. Both exchanges have highly international clienteles, more than 95 per cent of the LME's turnover and 50 per cent of the IPE's coming from international houses. The LME's activities contribute £250 million to the UK balance of payments.[29]

Asset management

The UK has a large asset management industry, the lion's share of which is conducted in London, although Edinburgh and Leeds are also important centres. Institutional equity holdings, one measure of the scale of activity, was $1 trillion in the mid-1990s, placing London second only to Tokyo.[30]

The pension fund management industry in London is highly concentrated, just five firms handling two-thirds of the £300 billion of UK pension fund assets managed by outsiders – Mercury Asset Management, Schroders, PDFM (Philips and Drew Fund Management), Gartmore, and Morgan Grenfell Asset Management.[31] The 1990s saw a spate of purchases of independent UK fund managers by Continental European banks eager to acquire international asset management expertise. Dutch bank ABN-Amro, for instance, purchased two British fund management companies in 1996 as the core of its asset management unit. In September 1997, it upgraded the London operation to an equal footing with Amsterdam, anticipating rapid expansion.

London's fund management industry preponderantly services an institutional clientele, in contrast to the Continental industry, led by the Swiss, which deals first and foremost with private clients. Other notable characteristics are a preponderance of equity business, and the large-scale ownership of foreign equities. These factors give London a dominant lead over other European centres in competition for the management of international funds. In the mid-1990s, four-fifth of funds managed in Europe for foreign institutional clients were managed in London.[32] During the 1990s, the volume of foreign clients' funds managed by UK fund managers has soared, their overseas earnings doubling from £202 million in 1990 to £445 million in 1996.[33]

Bullion

London has been the world's leading bullion market since the nineteenth century. There is no formal marketplace like the stock market or the futures exchanges, but twice a day representatives of the world's five leading bullion-dealing firms meet in a deep-carpeted, oak-panelled room at Rothschilds merchant bank where they 'fix' an official price at which they deal with each other. This smooths price fluctuations and dampens disruptive violent swings. Other market participants trade at open-market prices determined by supply and demand.

At the beginning of 1997, daily settlements of gold bullion in London were $10 billion – a volume equivalent to the combined reserves of the EU's central banks or nearly double South Africa's annual production.[34] In fact, some traders argue that market turnover is three or even five times greater, the statistical approach adopted substantially under-recording the volume of business. 'We have a serious market with a lot of depth and deserving of more attention,' the vice-chairman of the London Bullion Market Association told the *Financial Times*. 'Potential investors will not be able to dismiss this as a Mickey Mouse market.'[35]

Insurance

London is a major centre for insurance, notably marine, aviation, international reinsurance, and large commercial risks. General insurance business is conducted through Lloyd's of London and by large insurance companies. In 1996, the overseas earnings of the UK insurance industry was £6.1 billion ($10 billion).

Lloyd's of London is an insurance marketplace whose capital has traditionally been provided by a large number of individual members who assume unlimited liability for claims. Recently, companies have also been allowed to join Lloyd's. Lloyd's itself does not provide insurance, though it maintains a fund to support syndicates that might otherwise default and thus damage the reputation of the institution. The business conducted at Lloyd's is preponderantly international, three-quarters of its earnings coming from overseas.

Besides the international business, London serves a substantial UK insurance market. The bulk of life insurance business is domestic, and there is a not insignificant volume of home general insurance.

Marine services

Marine services – marine insurance, shipbroking, ship classification and accounting, and legal and consultancy services – form an important part of the matrix of London's international financial and business services.

These are substantial activities generating an aggregate added value of more than £1 billion – more than New York, Tokyo, Singapore, Hong Kong, Oslo, Piraeus or any other shipping centre.

London's position is a legacy of its former pre-eminence as the world's foremost shipping nation – in the 1920s the UK's merchant fleet was 30 per cent of the world fleet, although by the 1990s it was a mere 3 per cent. London's continued position is explained by a number of factors: the high repute of its institutions; the liquidity and sophistication of its long-established markets; the comprehensive spread of marine services, including an unrivalled expertise in maritime law; and long-standing close ties with Greek ship owners, many of whom are based in London.

The focus of these activities is the Baltic Exchange, which celebrated its 250th anniversary in 1994. It almost didn't make it, being wrecked by an IRA bomb in 1992. Despite the devastation, the Baltic's 2000 brokers were able to continue trading without interruption and so avoid clients taking their business to other centres. As a result, the exchange was able to sustain its commanding market share of 50 per cent of the tanker and 30–40 per cent of dry bulk chartering business worldwide.[36] The Baltic Exchange generated net overseas earnings of £260 million in 1996, and Lloyd's Register of Shipping a further £57 million.[37]

Bank of England and the Financial Services Authority

The Bank of England is both the City's traditional policeman and guardian. Wearing its policeman's helmet, it has had both an official responsibility for the banking system and has kept an informal eye on City firms and City markets. Such was its influence and intimacy with the City that a discreet word from an official was often sufficient to avert problems. Responsibility for bank supervision was transferred to the Financial Services Authority (FSA) in autumn 1997, the Bank's remit being limited to monetary policy and setting interest rates (see Chapter 5). But the Bank is still the principal spokesman for the City's viewpoint to the government, remaining closely in touch with the financial markets.

The FSA is the new unitary regulatory body with responsibility for policing the financial services industry, a sector that by the broadest measures accounts for nearly one-fifth of Britain's GDP.[38] It combines duties previously discharged by nine regulatory entities; banking supervision, from the Bank of England; insurance regulation, from civil servants; and, from various self-regulatory organisations, the oversight of fund managers, personal investment products and securities houses. Explaining the decision to merge these bodies into a single authority, the Chancellor, Gordon Brown, told Parliament: 'The distinctions between different types of financial institutions – banks, securities firms and insurance companies – are becoming increasingly blurred. Many of today's financial institutions are regulated by a plethora of different supervisors. This increases the cost and reduces the effectiveness of supervision.'[39] But some international bankers are less happy, fearing that politically sensitive consumer protection will take precedence over the requirements of the wholesale financial markets. This could prove detrimental to London's standing as an international financial centre.

LONDON VERSUS FRANKFURT

The introduction of the European single currency – the euro – is intensifying the struggle between Europe's financial centres. The race is on to become the leading wholesale market for the euro and euro products, the hub for trading euro currency, euro-denominated derivatives and euro-denominated securities. Paris and Frankfurt have recognised this once-in-a-generation opportunity to grab market share and are energetically marketing their services (see Chapter 8). Euribor, a new Europe-wide benchmark for interbank interest rates is a challenge to Libor, the London benchmark. The supplanting of Libor would be a psychological blow and might boost Frankfurt's interest rates products.

In London, the Bank of England has taken the lead in spearheading the City's preparations for the euro. A significant supporting role has been played by the Corporation of London's Policy and Resources Committee, which actively promotes the City of London as an international financial services centre.

The Bank of England has established working parties on technical aspects and led discussions on wholesale market issues, such as conversion processes and redenomination of bonds. Its publication *Practical Issues Arising from the Introduction of the Euro* quickly became required reading for bankers and others affected by the new currency. In early 1998, the Bank despatched a roadshow around the world's major financial centres, headed by deputy governor David Clementi. 'The key message,' says Clementi, 'is that while the euro is not our domestic currency, it must be the central currency for the wholesale markets in London. We are in the curious position that the euro is not our domestic currency but it is a wholesale currency. I wouldn't say it is an advantage. Our job is to make sure it is not a material disadvantage.'[40]

Clementi, a former investment banker with Dresdner Kleinwort Benson, argues that the crucial factor is where market and trading activity are centred. 'The one thing you do need is to centralise your traders. You can't have people all over the place betting the bank,' says Clementi. 'It's very hard to control. At the simplest level, it's harder to spot when a trader comes back from lunch having had too much to drink. There's a limit to how much damage a salesman can do when he's had too much to drink, but not a trader.'[41] Once a bank has located its trading in a particular place, other functions such as information technology, bookkeeping and senior management will follow.

In the normal course of events, the advent of the euro ought to be to the advantage of the largest financial centre because of the operation of the economies of scale discussed above. Indeed, there is every likelihood that dealing in the euro will concentrate in the world's biggest foreign-exchange markets, and that the losers will not be London, Frankfurt or Paris, but Europe's smaller regional financial centres – Milan and Madrid for instance – where inter-European foreign exchange cross-trades are bread-and-butter activities.

Views vary about the effect on the City of Britain's non-participation in the euro. Many argue that it will make little difference, at least in the short term. 'The critical mass of people, infrastructure and firms is here (London) and it is almost inconceivable that this could unravel,' says Stephen Kingsley, partner at accountant Arthur Andersen. 'London with the UK in or out of the euro will still be the primary centre in this time zone.'[42] 'In the next five years there will be very great benefits to London,' says a senior City figure. 'But in the long run, if we are not in Emu, there is the risk that activity will gravitate towards one or other of the alternative European centres'.[43]

In a Nutshell

International financial centres are cities that specialise in the provision of international financial services. Their function is to intermediate international financial flows. This is undertaken by the financial markets and the financial firms located in them. Financial services concentrate in financial centres because of the powerful effects of economies of scale and economies of agglomeration.

London – where the financial services sector is often known as 'the City' – is the world's leading international financial centre. More people work in international financial services in London than in any other centre, and it has the highest number of foreign banks. The principal international financial ⇨

---

activities conducted in London are international banking, securities and derivatives trading, foreign exchange trading, capital raising, asset management, insurance and marine services.

The advent of the European single currency – the euro – is a challenge for London and presents an opportunity for rivals Frankfurt and Paris to win market share. On the other hand, London's leading position in the international financial wholesale markets may well mean that euro business gravitates to the City.

FURTHER READING

Coggan, Philip, *The Money Machine: How the City Works* (London, Penguin, 1995)

Courtney, Cathy, and Thompson, Paul, *City Lives: The Changing Voices of British Finance* (London, Methuen, 1996)

Kynaston, David, *LIFFE: A Market and its Makers* (Cambridge, Granta Editions, 1997)

Michie, Ranald, *The City of London: Continuity and Change, 1850–1990* (London, Macmillan, 1992)

Roberts, Richard (ed), *Global Financial Centres: London, New York, Tokyo* (Aldershot, Edward Elgar, 1994)

NOTES AND REFERENCES

In the list below for this chapter, any reference to an author alone should be taken to be a reference to his/her work in 'Further reading' above.

1 *London's Size and Diversity*, (Corporation of London, 1996)
2 British Invisibles, *The City Table, 1996*
3 British Invisibles, *The City Table, 1996*
4 Final Report, *City Research Project* (Corporation of London, 1995)
5 Plender, John and Wallace, Paul, *The Square Mile: a Guide to the New City of London* (London, Century Publishing, 1985)
6 *The Banker*, November 1986
7 'Overseas banks boost presence', *Financial Times*, 17 March 1997
8 *International Banking in London*, *Financial Times* supplement, 27 November 1997
9 Final Report, *City Research Project*, (Corporation of London, 1995
10 *The Banker*, November 1997
11 *The Banker*, November 1997 adjusted by estimates for amalgamations
12 Davis, E.P., and Latter A.R., *London as an International Financial Centre, Bank of England Quarterly Bulletin*, vol 29 (1989)

13 Deutsche Bank, *Annual Report*, 1995

14 *Sunday Times*, 4 February 1996

15 *Evening Standard*, 26 November 1996

16 *Financial Times*, 8 October 1997

17 'Cats that got the cream', *Euromoney*, February 1996

18 British Invisibles, *UK Financial Trends & World Invisible Trade 1997*

19 *Stock Exchange Fact Book*, 1997

20 *Sunday Times*, 14 September 1997

21 *Sunday Telegraph*, 24 September 1995

22 'Give or take a trillion', *Financial Times*, 20 September 1993; *Financial Times*, 13 March 1996

23 *Sunday Telegraph*, 24 September 1995

24 *Independent*, 20 September 1995

25 *Financial Times*, 19 September 1997

26 'Ready, set . . . Euro!', *Futures*, January 1997

27 *Financial Times*, 11 March 1998

28 *Financial Times*, 4 October 1997

29 Final Report, *City Research Project*, (Corporation of London, 1995)

30 British Invisibles, *UK Financial Trends & World Invisible Trade 1997*

31 *Financial Times*, 13 October 1997

32 Final Report, *City Research Project*, (Corporation of London, 1995)

33 British Invisibles, *The City Table 1996*

34 *Financial Times*, 30 January 1997

35 *Financial Times*, 30 January 1997

36 The Baltic Exchange, *The Baltic Exchange* (Pamphlet, 1997)

37 British Invisibles, *The City Table 1996*

38 *The Economist*, 4 October 1997

39 *Independent*, 21 May 1997

40 *Financial Times*, 20 January 1998

41 *Financial Times*, 20 January 1998

42 *Financial Times*, 18 November 1996

43 *Financial Times*, 14 May 1998

Box 6.1: Offshore financial centres

Offshore financial centres intermediate financial flows between non-resident borrowers and non-resident depositors. They emerged in the 1960s to service the rapidly expanding eurocurrency market.

All eurocurrency business is offshore business. Thus much of the ⇨

international banking conducted in London, Switzerland and Luxembourg might be classified as offshore business. So too are transactions routed via international banking facilities, special accounts established separately from domestic accounts that are exempt from banking restrictions applying in the domestic market, for instance on interest payments or reserve requirements. The operation of international banking facilities in New York, Tokyo and Singapore is discussed in Chapters 7 and 8.

The term 'offshore financial centre' usually refers to a set of tax havens where low tax or zero tax is levied on transactions between non-residents. The list of such offshore financial centres includes the Bahamas, Barbados, Bermuda, the Cayman Islands, the Netherlands Antilles, the New Hebrides (Vanuatu), the Seychelles, Jersey, Guernsey and the Isle of Man. In aggregate, external lending booked in offshore financial centres in the mid-1990s was 23 per cent of total international external lending.

For banks, the advantages of routing transactions through offshore financial centres are their minimal regulatory requirements and low taxes. For the offshore centres, often far-flung islands with narrowly based local economies, the establishment of a financial services sector yields jobs, licensing fees and other economic benefits.

Successful offshore financial centres have various special characteristics:

- minimal regulation of inflows and outflows of funds
- segregation of international financial flows from the local financial system
- financial secrecy
- low taxes
- financial stability and an effective central banking authority
- good international communications and transportation
- convenient time-zone location
- availability of skilled labour

Caribbean islands constitute a notable cluster of offshore financial centres. Proximity to the US is the explanation of this pattern, US banks being the leading users of their facilities. In the 1970s, they were an important conduit for international lending to Latin America. The 1980s saw a slowdown in the growth of offshore centres because of the opening of international banking facilities in the US in 1981 and the onset of the debt crisis in 1982. But a significant volume of transactions continued to be routed through them. In 1996, outstanding external lending booked in the Cayman Islands and the Bahamas (the most important of the Caribbean offshore financial centres) was $456 billion and $174 billion respectively, representing 9 per cent and 4 per cent of total net international bank lending.

Box 6.2: The meaning of LIFFE

Trading financial derivatives began in Chicago in 1972 and soon mushroomed. Six years later, London's International Commodities Clearing House decided it was time to establish a financial derivatives market in London to serve the European time zone. The running was taken up by John Barkshire, chairman of money brokers Mercantile House, who became chairman of the working party set up in 1980 to develop the project, cajoling a cautious Bank of England into lending its support in March 1981. The outcome was the London International Financial Futures and Options Exchange (Liffe), broadly modelled on the successful Chicago Mercantile Exchange.

Liffe opened for business in September 1982. Progress was spectacular, the growth of transactions averaging 50 per cent per annum from 1982 to 1994. Between 1988 and 1994, total trading volumes rose tenfold. In March 1992, encouraged by the Bank of England, Liffe merged with the rival London Traded Options Market, and in September 1996 it absorbed the London Commodity Exchange (LCE), consolidating its position as Europe's leading futures and options exchange.

Liffe has pursued a policy of aggressive innovation in new derivative instruments, but it has not all been plain sailing. The exchange began with three interest-rate futures contracts and four currency futures contracts. Despite London's position as the world's leading foreign exchange market, the currency contracts proved uncompetitive with the established markets in Chicago and Philadelphia, and Liffe's time-zone advantage was not sufficient to outweigh the higher cost of trading in its smaller and thus less liquid market. Futures contracts in US treasury bonds and Japanese government bonds, introduced in 1984 and 1987 respectively, also failed to live up to expectations. But the 10 year German government bond (*bund*) futures contract, established in 1988, and the short-term Euromark contract proved spectacularly successful. However, in 1998 the rival bund contract offered by Frankfurt's Deutsche Terminbörse overtook the volume of business in the Liffe contract, prompting Liffe to shift from 'open-outcry' trading to screen-based trading.

Success with Deutschmark contracts encouraged the introduction of other European products, and the early 1990s saw a substantial shift in the pattern of business away from dollar contracts into European ones. Many of the new contracts were launched in direct competition with Continental markets, it usually being the case that the market pioneering a contract and first establishing good liquidity is the market that achieves dominance. In 1998, Liffe launched the first 10 year interest rate futures contract denominated ⇨

in the euro, a rival product to bund features.

In addition to interest rate and currency products, Liffe also developed a variety of equity-related derivative products: about 70 individual equity options; FT-SE 100 Index futures and options; and the FT-SE Mid-250 future. The merger with the LCE brought contracts on coffee, cocoa, sugar, grain, potatoes and the Baltic Freight Index. This is a uniquely comprehensive product range, being the only exchange to offer trading in futures and options on financial, commodity and stock market index products, as well as options on individual equities.

The reasons for Liffe's success are the time-zone factor, its dynamic development of new products, its diversity of products, the size and liquidity of the market, the price integrity of its contracts, and technical innovation. It has attracted a broad international membership: among the 222 member firms, which include most of the world's leading financial institutions, almost three-quarters are non-UK firms: 29 per cent are based in Continental Europe; 20 per cent in Japan; 19 per cent in the US; and 4 per cent in the rest of the world.

'Our markets are easy to use, safe to use, and cheap to use, and the systems that support them are robust,' says Liffe chairman Jack Wigglesworth. 'In a sense, companies, banks and institutions like pension funds have a duty to use these markets. By not using them they are in effect speculating in a benign way. There have been cases in the United States where the trustees of institutions have been charged with not properly protecting their assets because they have not been using financial futures. I think this is a very valid point.' ('Profile of LIFFE chairman Jack Wigglesworth', *Evening Standard*, 26 June 1995.)

CHAPTER 7

New York and Tokyo as Global Financial Centres

INTRODUCTION

London, New York and Tokyo – the three global financial centres – constitute a top tier in the hierarchy of international financial centres. Each is the principal centre in its time zone. These global centres provide a wide range of services to a worldwide clientele. In *international* financial business, the scale of activities in London surpasses that of New York and Tokyo by virtually every measure. But the size and scope of financial activity in New York and Tokyo is greatly boosted by also being the most important *domestic* financial centres of the world's two largest economies and major international currencies.

Box 7.1: The rise and fall of international financial centres

Antwerp was the earliest city to fulfil the functions of an international financial centre in a recognisably modern way in the sixteenth century. Its downfall came when it was overrun by Spanish troops in 1585.

With the demise of Antwerp, Amsterdam took over as Europe's leading port and international centre for the next two centuries. Trade was financed by way of bills of exchange, the buying and selling of this paper being the basis of the money market. A bond market also developed, providing long-term loans to governments and large colonial trading companies. In the early eighteenth century, London overtook Amsterdam in size as a port, yet Amsterdam retained its pre-eminence as an international financial centre. But the curtain came down in 1795, when the Netherlands were conquered by the French.

London, already the world's biggest port, at that stage became the ⇨

---

leading international financial centre. During the nineteenth century, much of world trade was financed in London and it was the most important location for the issue and trading of international bonds. It also hosted the leading commodity markets, physical and later financial, and was foremost in shipping and insurance services. London's pre-eminence was bolstered by the evolution of sterling into the first global currency, the principal international medium for transactions and reserves, and by the Bank of England's pioneering development of central banking.

Paris became a significant international bond and banking centre from the 1840s, French government policy being that it should become the Continental counterpart to London. The plan was probably fanciful, but the devastation caused by the Prussian siege of Paris during the Franco-Prussian War of 1870, and the subsequent Paris Commune of 1871, put paid even to the pipe dream.

Berlin emerged as an important centre from the 1870s, initially financing German industrialisation but later undertaking international business too. The early years of the twentieth century also saw the start of an international capital market in New York.

During World War I, London, Paris and Berlin all ceased to function as international financial centres. New York took over as the leading international bond market and banking centre, and the US dollar became a major international currency for the first time. The Allied victory allowed London to mount a revival in the 1920s, and that decade saw an intense rivalry for business between the two centres, London and New York, and their respective currencies.

International trade and international financial transactions slumped drastically in the 1930s with the onset of the world economic depression. Disillusion with sterling and the dollar after their departures from the gold standard in the early 1930s led international money seeking a safe haven to Switzerland, where banking business boomed. World War II provided another boost to business, subsequently a highly controversial subject. Switzerland was established as a leading international financial centre, a position it retains.

Berlin's role as a financial centre came to an end with World War II, becoming in the post-war era a divided city within the Soviet zone. Frankfurt, which had a long history as a regional banking centre, took over as the leading German financial centre.

After World War II, New York and the US dollar began to rule the roost. However, in the early 1960s the worsening US balance of payments, principally as a result of the Vietnam War, led to restrictions to curb capital outflows. This gave a big fillip to the burgeoning euromarkets, which had begun in London a few years earlier. In the 1950s, a significant volume ⇨

of international trade was still conducted in sterling, and London retained many of its pre-war financial institutions and a global outlook. These provided the bedrock for its re-emergence as an international financial centre from the late 1950s. This re-emergence was based on London's leading role in the development of the eurodollar and eurobond markets. In the 1970s, London's position was boosted by the boom in petro-dollar recycling, which further enhanced its standing as the leading international banking centre.

In the early decades of the century, Shanghai was the leading financial centre of Asia. This role came to an end in 1937 when the city was occupied by the Japanese. Liberation by the Peoples' Army placed the Chinese Communist Party in charge and put paid to a revival of international banking business for more than a generation. The beneficiary was Hong Kong, which emerged as an important regional centre. In the 1970s and 1980s, Tokyo, the financial centre of the world's second-largest economy, also emerged as an important international financial centre.

Beirut was the financial capital of the Middle East in the 1950s and 1960s, but its role as an international financial centre came to an end with the onset of the Lebanese civil war in 1975.

In the 1960s and 1970s, there were hopes that Panama City would become the international financial entrepôt of Latin America. Instead, under the rule of dictator General Manuel Noriega, it became the global capital for the laundering of drug money. Respectable banks took their business elsewhere and the lofty aspirations came to little.

The lesson of history is that, once established, leading international financial centres will retain their positions unless affected by an external shock that profoundly dislocates business. As firms depart a stricken centre, the external economies of scale and agglomeration go into reverse and the centre's competitive advantage rapidly dissipates. Over the centuries, the foremost source of such shocks, which have promoted shifts in the locus of financial activity from one centre to another, has been war.

NEW YORK

New York, where the financial services industry is often referred to as 'Wall Street' – a winding canyon in the heart of the traditional downtown financial district – is both the foremost financial centre of the world's biggest economy and an important international financial centre. The scale of its capital and money markets dwarfs other centres, although the bulk of securities quoted and transactions undertaken are domestic rather than international. New York ranks first amongst international financial centres in stock market capitalisation, and second or third by five of the other seven indicators in Table 7.1

Table 7.1: New York as an international financial centre: some indicators

	Volume/ number	World rank
International banking		
Cross-border bank lending[a]		
(US – 1996)	$821 billion	3
Foreign banks present[b]		
(New York – 1995) branch, subsidiary, rep. office etc.	326	3
Capital market		
Equity market capitalisation[c]		
(US – 1995)	$6857 billion	1
International equities turnover[d]		
(NYSE + Nasdaq – 1996)	$454 billion	2
Asset management		
Institutional equity holdings[e]		
(New York – 1995)	$896 billion	3
Money markets		
Foreign exchange turnover[f]		
(US – 1995) net daily turnover	$244 billion	2
Derivatives contracts[g]		
(NYMEX – 1997) average monthly volume	7 million	4

Sources:
[a] IMF, *International Financial Statistics* (Washington D.C., August 1997).
[b] Jao, Y.C., *Hong Kong as an International Financial Centre* (Hong Kong, City University of Hong Kong Press, 1997).
[c] *Emerging Stock Markets Factbook 1996* (Washington D.C., International Finance Corporation, 1996).
[d] *London Stock Exchange Fact File* London, London Stock Exchange, 1997).
[e] British Invisibles, *UK Financial Trends & World Invisible Trade 1997* (London 1997).
[f] Bank for International Settlements, *Triennial Survey of Foreign Exchange* (Basle, BIS, 1995).
[g] Liffe, *World Volumes* (London, August 1997).

Development of New York as a financial centre

New York emerged as America's most important financial centre in the years following the end of the Civil War in 1865. It was the focal point for raising finance to build the railroad system that united the country and for investment in industrialisation. By the turn of the century, it had a coherent array of financial markets and a boisterous bevy of brokers and bankers. Its coming-of-age party was the first-ever billion-dollar deal, a $1.4 billion issue (about $25 billion in today's money) that created the giant US Steel Corporation in 1901.

A few international loans were issued on Wall Street in the 1900s, but it was World War I that transformed New York into the world's leading international capital market. The British and other Allied governments turned to the New York market to raise vast sums to finance their armies. Foreign business continued to be big business in the 1920s, New York remaining the leading international capital market despite competition from London. But foreign loans were just a sideshow compared with the boom in domestic stock prices. In October 1929 came the Wall Street crash, and then its dismal aftermath.

Table 7.2: Volume of transactions on New York Stock Exchange, 1900–96

	Daily average turnover (millions of shares)		Daily average turnover (millions of shares)
1900	0.5	1980	44.9
1910	0.6	1985	109.2
1920	0.8	1990	156.2
1930	3.0	1991	178.9
1940	4.0	1992	202.2
1950	2.0	1993	264.5
1960	3.0	1994	291.3
1965	6.2	1995	346.1
1970	11.6	1996	441.9
1975	18.6		

Source: New York Stock Exchange Fact Book 1997.

With the economy in depression, the 1930s were not a prosperous decade on Wall Street. Another problem was the anger of investors who had suffered losses in the crash and blamed Wall Street financiers. The outcome was a tightening of the regulatory framework within which they operated. In 1934 there was legislation establishing the Securities and Exchange Commission to police the securities industry, and the Glass-–Steagall Act of 1933 that required the complete separation of investment banking from commercial banking. Henceforth, an American bank could be either a commercial bank that took deposits and made loans or an investment bank that engaged in the origination and distribution of securities, but not both.

After World War II, the US dollar was the world's leading currency and Wall Street the foremost source of finance for international transactions. As international trade grew and US corporations expanded overseas the international dimension of Wall Street's business increased. Domestic banking and securities business grew too, but there was no boom. Average daily share turnover on the New York Stock Exchange was actually lower in 1950 and 1960 than in 1940 (Table 7.2), but activity picked up in the 1960s and grew rapidly in the 1970s. A significant milestone was the abolition of the New York Stock Exchange's 183-year-old system of fixed brokerage commission rates on 'Mayday' 1975. This measure of deregulation stimulated increased competition and innovation in the securities industry.

The US economy was in recession at the beginning of the 1980s, but growth resumed in 1983. Anticipating the revival, the stock market rose from August 1982 to October 1987, the Dow Jones Industrial Average (the leading stock market index) increasing from 900 to 2,700. The crash of 1987 led to the loss of 50,000 jobs on Wall Street as banks and securities houses slashed costs. Unlike 1929, it was not followed by an international slump, yet there was a slowdown and by 1991 the US economy was in recession. Growth resumed in 1992 and the financial markets picked up too. In fact, the Dow Jones Industrial Average had already overtaken its 1987 peak and had set off on a record bull run, reaching 8,000 in 1997. By the summer of 1996, employment on Wall Street in the securities industry was 257,000, only a few thousand less than at the peak of the 1980s' bull market. Total employment in New York in finance and insurance, both domestic and international, was 443,000 by the mid-1990s.

Key characteristics of New York as a financial centre

David C. Batten, managing director of investment bank First Boston, has identified half-a-dozen key characteristics of New York as a financial centre:[1]

- *Diversity of markets*   New York is host to eight separate major financial markets:
  — US government securities
  — corporate bonds and paper
  — equities
  — municipals
  — securitised assets
  — money markets
  — foreign exchange
  — swaps

The large commercial banking sector and the investment banks are also vital institutions.

- *Size and quality of markets* The US equity and bond markets are the largest and most sophisticated in the world. Outstanding US public debt exceeds the combined total for Japan, Germany, France, the UK, Italy, the Netherlands and Belgium.
- *Range of strategies and maturities available to issuers of securities* Strategies: for example, there are over 50 forms of securitised mortgage on offer. Maturities: the range of average maturities is double that available in the eurobond market.
- *Role of institutional investors* The US markets are driven by institutional investors – mutual funds, insurance companies, pension funds, and bank trust departments. Direct investment by individuals is relatively unimportant: households have been net liquidators of equities since 1958. However, investment via mutual funds is booming.
- *Creativity and innovation* The New York capital and money markets are the cutting edge of financial innovation, the products created there being imitated around the world.
- *Competitive pressure* The constraints of the Glass–Steagall Act on diversification have resulted in a much greater concentration of business than is found in the euromarkets, with the same handful of large, aggressive investment banks operating at the forefront of virtually every financial market.

The capital market

The US has the world's largest capital market. In 1996, the market value of listed domestic equities on the New York Stock Exchange was around $6,700 billion, compared with $3,000 billion for Tokyo and $1,700 for London.[2] The composition of the US capital market is shown in Table 7.3. In descending order, the largest components are:

- equities (shares)
- mortgages – part private and part government agencies, notably the Government National Mortgage Association
- US treasury debt
- corporate bonds

US tax laws favour corporate financing by bond issues, providing opportunities for innovative investment bankers to engineer new products, most notoriously Michael Milken, apostle of the 'junk bond' (see

Chapter 10). The efficiency and competitive pressure of the New York market means that the cost to a borrower of a sustained bond issue is cheaper than in London or Tokyo, the respective costs being 0.98 per cent, 1.08 per cent and 3.5 per cent.

Table 7.3: US capital market, 1995

	$ billion
Equities	8,345
Bonds	
Mortgages	4,724
US treasury debt	2,531
Corporate	2,478
Municipal	1,301
Business loans	1,116
Consumer credits	946
Foreign	282
Total	13,378

Source: The Economic Report of the President, 1996.

Since the mid-1990s, there has been a rapid rise in the number of foreign companies listed on the New York Stock Exchange (NYSE). By autumn 1997, there were 326, up from 200 in 1995, and it was predicted that there would be 600 by the year 2000, 20 per cent of the total listing. This is an important development, likened by NYSE chairman Richard Grasso to the rise of modern industrial enterprise a hundred years earlier.[3] It was driven by the international diversification of US investment funds, whose holdings of foreign equities doubled over the years 1992–97 and were expected to double again in 1997–2002. Being able to invest in foreign companies via the NYSE provides a familiar and reassuring route for US investors. And, for foreign companies, it gives access to the vast US capital market since many US pension funds are restricted by their rules to holding only US-listed securities. Over half of the new arrivals in 1996 came by way of an initial public offering, raising a total of $6.4 billion.

Money markets
The US money market, focused on New York, is the largest in the world. In 1994, the volume of outstanding money-market instruments was $2,320 billion, up from $1,508 billion in 1985.[4] Whereas the capital market

provides long-term finance for investment, the money market furnishes short-term funds for government agencies and corporations. The New York money market is used by banks and corporations to adjust short-term liquidity. It also plays a crucial role in the conduct of US monetary policy by the central bank. Through 'open-market operations' – the sale or purchase of government securities by the central bank – the Federal Reserve Bank of New York is able to influence US short-term interest rates, giving effect to the decisions of the monthly meetings of the Open Markets Committee of the board of governors of the Federal Reserve System in Washington (see Chapter 5).

New York is second only to London as a centre of foreign-exchange dealing. Between 1986 and 1995, average daily turnover of foreign exchange transactions increased from $58 billion to $244 billion.

International banking

Foreign banks are a significant dimension of New York as an international financial centre. In 1971, 73 foreign banks had a presence in New York. The 1970s saw a large increase in their number, mostly through European and other OECD countries participating in the booming business of petro-dollar recycling and lending to emerging economies. By 1980, the number of foreign banks had increased to 240. The 1980s saw a new influx, notably from developing countries and Scandinavia, as well as Japanese regional banks. 'Most Japanese banks have established themselves in London and are now turning towards New York, a logical sequence,' explained a Japanese banker in New York in 1987.[5] By then, foreign banks in New York numbered 358, employing 29,000 staff.[6]

That level marked a peak: in 1997, the foreign banks numbered 314.[7] The fall was due to disappearances through amalgamations and the closure of costly Manhattan offices, many foreign banks finding that making money out of their New York operations, or even managing them, was problematic. 'You can build revenue easily enough, but making a profit is a different matter,' says Simon Robertson, former chairman of Kleinwort Benson.[8]

The foreign bank with the largest staff in New York is the UK-based Hongkong and Shanghai Bank, employing 2,300. Other European banks with a significant presence are the European American Bank, which is a Dutch bank with 1,900 staff, Union Bank of Switzerland, 1,800, Deutsche Bank, 1,500, Swiss Bank Corporation, 760, Credit Suisse, 600, Crédit Lyonnais, 600 and Banque National de Paris and Paribas, 500 staff each. Since the mid-1990s, many leading European banks with global aspirations have been seeking to build up their deal-making capabilities in the

US by hiring experienced bankers and traders and purchasing niche investment-banking businesses.

The 64 Japanese banks resident in New York are numerically the largest national contingent of foreign banks. The biggest are the Industrial Bank of Japan with 950 staff, the Bank of Tokyo-Mitsubishi 450, and Dai-Ichi Kangyo Bank and Sanwa Bank, 350 staff each. Their number suffered a spectacular depletion in 1995 when Daiwa Bank, the fifteenth-largest bank in Japan and forty-first-largest worldwide, was banned from doing business in the US after it was revealed that bank officers had covered up bond trading losses of $1.1 billion run up over an 11-year period (see Chapter 10).

Latin American bank nameplates are numerous in New York – 14 from Brazil, six from Argentina, six from Venezuela, and six from Mexico – but many are representative offices with only a handful of staff.

International Banking Facilities (IBFs) are an accounting device that allows US banks and the US branches of foreign banks to compete for international deposit and lending business in offshore dollars. IBFs permit offshore dollar deposits to be taken without infringing domestic reserve requirements or interest-rate restrictions. Earnings from IBFs are also exempt from state taxes, although subject to federal tax. They were first proposed in the 1960s, in response to the restrictions on foreign lending imposed on US banks by the government, as a measure to mitigate balance-of-payments problems; but the Federal Reserve vetoed the proposal, fearful that leakage of funds between the domestic and offshore markets would undermine domestic monetary policy. Pressured to permit IBFs in order to promote New York's competitive position in international banking, the Federal Reserve eventually relented in 1981.

Box 7.2: Are financial centres an endangered species?

Modern communications technology makes information almost instantly available. In fact, this is not such a novel wonder of the age as is often assumed. In terms of time savings, the mega technological communications revolution happened well over a century ago when the introduction of the electric telegraph transformed international financial trading. The opening of the transatlantic cable in 1866 cut communications time between London and New York from three weeks to seconds. It hardly needs saying that firms in a financial centre with telegraph communications had a massive advantage over firms without them. ⇨

It is the wide dispersion and profusion of information that is different about today's communications technology. The telegraph was a technology that reinforced the importance of financial centres. But modern technology means that price information and trading facilities are as readily accessible from the side of a swimming pool on the Côte d'Azur as in a bank dealing room.

Does this mean that financial centres are being made dinosaurs by technology? No, because many financial operations still involve close contact between bankers, lawyers, accountants and others, such as M & A work, capital raising for governments or companies and asset management. Financial innovation is stimulated by personal contact with other experts and commercial rivals. However, some 'back office' administrative tasks, such as settling trades and handling cash settlements are being dispersed to cheaper locations.

Technology is but one aspect of the spectrum of factors that influence the location of financial firms. In fact, by making information instantly available everywhere, it becomes a neutral factor. Today, the problem is how to *interpret and use* the vast volume of information flows communications technology makes available. Nowadays, it is access to a pool of specialist skilled personnel who can analyse and act on the information that is the vital external economy provided by international financial centres. Despite the theoretical centrifugal impact of technology, international financial centres will be important for the foreseeable future.

In the first year, IBF assets jumped from $55 billion to $152 billion and subsequently grew at 20 per cent per annum. The development of a growing volume of offshore funds in IBFs strengthened the hand of the US authorities in relation to the supervision and regulation of the eurocurrency market and international banking. There are around 600 IBFs, principally in New York, California and Florida.

TOKYO

Introduction

Tokyo is the Asia–Pacific time zone's foremost financial centre. Some 522,000 people work in finance and insurance in Tokyo, more than in London or New York, but most are engaged in domestic business.[9] In fact, as a global financial centre, Tokyo ranks behind London and New York in all but one of the seven indicators of international financial activity in Table 7.4.

Table 7.4: Tokyo as an international financial centre: some indicators

	Volume	World rank
International banking		
Cross-border bank lending[a]		
(Japan – 1996)	$1123 billion	2
Foreign banks present[b]		
(Tokyo – 1995) branch, subsidiary, rep. office etc.	153	6
Capital market		
Equity market capitalisation[c]		
(Japan – 1995)	$3667 billion	2
International equities turnover[d]		
(Toyko – 1996)	$1 billion	9
Asset management		
Institutional equity holdings[e]		
(Tokyo – 1995)	$1524 billion	1
Money markets		
Foreign exchange turnover[f]		
(Japan – 1995) net daily turnover	$161 billion	3
Derivatives contracts[g]		
(TIFFE/TSE – 1997) average monthly volume	3 million	7

Sources:
[a] IMF, *International Financial Statistics* (Washington D.C., August 1997).
[b] Jao, Y.C., *Hong Kong as an International Financial Centre* (Hong Kong, City University of Hong Kong Press, 1997).
[c] *Emerging Stock Markets Factbook 1996* (Washington D.C., International Finance Corporation, 1996).
[d] *London Stock Exchange Fact File* (London, London Stock Exchange, 1997).
[e] British Invisibles, *UK Financial Trends & World Invisible Trade 1997* (London, 1997).
[f] Bank for International Settlements, *Triennial Survey of Foreign Exchange* (Basle, BIS, 1995).
[g] Liffe, *World Volumes* (London, August 1997).

Like New York, Tokyo is both the leading domestic financial centre and an important international financial centre. Although for decades Japan's foremost domestic centre, it was not until the 1970s that Tokyo began to emerge as an international financial centre, as Japan became an economic superpower. Propelled by Japan's enormous financial surpluses, Japanese financial institutions experienced exponential growth. By the mid-1980s, six of the ten largest banks in the world were Japanese. The 1980s saw the establishment of overseas offices by the big Japanese banks and securities houses in London, New York and other centres.

The 1990s were years of crisis in the Japanese financial system. The problems prompted reform: sounder banking practices, and deregulation. The 'Big Bang' reform programme announced by the government in June 1997 was a blueprint for nothing less than a complete overhaul of the country's financial system by 2002.[10]

Development of Tokyo as a financial centre

Japanese economic development began after the political upheavals known as the Meiji Restoration in 1868. Led by a government with a mission to modernise, Japan developed a financial system to serve the country's economic development. Within two generations, Japan was transformed from feudalism to an industrial society with an overseas empire. Defeated and devastated in World War II, the financial system was deployed to rebuild Japan's war-torn economy. Assisted financially and technologically by the US, Japan achieved an annual GNP growth rate of 11 per cent in the 1960s, becoming the world's second-largest economy.

Despite Tokyo's size and importance as a domestic financial centre, it did not develop into an international financial entrepôt like London and New York in the 1960s. Japan's financial markets were instruments of government economic policy, and the operation of market forces was carefully controlled. Regulations and restrictions made it difficult for foreign banks to undertake banking activities or participate in the securities market. Foreign-exchange controls constrained foreign borrowers and investors; besides that, in the 1950s and 1960s international financial flows to Japan were capital imports in order to finance Japanese industry.

The 1970s saw financial liberalisation and the beginnings of Tokyo's emergence as an international financial centre. The first yen-denominated issue for a foreign borrower – known as 'samurai bonds' – in December 1970 was the turning point.[11] The borrower was the Asian Development Bank, and the following year saw a samurai bond issue by the World Bank (see Chapter 5). Private corporations and governments followed the lead set by these international financial institutions and Tokyo emerged as a significant international capital market. The country's huge financial reservoir, a result of high personal savings rates and trade surpluses, and the generally low interest rates, made borrowing in Tokyo attractive to foreigners.

The 1980s saw further liberalisation and Tokyo's emergence as a fully-fledged international financial centre. Banking licences became more readily available for foreign banks, and from 1982 they were permitted to trade short-term bonds and to participate in bond-repurchase business. In 1986, the Tokyo Stock Exchange's exclusion of foreign firms was repealed, and six foreign firms were admitted. By 1996, 92 foreign commercial banks had offices in Japan, as well as 67 securities firms or investment banks.[12]

The establishment of the Japanese Offshore Market (JOM), modelled on New York's International Banking Facilities, also in 1986, was an important step in the internationalisation of the yen and Japan's financial markets. External deposits and credits booked through the JOM were free from domestic reserve requirements and interest-rate restrictions, permitting Japanese banks in Tokyo to compete in offshore banking business. JOM business grew rapidly, boosting the volume of Japan's international lending, which increased from $434 billion in 1986 to $1,140 billion in 1996 (see Table 7.5).[13]

Table 7.5: Japan's international lending, 1986–97

	$ billion					
	1986	1993	1994	1995	1996	1997
Japan Offshore Market	89	507	574	667	573	561
Other lending	345	412	434	550	550	537
Total	434	919	1,008	1,217	1,123	1,098

Source: BIS, *International Banking and Financial Market Developments*, statistical annex.

The Japanese financial system

The configuration of the Japanese financial system reflects its original purpose of encouraging saving to fund politically driven and directed industrialisation and post-war reconstruction. At the centre is the Ministry of Finance, which has responsibility for the supervision of Japanese financial institutions. Banks and bank-like entities – not markets – were the chosen instruments of the Ministry's officials. Japanese financial institutions and their specialist functions are listed below:[14]

- Ministry of Finance.
- Bank of Japan.
- Domestically licenced banks:
  — banking accounts (174): city banks (10); regional banks (129); trust banks (32); long-term credit banks (3);
  — trust accounts (52);
  — accounts of overseas branches (373).
- Financial institutions for small business: *sogo* banks; *shinken* banks;

credit co-operatives etc.
- Financial institutions for agriculture, fishery and forestry: credit; federations of agricultural co-operatives; credit federations of fishery co-operatives etc.
- Foreign banks in Japan (92).
- Post Office Bank – 23,000 branches.
- Insurance companies.
- Securities houses – 3 large firms; around 230 small firms.
- Government financial institutions.

The Bank of Japan, the central bank, is the financial system's lender of last resort and the government's fiscal agent, and it implements government monetary policy (see Chapter 5). The 173 banks with banking accounts at the Bank of Japan comprise:

- 9 city banks (national commercial banks), with headquarters in Tokyo and branches in other major cities: Asahi Bank, Bank of Tokyo-Mitsubishi, Daiwa Bank, Dai-Ichi-Kangyo Bank, Fuji Bank, Sakura Bank, Sanwa Bank, Sumitomo Bank, and Tokai Bank. A tenth city bank, Hokkaido Takushoku Bank, collapsed in November 1997. The nine provide short-term funds to the corporate sector.
- 129 regional banks, which supply the short-term borrowing requirements of small and medium-sized firms.
- 32 trust banks.
- 3 long-term credit banks: Industrial Bank of Japan, Long-term Credit Bank of Japan, and the Nippon Credit Bank. They furnish long-term funds for industry, and used to have a monopoly on issuing long-term bonds.

As in the US, the Japanese financial system features the separation of commercial banking and securities underwriting – Article 65 of Japan's legal code. Since the beginning of financial liberalisation in 1970, Japan's financial markets have assumed greater importance in the Japanese financial system, almost doubling in overall size over the decade 1985–94.

The capital market
There are nine stock exchanges in Japan. The Tokyo Stock Exchange, established in 1878, is much the biggest, accounting for 85 per cent of activity, but the Osaka Securities Exchange is a significant rival. The Japanese equity market is second only to the US market. There is also a substantial bond market, the volume of fixed-interest securities being

boosted in the mid-1970s by government issues to fund deficit spending in order to relieve the recession that followed the oil price rise of 1974. Another stimulus was the consent of authorities to the inauguration of a bond repurchase market, the *gensaki* market, in 1976. This allowed outflows of funds from regulated bank deposits into the more remunerative bond market.

Table 7.6: Japan financial markets, 1985–94

	¥ trillion	
	1985	1994
Equity market	190	358
Bond market	103	179
Money market	37	104

Source: Bank of Japan, *Comparative Economic and Financial Statistics: Japan and Other Major Countries*, 1996.

Securities underwriting and broking is dominated by the 'Big Three' securities houses: Daiwa Securities; Nikko Securities; and Nomura Securities. A fourth big broker, Yamaichi Securities failed in November 1997 (see Chapter 4). All were caught up in the *sokaiya* scandal of 1997, which resulted in fines and resignations. The penalties imposed by the authorities included temporary trading bans, which allowed foreign securities firms to boost their market share at least temporarily. In August 1997, for the first time, the combined share of the 21 foreign securities houses with seats on the Tokyo Stock Exchange surpassed the share of the big four Japanese houses, the respective proportions being 32 per cent and 26 per cent.[15] There are also around 230 small brokerage firms. In 1997, the Tokyo staff of Japanese securities houses numbered 106,000 and foreign firms employed 7,000.[16]

Foreign equities were first listed in Tokyo in 1972, when Dow Chemical and five other US firms achieved a listing. The 1980s saw a rapid expansion of foreign firms listed on the foreign section of the Tokyo Stock Exchange (TSE), numbering 127 companies from ten countries by 1991. The 1990s, however, have seen a substantial de-listing of foreign firms, and by 1998 the number had dropped to 60.[17] The reason was the 53 per cent fall in the volume of shares traded on the TSE over the decade 1988–98. Tokyo was even losing its position as a place to trade Japanese equities: by 1997, turnover of Japanese equities in London, where charges were much lower, amounted to 18 per cent of Tokyo's volume. In an attempt to revitalise the market and halt the exodus from the foreign section, the TSE announced in autumn 1997 a relaxation of the listing rules and an extension of trading hours.[18]

Money markets

Japan's money market in overall terms is a complex matrix of players, financial instruments and subsidiary markets. The players include the full gamut of banks listed above, especially the large city and regional banks. Insurance companies and securities houses are also participants, as are a number of government financial institutions, notably the Japan Development Bank and the Export Import Bank of Japan, ten financial corporations – known as *koko* – and the Post Office with 23,000 units that operate like banks. There are also six specialist brokers – *tanshi* – that provide links between the principals.

The instruments employed in the various markets are: call money; bills of exchange; negotiable certificates of deposit; finance bills and short-dated government securities; commercial paper; and euro-currencies. *Gensaki* transactions – sale and repurchase agreements in government securities, certificates of deposit and commercial paper – are also important, as are currency swaps. The markets in which these instruments are traded are: the interbank yen call-money market; the bill discount market; the certificate-of-deposit market; the secondary commercial paper market; the *gensaki* market; the Tokyo dollar market; and the offshore market.

Traditionally, the Japanese money market was a tool of economic policy controlled by the Bank of Japan. Its principal means of directing the market was credit rationing, but from 1971 open-market operations, a more flexible device, were increasingly used. The traditional money-market instruments were bills of exchange and call money, representing borrowings of funds between banks. To promote more active competition for loan funds, the Bank of Japan authorised the creation of new money-market instruments. In 1979, banks were permitted to issue negotiable certificates of deposit. Treasury bills were introduced in 1986, and yen commercial paper in 1987. The outcome was a rapid expansion of the money markets, which grew from ¥37 trillion in 1985, to ¥104 trillion by 1994.[19]

Trading in financial derivatives in Tokyo began in October 1995 with the introduction of a ten-year government bond future on the TSE. Stock index and equity futures and options contracts were subsequently introduced. In June 1989, the Osaka Securities Exchange stole the lead in index products by introducing an options contract on the Nikkei-225 index, a leading equity-market index. The TSE responded with its Topix index options. While bond and equity products were introduced on the existing stock exchanges, a new exchange, the Tokyo International Financial Futures Exchange (TIFFE), was established in 1989 to trade currency and money market products.

Derivatives provide Japanese investors with vital instruments for hedging risk in the equity, money and currency markets. Yet the development of derivatives trading in Japan has been hampered by legal restrictions, absent in the US and Europe. Another constraint has been the decision to separate the trading of stock-market-derived products and currency and equity-market products. This was to protect the entrenched positions of the securities houses and banks in relation to their principal spheres of activity. As a result of such factors, the rate of growth in the 1990s has been slow relative to other financial centres. Steps are being taken to cut the level of margin that brokers must deposit on behalf of clients, the high-margin requirements being the main reason why much dealing in the Nikkei-225 contract moved offshore to the Singapore International Monetary Exchange (Simex) in the early 1990s.[20]

Tokyo ranks third, after London and New York, as a centre for foreign-exchange trading. Although the overall volume of Tokyo's foreign-exchange trading grew from $115 billion per day in 1989 to $161 billion per day in 1995, relative to the other global centres its position slipped. In 1989, Tokyo accounted for 27 per cent of the total foreign-exchange business of the three global financial centres; but by 1995 this had reduced to only 19 per cent. In both derivatives and foreign exchange, deregulation and liberalisation are expected to create more active markets.

The Japanese financial crisis of the 1990s

In 1990, after a heady run in which share prices increased threefold in three years, the Tokyo stock market plunged. Prices continued to drop and, by 1992, the Nikkei-225 index was less than half its 1989 peak. By then, Japan was mired in its longest post-war recession, causing traumas for banks, brokers, insurers and mortgage institutions.

The downturn adversely affected Tokyo's position as an international financial centre. Foreign demand for Japanese equities disappeared, and foreign banks scaled down their securities operations on the Tokyo stock market, some US institutions pulling out of equities operations there completely. Japanese banks reined back their international lending: in 1990, loan growth overseas by Japanese banks was three times as high as in the domestic market; in 1991, and 1992, it was negative.[21] This came about because, as share prices fell, the banks' capital bases were eroded, causing them to cut back lending to maintain internationally agreed loan-to-capital ratios. Falling share prices also adversely affected the returns made by Japanese banks, which had become accustomed to topping up their profits by realising some of the gains on their investments.

In the winter of 1994–95, a further set of shocks buffeted Japan's beleaguered financial sector. The bungled privatisation of Japan Telecom and Japan Tobacco, the so-called 'double JT fiasco', sent the stock market plummeting again. Doubts about the authorities' judgment were compounded by the Bank of Japan's proposal to use public funds to rescue two failed credit institutions that had got into trouble through incompetence and corruption. Confidence was further shaken by the Kobe earthquake of 17 January 1995, which came with a massive price tag for reconstruction.

A Japanese banking crisis began in summer 1995, when a string of small credit institutions collapsed, Hyogo Bank being the first listed bank to fail for half a century. During the 'bubble economy' of the late 1980s, banks lent prodigiously to property companies and stuffed their balance sheets with soaring equities. With the falls in property and share prices, they found themselves awash with bad debts and devalued assets – by the end of 1997 the banking system's aggregate bad debts were officially estimated at ¥29,000 billion ($219 billion).[22] In the financial year 1995–96, the big city banks wrote off more than ¥10,000 billion in bad debts, resulting in combined pre-tax losses of ¥3,000 billion.

Several Japanese banks announced that they were 'reviewing their global ambitions' – code for retrenchment in international lending. Amongst the big securities houses, Nikko and Daiwa scaled down their overseas operations and Nomura restructured;[23] Yamaichi disappeared following its closure. In Japan, some intrepid foreign banks perceived opportunity in the disarray amongst the Japanese banks and the fears of foreign rivals. 'Other banks are rationalising or moving away. This gives us a chance to go in the front door of a lot of companies where we weren't able to go before,' explained an HSBC spokesman whose bank was beefing up its presence in Tokyo.[24] The demise of Yamaichi Securities provided an opportunity for Merrill Lynch to set up a retail brokerage network in Japan, the first foreign firm to do so. In December 1997, it announced its intention to establish about 50 brokerage outlets, some of them former Yamaichi branches, and to hire some ex-Yamaichi staff. Merrill Lynch's move reflects the growing demand for Western investment products and a mistrust of ailing local banks and brokers by Japanese investors.

Liberalisation and deregulation

The banking crisis prompted reform. In June 1997, the government produced a timetable for a Japanese 'Big Bang': a programme of liberalisation and deregulation ambitiously aimed at propelling Japan's equity market to the size and sophistication of New York's by the year 2002.[25] The key points of the Big Bang plan are:

- abolition of fixed commissions on equity sales and insurance premiums
- banks, stockbrokers and insurance companies to be permitted to undertake each other's activities
- financial holding companies to be allowed, doing away with the separation of banks and securities houses
- pension fund managers to be able to invest more in equities
- asset managers to be required to disclose the market value of their investments to allow appraisal of their performance
- licensed foreign exchange banks to lose their monopoly
- movement towards international accounting standards so that investors can assess the real value of financial institutions
- Bank of Japan to be given nominal independence to set interest rates
- powers of the Securities and Exchange Surveillance Commission to be strengthened and penalties raised

The plan was widely welcomed, even by the stockbroking industry. But it also attracted criticism on several counts. First, how would the authorities cope with the large number of collapses of financial firms that would result from the competition unleashed by deregulation, particularly amongst the country's 230 second-tier stockbrokers and many small banks? Second, the inadequacy of the plans to strengthen the supervision of the financial sector 'If you don't have proper inspection and supervision,' warns a senior analyst at James Capel Pacific, 'you won't have a Big Bang but a catastrophic explosion.'[26]

Finally, the failure to address the problem of Post Office subsidised savings accounts is an unresolved issue. The Japanese Post Office, the world's largest savings bank with 23,000 branches, is the linchpin of Japan's system of gathering savings from individuals for investment. Traditionally, it has offered depositors higher rates than banks and better yields than equities. Under current arrangements, no rational investor would move his savings from the Post Office to equities, blocking the development of other parts of the financial system.

Nevertheless, the reform plan is a radical step and deregulation is firmly on Japan's financial agenda. Ultimately, it is expected to promote a restructuring of Japanese banking, securities and insurance activities along the universal banking model common in Continental Europe, under single holding companies.[27] The opportunities presented by liberalisation and deregulation led foreign banks and insurance companies to boost their presence in Japan through alliances with Japanese partners. Examples include: US insurance giant American International Group with Mitsubishi Trust and Banking; Swiss Bank Corporation and Long-Term Credit Bank; and Bankers Trust with Nippon Credit Bank. Barclays Bank also tried this route: 'Deregulation is going to offer some exciting opportunities,' said a spokesman announcing a tie-up with Hokkaido Takushoku Bank in June 1997.[28] He was right about the excitement – the Japanese bank failed a few months later.

The East Asia financial crisis that began in summer 1997 was a difficult context in which to pursue reform. And yet the fragility of many Japanese banks and brokers, having huge bad debts and troubled business franchises and making losses, and of the Japanese financial system itself, makes reform essential and urgent. The process is likely to be problematic and painful.

In a Nutshell

London, New York and Tokyo, the three global financial centres, are each the principal financial centre in their respective time zones, providing a wide range of services to a worldwide clientele. In international financial business, the scale of activities in London surpasses that of New York and Tokyo by virtually every measure. But the size and scope of financial activity in New York and Tokyo is greatly boosted by also being the most important domestic financial centres of the world's two largest economies and major international currencies.

New York, where the financial services sector is often referred to as 'Wall Street', hosts the world's largest and most creative capital market and money market. International bank lending, foreign exchange dealing and derivatives trading are also major activities. Tokyo became an important international financial centre in the 1980s. Japan's economic problems and structural rigidities in the financial sector have restrained its development in the 1990s. It is anticipated that liberalisation and deregulation of the financial sector will lead to renewed dynamism.

FURTHER READING

Roberts, Richard, 'The Economics of Cities of Finance', in Diederiks H. A. and Reeder D. (eds), *Cities of Finance* (Amsterdam, North-Holland, 1996)

Roberts, Richard (ed), *International Financial Centres: Concepts, Development and Dynamics* (Aldershot, Edward Elgar, 1994)

Roberts Richard (ed), *Global Financial Centres: London, New York, Tokyo* (Aldershot, Edward Elgar, 1994)

E. P. Davis, 'International Financial Centres – An Industrial Analysis', *Bank of England Discussion Paper*, no. 51, (1990)

McGahey, Richard; Malloy, Mary; Kazanas, Katherine and Jacobs Michael, *Financial Services, Financial Centers: Public Policy and the Competition for Markets, Firms and Jobs* (Boulder Col., Westview Press, 1990)

Hayes, Samuel and Hubbard, Philip *Investment Banking: A Tale of Three Cities* (Boston Mass., Havard Business School Press, 1990)

Alletzhauser, Al *The House of Nomura* (London, Bloomsbury, 1990)

Taggart Murphy, R., *The Real Price of Japanese Money* (London, Weidenfeld & Nicolson, 1996)

NOTES AND REFERENCES

In the list below for this chapter, any reference to an author alone should be taken to be a reference to his/her work in 'Further reading' above.

1 Batten, David C., 'Characteristics of the New York Financial Markets', in Swiss Bankers' Association, *International Financial Centres: Structure, Achievements and Prospects* (Swiss Bankers Association, Basle, 1987)

2 *London Stock Exchange, Fact File, 1997* (converted at £1:$1.65)

3 *Financial Times*, 24 September 1997

4 Bank of Japan, *Comparative Economic and Financial Statistics: Japan and Other Major Countries*, 1996

5 *The Banker*, March 1987

6 *The Banker*, March 1987

7 *The Banker*, March 1997

8 'Rush for the big league', *Financial Times*, 11 July 1996

9 *Japan Statistical Yearbook 1997* (occupational census 1991).

10 *Financial Times*, 16 June 1997

11 Japan Securities Research Institute, *Securities Market in Japan 1996*

12 Japanese Ministry of Finance, Securities Bureau, *33rd Annual Report*, 6 March 1996

13 Bank for International Settlements, *Annual Report*, 1996, statistical annex

14 Bank of Japan, *Economic Statistics Monthly*, December 1996

15 *Financial Times*, 4 September 1997

16 *Financial Times*, 21 August 1997

17 *Financial Times*, 18 September 1997

18 *Financial Times*, 18 September 1997

19 Bank of Japan, *Comparative Economic and Financial Statistics: Japan and Other Major Countries*, 1996

20 Lapper, Richard, 'Restrictions set to ease', *FT Survey of Japanese Finance, Financial Times*, 25 March 1997

21 Jackson, Tony, 'Confidence crisis', *Financial Times*, 13 July 1992

22 *Financial Times*, 1 December 1997

23 *Financial Times*, 2 September 1997

24 'Foreign banks build up Tokyo finance houses', *Reuters News Service*, 18 October 1996

25 Dawkins, William, 'A big bang in slow motion', *Financial Times*, 10 December 1996

26 Dawkins, William, 'A big bang in slow motion', *Financial Times*, 10 December 1996

27 Plender, John, 'Fears of collateral damage', *Financial Times*, 1 April 1997

28 *Financial Times*, 18 June 1997

CHAPTER 8

Frankfurt, Paris, Hong Kong and Singapore as International Financial Centres

INTRODUCTION

This chapter surveys a further four leading international financial centres: Frankfurt, Paris, Hong Kong and Singapore. Each conducts international financial business on a worldwide basis, but on a smaller scale than the global centres of London, New York and Tokyo and with more regional focus. All face strong competition and new challenges. For Frankfurt and Paris, the issue of the moment is the introduction of Europe's single currency, the euro, in 1999. Both are striving to reap maximum benefits from the opportunities thrown up by this development, competing fiercely with each other and with London and other European financial centres. For Hong Kong and Singapore, the topical questions are the effects of Hong Kong's return to Chinese sovereignty in July 1997 and the impact of the East Asia financial crisis that began in 1997. In each case, there is much at stake and much to play for.

FRANKFURT

Frankfurt-am-Main has been an important financial centre since the Middle Ages. Briefly eclipsed by Berlin in the early decades of the twentieth century, it has been Germany's leading financial centre since the end of World War II. Some 59,000 people work in banking and a further 7,000 in insurance in Frankfurt, 12 per cent of the city's workforce.[1] The indicators shown in Table 8.1 confirm the generally held perception that 'Finanzplatz Frankfurt' is Continental Europe's foremost international financial centre, being ahead of Paris on five out of the seven indicators, and ahead of Switzerland on four. However, it lags behind London on all of them.

Table 8.1: Frankfurt as an international financial centre: some indicators

	Volume	World rank
International banking		
Cross-border bank lending[a]		
(Germany – 1996)	$606 billion	6
Foreign banks present[b]		
(Frankfurt – 1995) branch, subsidiary, rep. office etc.	277	4
Capital market		
Equity market capitalisation[c]		
(Germany – 1995)	$577 billion	4
International equities turnover[d]		
(Germany – 1996)	$23 billion	4
Asset management		
Institutional equity holdings[e]		
(Frankfurt – 1995)	$157 billion	8
Money markets		
Foreign exchange turnover[f]		
(Germany – 1995) net daily turnover	$76 billion	7
Derivatives contracts[g]		
(DTB – 1997) average monthly volume	9 million	3

Sources:
[a] IMF, *International Financial Statistics* (Washington D.C., August 1997).
[b] Jao,Y.C., *Hong Kong as an International Financial Centre* (Hong Kong, City University of Hong Kong Press, 1997).
[c] *Emerging Stock Markets Factbook 1996* (Washington D.C., International Finance Corporation, 1996).
[d] *London Stock Exchange Fact File* (London, London Stock Exchange, 1997).
[e] British Invisibles, *UK Financial Trends & World Invisible Trade 1997* (London, 1997).
[f] Bank for International Settlements, *Triennial Survey of Foreign Exchange* (Basle, BIS, 1995).
[g] Liffe, *World Volumes* (London, August 1997).

Banking

Frankfurt is host to more than 400 banks, including some 250 foreign banks.[2] It is the location of the headquarters of the Deutsche Bundesbank, the German central bank, and the European Central Bank (see Chapter 5). Despite some consolidation, the German domestic banking system remains fragmented, comprising private-sector universal commercial banks, savings banks, credit associations, and a variety of specialised credit institutions such as mortgage banks, postal banks and building-

and-loan associations. It is widely recognised that Germany is over-banked – there are more than 37,000 bank offices, one per 2,150 inhabitants, which is almost double the density in the US. The announcements in summer 1997 of the merger of the Bankgesellschaft Berlin with the Noddeutsche Landesbank, and the Bayerische Vereins-bank with the Bayerische Hypotheken und Weschelbank was interpreted by some as heralding the onset of a shakeout, yet others were sceptical. 'We can only talk about structural changes when people's powers of imagination reach far enough to allow German public sector banks to combine or link up with co-operative or private sector banks,' a cautious Hilmar Kopper, former Deutsche Bank chairman, told the *Financial Times*. 'So far, the imagination is lacking for this now.'[3]

Every type of bank plays a part in the German financial system, but it is the private-sector universal commercial banks and some of the publicly owned regional savings banks that are most active in the Frankfurt financial markets and that are the international players. First and foremost are Frankfurt's big three universal commercial banks, Com-merzbank, Deutsche Bank and Dresdner Bank, whose skyscraper head-quarters have earned the city the nick-name 'Mainhattan',[4] plus the Munich-based Bayerische Hypo-und Vereinsbank. The leading second-tier players are Frankfurt's Kreditanstalt für Eiederaufbau, DG Bank, and BHF-Bank, the Dusseldorf-based Westdeutsche Landesbank Girozen-trale, the Berlin-based Bankgesellschaft Berlin, the Munich-based Bayeri-sche Landes Bank, and the Hanover-based Norddeutsche Landesbank. Also significant is the privately owned Cologne-based investment bank Sal. Oppenheim.

Most of the top 100 international banks have a presence in Frankfurt, usually a subsidiary or branch. Around 130 lesser foreign banks execute their business through representative offices, although this considerably restricts their activities.

The capital market
The Deutsche Börse – the Frankfurt Stock Exchange – is much the most important of Germany's eight regional bourses. Frankfurt handles around 80 per cent of the volume of all German equity trading and 75 per cent of bond trading.[5] In May 1995, the three leading German bourses, Frankfurt, Dusseldorf and Munich announced a merger, a move that was expected eventually to lead to the closure of the smaller exchanges. Since 1991, the Deutsche Börse has been the supplier of automated trading services to the other bourses.

A new electronic trading system known as 'Xetra' was introduced at the end of 1997. The new system cut the cost of transactions by half and increased liquidity by automatically matching buyers and sellers. It is envisaged that the more efficient bourse will encourage more of Germany's plentiful private companies to go public to raise finance for investment more cheaply than through traditional bank lending. It also enhances the Frankfurt market's appeals to investors by increasing transparency and making it easier to spot transgressions. Foreign investors will have remote access by computer. 'What's important is what it means for Germany as a financial centre,' says the DTB's Werner Seifert. 'Xetra is much more than simply a trading system.'[6]

Fixed-interest securities are the most important element of the German capital market, bond turnover being about three times equity turnover in 1996.[7] There are two types of bond issuer – the public authorities, notably the federal government, whose bonds are called *bunds*, and the banks. The almost complete absence of corporate bonds, because of unfavourable taxation, is a notable feature of the market. Banks are the main trading members of the Frankfurt exchange, although there are some specialist broking firms. Frankfurt's combined bonds and equity turnover of DM5,800 billion ($3,400 billion) in the nine months of January–October 1996 was third-largest amongst world securities exchanges.[8]

Traditionally, the stock market has played a far smaller role in financing companies than in the US, Japan or the UK. 'I'm afraid we are still sort of an emerging country in this respect,' says Rolf Breuer, chairman of the Deutsche Börse supervisory board, '– on our way, but far from having reached a situation where the size and importance of the equity market reflect the strength of the underlying market.'[9] Recent years have seen efforts by financial leaders to foster an 'equity culture' amongst German investors, a notable milestone being the highly successful DM20 billion Deutsche Telekom privatisation issue of November 1996, which boosted Germany's four million individual shareholders by a further one-and-a-half million.[10] The Neuer Markt – New Market – launched in February 1997 to serve small, innovative, high-tech companies, is meeting a real need. There are also moves afoot to make legal reforms that will encourage the development of fully funded Anglo-Saxon-type pension funds. This would be a big boost both for demand for equities and for asset management services, asset management being the least developed aspect of Frankfurt as an international financial centre.

Another development driving the German capital market towards the Anglo-Saxon model was the launch of Germany's first hostile takeover bid in spring 1997. Backed by Deutsche Bank, Dresdner Bank and

Goldman Sachs, engineering corporation Krupp-Hoesch made an offer for steelmaker Thyssen. The move was completely out of keeping with German social market practices and provoked a furious reaction from trade unionists and politicians, besides Thyssen executives. Such was the outcry that Krupp-Hoesch backed off and dropped the bid, but the precedent has been set.

The money markets

The Frankfurt money market is an interbank market, where banks deal in short-term debt instruments. There is no institutional or physical structure, dealing being done by telephone between the banks. The Bundesbank is active in the money market, buying and selling securities in order to influence interest rates and the money supply.

The Deutsche Terminbörse (DTB) – German Futures Exchange – is Frankfurt's financial futures and options market. The DTB opened for business in 1990, and since 1995 has been run by the Deutsche Börse. Business grew rapidly from the outset, and by 1996 turnover was 77 million contracts, behind only the Chicago exchanges and London's Liffe. The DTB dominates German equity instruments, notably DAX (the equity market index) products, which constitute 60 per cent of turnover. In interest rate products it competes with Liffe, the London derivatives market having taken the lead when it launched a ten-year *Bund* futures contract in September 1988, two years ahead of the DTB. This contract was soon Liffe's most successful product, much to Frankfurt's chagrin. But in 1998, the DTB's 10-year bund contract overtook Liffe's, capturing 80 per cent of the market.

From the outset, the DTB adopted an electronic screen-based trading system, rather than the traditional 'open outcry' trading system used in Chicago and London. Screen-based trading has proved substantially cheaper than open outcry and its liquidity shortcomings are being overcome. 'Cost is becoming a key issue for clients,' says a continental European derivatives salesman. 'Today, large trades can be executed on an electronic system just as easily as in open outcry.'[11] The electronic system also allows the DTB to offer its services directly in other financial centres, as traders everywhere are linked through DTB screens. The DTB's capture of a dominant share of trading in the 10-year German *bund* futures contract puts it in a strong position to establish its 10-year euro-denominated bond futures contract as the benchmark contract for the new European currency.

The European Union's Investment Services Directive, which came into effect in January 1996, permitted EU members free access to each others' financial markets. The DTB seized the opportunity to create a network of terminals across the continent, linked to its electronic trading system. They provide ready access to German derivative instruments, making it harder for Liffe or other rivals to compete in such products and creating the basis for expanding into other products, notably the euro.

Jockeying for position in the run-up to the start of use of the euro in 1999 led the DTB to forge alliances with the Swiss and French derivatives exchanges. A full merger between the DTB and Soffex, the Swiss exchange, was announced in autumn 1997, to form a single market called Eurex. This was a significant departure, the first time that two large derivatives markets in different countries had pooled their trading and clearing. Then a tie-up was announced between Eurex and the French exchange Matif, the parties operating as a single market with a common product range and unified screen-based trading facilities. 'Eurex is open to other exchanges,' says a spokesman. 'It definitely sees itself as a nucleus for a European exchange.'[12]

'Finanzplatz Frankfurt'

Since 1994, Frankfurt has been host to the European Monetary Institute, the forerunner of a European Central Bank (ECB). Proximity to the institution that will set the euro-zone's monetary policy confers advantages to banks with a presence in Frankfurt, argues Deutsche Bank chairman Rolf Breuer. 'We in Frankfurt have decided to play on that – in a friendly competitive manner. We will try to establish close connections with the decision-makers in the ECB and thus cultivate a better market feeling for the decisions to be made.'[13] Yet in 1995, his own bank and Dresdner Bank shifted their international capital markets activities to London, a reminder of Frankfurt's limitations. 'London,' comments former Dresdner chairman Jürgen Sarrazin, 'is the centre for investment banking, and you can't transplant it.'[14]

The promotion of Frankfurt as a financial centre is undertaken by the Wirtschaftsförderung Frankfurt, an entity of the local government authority, whose initiatives include the provision of Japanese and Korean language schools to persuade banks and corporations from these countries to locate in the city. The Finanzplatz Association, formed in 1996, is a private-sector initiative to promote Frankfurt, backed by the Deutsche Börse and a group of bankers. It focuses on practical problems, such as a shortage of specialists in derivatives and securitisation, and lobbies the Bundesbank and government about regulations and imposts that make Frankfurt uncompetitive. It has been rewarded by a more supportive stance from the Bundesbank, although complaints about *reformstau* – a reform backlog – persist.[15] The Bundesbank has added its voice to the protests, arguing that the unfairness and complexity of Germany's tax system discourages business activity and job creation.[16] As attention focuses on the new opportunities stemming from the euro, the struggle between Frankfurt and its rivals, both London and Paris, is intensifying.

PARIS

In the nineteenth and early twentieth centuries, Paris was Continental Europe's most important international financial centre, although it never developed the worldwide scope of London's markets. Then, as now, the government played a major role in determining the form of French financial institutions and in promoting Paris as a financial centre, for political as well as economic reasons. Widespread nationalisation of the banking system by a Socialist administration in the early 1980s was a setback for Paris as an international financial centre, being out of step with the trends towards the liberalisation, deregulation and globalisation of financial markets. London's Big Bang, beginning in 1983, highlighted the over-regulation and international uncompetitiveness of the Paris markets. Moreover, Frankfurt and Switzerland were actively competing for Continental clients. In 1986, the French government executed an abrupt about-turn. It initiated a programme of bank privatisation and a set of reforms to boost the position of Paris as an international financial centre – 'Paris Europlace' – that have continued into the 1990s. Paris Europlace even assumed a physical expression – the glittering towers of the new financial district 'La Défence.'

Paris ranks perhaps fifth or sixth amongst the world's international financial centres by the indicators listed in Table 8.2, although Paris Europlace publications put it firmly in fourth place.[17] Amongst European centres, it is behind London on every measure and trails Frankfurt on five of the most significant seven. But it is ahead of Switzerland on four indicators, and well ahead of the lesser European financial centres such as Amsterdam, Brussels, Madrid and Milan. The EMU process offers new opportunities for Paris that are being energetically pursued.

Table 8.2: Paris as an international financial centre: some indicators

	Volume	World rank
International banking		
Cross-border bank lending[a]		
(France – 1996)	$683 billion	4
Foreign banks present[b]		
(Paris – 1995) branch, subsidiary, rep. office etc.	114	7
Capital market		
Equity market capitalisation[c]		
(France – 1995)	$522 billion	5
International equities turnover[d]		
(France – 1996)	$7 billion	5
Asset management		
Institutional equity holdings[e]		
(Paris – 1995)	$261 billion	5
Money markets		
Foreign exchange turnover[f]		
(France – 1995) net daily turnover	$58 billion	8
Derivatives contracts[g]		
(Matif – 1997) average monthly volume	6 million	5

Sources:
[a] IMF, *International Financial Statistics* (Washington D.C., August 1997).
[b] Jao, Y.C., *Hong Kong as an International Financial Centre* (Hong Kong, City University of Hong Kong Press, 1997).
[c] *Emerging Stock Markets Factbook 1996* (Washington D.C., International Finance Corporation, 1996).
[d] *London Stock Exchange Fact File* (London, London Stock Exchange, 1997).
[e] British Invisibles, *UK Financial Trends & World Invisible Trade 1997* (London, 1997).
[f] Bank for International Settlements, *Triennial Survey of Foreign Exchange* (Basle, BIS, 1995).
[g] Liffe, *World Volumes* (London, August 1997).

Banking

The French banking sector comprises 1,445 French and foreign-owned establishments.[18] Seven out of the world's top 50 banks are Paris-headquartered French banks, and five of Europe's ten largest banks, by assets, are French. The leading commercial banks, notably the Banque National de Paris, Société Générale and Crédit Lyonnais, and the French-style investment bank Paribas are important international players contributing significantly to France's rank of fourth in cross-border lending. The major French banks are 'universal' banks – offering both retail and investment banking services – but there are also smaller banks specialising in activities such as mergers and acquisitions or capital markets. The substantial co-operative and mutual banking sector, led by Crédit Agricole, Groupe Caisse d'Epargne and Crédit Mutuel are more domestically focused, but enhance the breadth and depth to the markets.

There are some 400 non-resident banks and financial institutions in Paris, more than any other European city except London. Foreign banks are active in the money markets, especially in derivatives, and provide specialist banking services for international corporations. Since the mid-1980s, French banks have invested $500 million abroad, creating the second-largest banking network worldwide.

The mid-1990s were difficult years for the French commercial banks; they suffered heavy losses from the slump in property values and bad debts. Most controversial of all was Crédit Lyonnais, at the time the world's biggest bank outside Japan, which was bailed out by French taxpayers at a cost of some $10 billion after an extraordinary saga of incompetence, corruption and political interference.[19]

An urgent need for sweeping reforms and restructuring in the French banking sector was the conclusion of a highly critical report produced by the French Senate in November 1996. It identified problems of poor credit judgment, structural rigidities, overstaffing, and inflexible labour laws. 'The banking sector is facing a crisis without precedent,' commented the report's secretary.[20] And his alarmist words were vindicated by the government's failure to find a buyer to privatise the bank Union Européenne de CIC.

The capital market
The Paris Bourse is the focal institution of the capital market. It is much the most important of the seven French stock exchanges run by the Société des Bourses Françaises (SBF). Although a commercial profit-making company, the SBF operates under the control of the Ministry of Economy and Finance. It is regulated by the Commission des Opérations de Bourse.

The French capital market saw far-reaching reforms following the government's 1986 policy u-turn, making up for lost time in an attempt to make Paris competitive as an international financial centre. That year saw the creation of the Matif futures exchange and the beginning of the move to an automated screen-based trading system, CAC (*Cotation Assistée en Continue*). An equity options exchange, Monep, was established in 1987. In 1988, Paris had its own Big Bang: the abolition of the monopoly of the traditional broking firms, many of which were bought by banks; the end of the brokers' fixed commissions; and the introduction of 'dual capacity' – that is, securities firms acting as both brokers and market makers. So radical was the shake-up that the SBF was reported as having 'little to do' to comply with the provisions of the EU's Investment Services Directive of January 1996.[21]

Market turnover on the Paris Bourse is dominated by bonds, which comprise four-fifths of transactions. The French bond market has grown spectacularly since the mid-1980s, outstanding issues increasing from FF585 billion in 1985 to FF4,600 billion ($800 billion) in 1997.[22] The market covers a full range of maturities and is highly transparent and liquid. The French bond market constitutes around 40 per cent of Bourse-based transactions in the European bond markets. Trading volume has increased tenfold since the early 1980s; in 1996 trading turnover of bonds was FF60.2 trillion.

The Paris Bourse ranks fifth in size in terms of world equity market capitalisation. In the decade prior to 1997, total capitalisation almost doubled, boosted by 150 new listings and the privatisation of 26 large and prestigious companies, including France Telecom and Air France. In winter 1996, the SBF conducted its first mass-market advertising campaign to persuade French companies to seek a listing. Another initiative was the establishment of the Nouveau Marché, aimed at new, fast-growing, often high-tech companies. Yet there is a long way to go, stock market capitalisation in France (and Germany) being around 30 per cent of gross domestic product compared with 160 per cent in the UK.[23] The French equity market is already highly internationalised, non-French investors – first and foremost the big US pension funds – holding 35 per cent of equity capitalisation and accounting for 40 per cent of trading volume.[24]

The Bourse and the French authorities are seeking maximum advantage from the introduction of the euro. The ambition is to establish French government bonds, instead of German *bunds*, as the benchmark of euro-denominated bond trading after 1999.[25] Benchmark status will win prestige and business for Paris in the international capital markets and lower the cost of government borrowing. To this end, new government bonds covering the full spectrum of maturities have been developed to serve as benchmarks for the spread of euro securities.[26] From the first day of euro trading in 1999, all securities prices in Paris will be quoted in euros and all government debt will be redenominated in euros. Additional favourable factors are the sophisticated market in 'repos' – securities repurchase contracts that are attractive to investors – and Europe's most developed bond 'strips' market. 'Strips' are the different components of a conventional bond, separated and traded as distinct securities. 'Competition between France and Germany to win the benchmark status in the euro is becoming more aggressive all the time,' says a banker at ABN-Amro. 'At the moment it looks as if the French are gaining the advantage.'[27]

The SBF's advanced quotation system is selling well to other exchanges, providing both profits and close technical ties. Taking the battle to the Anglo-Saxon enemy, it has opened a telecommunications hub in the UK offering direct-access real-time dealing on the Paris Bourse, bypassing the London Stock Exchange's trading system, SEAQ International. 'What is SEAQ International?' muses SBF chairman Jean-Francois Théodore provocatively. 'It used to be very powerful. Now it is a ghost.'[28] Théodore's grand vision is of an alliance amongst the Paris, Frankfurt and Brussels stock exchanges to share technology and co-operate in the marketing of equities within the euro-zone to investors from outside the region. 'We have the feeling that we have the right cards in our hand,' says Théodore.[29]

The money markets

The French money market in overall terms has two elements: *le marché interbancaire* – the interbank market; and a broad-based market in short-term negotiable securities. The interbank market forms the core of the French money market. The commodity dealt in is balances at the Banque de France, the French central bank (see Chapter 5). The participants are market professionals – large commercial and investment banks and bank-type public savings institutions. The short-term securities market is open to all – banks, industrial and commercial corporations, insurance companies, mutual funds and high-net-worth individuals. It comprises all money-market operations between banks and other parties, and amongst other parties.

With a daily turnover of $58 billion, Paris ranked eighth in the world in the 1995 BIS survey of foreign exchange dealing. Amongst European financial centres it was fourth, behind London ($465 billion per day), Switzerland ($87 billion), and Frankfurt ($76 billion), but a long way ahead of Amsterdam ($26 billion), Milan ($23 billion) and Madrid ($18 billion). The advent of the euro will mean the elimination of the European currency cross-trades that constitute much of the foreign-exchange business of the smaller centres, and it is hoped in Paris that it will be a beneficiary of the transfer of trading to the major centres.

The Marché à Terme International de France (Matif), the Paris derivatives exchange, was set up in February 1986, one of the government-led measures to modernise the French financial markets. In fact, the chairman, Gérard Pfauwadel, was the French treasury official who drafted the legislation. The initial shareholders comprised about 100 banks and insurance companies, but in September 1997 the SBF, operator of the Paris Bourse as well as the much smaller Monep equity options market, acquired control. By linking with the Bourse, Matif aims to take advantage of its technological prowess, cut costs for members, and increase opportunities for new equity products. 'A strategic move to create critical mass on the eve of the new era of the euro,' explains SBF chairman Jean-Francois Théodore.[30]

Initially, Matif's growth was impressive, and by 1991 the volume of business was almost as great as London's Liffe, the longest-established and leading European derivatives exchange. But thereafter the rate of growth slowed, and from 1994 the volume of Matif contracts actually declined, being overtaken by the DTB in 1996.

As the countdown to EMU approached, it became widely agreed that the advent of the euro would mean reduced demand for hedging instruments such as futures and options and substantial overcapacity in the European derivatives market. Wary of being squeezed by its bigger rivals, in autumn 1997 Matif forged an alliance with Eurex, the new German–Swiss derivatives exchange emerging from the merger of DTB and Soffex. It was announced that the parties would operate as a single market with a common product range and a unified screen-based trading facility. 'What we are doing,' explained Jörg Franke, head of the DTB, 'is concentrating our markets into one single exchange to try to offer investors the most liquid trading system.'[31]

Asset management

Paris is a significant centre for asset management, ranking ahead of Frankfurt but behind London and Switzerland. Funds under management in summer 1997 totalled $536 billion.[32] The merger of French insurance companies Axa and UAP created the world's second-largest asset manager, with more than $400 billion under management. At the end of 1996, there were nearly 5,300 mutual funds, with assets totalling $500 billion. Legislation in November 1996 greatly enhanced the scope for private pensions raising the prospect of a major expansion of fund management in France.

Firms engaged in asset management in France include banks and other credit institutions, insurers, brokers, and asset management specialists. Money-market funds represent about 45 per cent of the market, bond funds about 30 per cent, balanced funds about 12 per cent, equity funds about 10 per cent, and hedge funds around 3 per cent.[33]

'Paris Europlace'

'The challenge ... is the euro,' says Matif's Gérard Pfauwadel. 'It is a question of do or die.'[34] The administration and French financial institutions are working hard to be equal to the challenge. French officials are insisting that the new European Central Bank conducts its money-market operations through the national central banks rather than through a single centralised market. This will allow the Banque de France to continue to trade on the Paris market, preventing business moving to Frankfurt. In fact, it is hoped that business will shift from the smaller and less well prepared European financial centres to 'Paris Europlace'. Europe's minnow-sized financial markets are expected to be disadvan-taged by the disappearance of products that constitute much of their trading activity, notably their own currency money market and derived currency and interest rate futures contracts. 'When the euro arrives,' says the president of Belfox, the Belgian futures and options exchange, 'we will lose all our interest-rate products. It is as simple as that.'[35]

France is further advanced in planning for the advent of the euro than any other country. 'The euro zone will be regarded by non-European investors as a single zone,' says the SBF's Jean-Francois Théodore, 'and all the indications are that, for instance, big US investors will very rapidly want to reallocate their investments accordingly and place their money in euros.' From the outset, all French treasury debt, stock market prices and derivative products are to be quoted in euros. The French government's decision to convert all public debt to euros should ensure the rapid formation of a euro-denominated money market, perhaps ahead of other European financial markets, allowing Paris to gain a permanent advant-age. 'We must not daydream and one can imagine that there will be room for everyone,' says Matif's Gérard Pfauwadel. 'There could be a division along product lines, with one market dominating interest rate products, another currencies, and yet another equities. One can also imagine markets being divided up by maturity segments. But ... in the best of worlds, we will be the global leader and Paris will become the euro's domestic market.'[36]

HONG KONG

Hong Kong ranks second after Tokyo as a financial centre in the Asia–Pacific region, but as an international financial centre it is ahead on several counts. It surpasses its rival Singapore on five of the seven indicators in Table 8.3, and is far ahead of all other Asian financial centres. Banking, finance and insurance are important activities in Hong Kong, employing 167,000 people in 1997, 5 per cent of the labour force, and up from 39,000 in 1975.[37] The financial services sector broadly defined – banking and insurance plus real estate and business services – employs 408,000, 12 per cent of the workforce.[38] This is a formidable level of activity, which generates strong competitive external economies of scale. But there are also significant uncertainties hanging over Hong Kong, in particular the effect of the transfer of sovereignty to China in July 1997 and the impact of the East Asia financial crisis that began in 1997.

Table 8.3: Hong Kong as an international financial centre: some indicators

	Volume/ number	World rank
International banking		
Cross-border bank lending[a]		
(Hong Kong – 1996)	$608 billion	5
Foreign banks present[b]		
(Hong Kong – 1995) branch, subsidiary, rep. office etc.	357	2
Capital market		
Equity market capitalisation[c]		
(Hong Kong – 1995)	$303 billion	9
International equities turnover[d]		
(Hong Kong – 1996)	$0.2 billion	15
Asset management		
Institutional equity holdings[e]		
(Hong Kong – 1995)	$71 billion	9
Money markets		
Foreign exchange turnover[f]		
(Hong Kong – 1995) net daily turnover	$90 billion	5
Derivatives contracts[g]		
(HKFE – 1997) average monthly volume	0.6 million	19

Sources:
[a] IMF, *International Financial Statistics* (Washington D.C., August 1997).
[b] Jao, Y.C., *Hong Kong as an International Financial Centre* (Hong Kong, City University of Hong Kong Press, 1997).
[c] *Emerging Stock Markets Factbook 1996* (Washington D.C., International Finance Corporation, 1996).
[d] *London Stock Exchange Fact File* (London, London Stock Exchange, 1997).
[e] British Invisibles, *UK Financial Trends & World Invisible Trade 1997* (London, 1997).
[f] Bank for International Settlements, *Triennial Survey of Foreign Exchange* (Basle, BIS, 1995).
[g] Liffe, *World Volumes* (London, August 1997).

A variety of internal and external reasons for Hong Kong's success as an international financial centre have been identified by Professor Y. C. Jao.[39] The important *internal* factors – those inherent to Hong Kong and over which it has some control – are: political and economic stability; economic freedom; a sound legal system and the rule of law; competent and responsive government; non-discriminatory treatment of foreign nationals; a favourable tax regime; an efficient and modern infrastructure; unimpeded news and information flows; a skilled workforce; use of English; and an effective but light-touch and low-cost regulatory regime. The favourable *external* factors – those constituting a favourable economic and political environment – are: its time-zone situation, lying between the European and North American time zones; its location in the rapidly growing Asia–Pacific region; specialisation in the fast-expanding global banking and finance industries; and the close connection with China.

Banking

Banking is the linchpin of Hong Kong's financial activities, with some 500 authorised institutions.[40] It is host to 357 foreign banks, more than any other centre except London, including 82 of the world's top 100 banks. Two-thirds of banking business is denominated in foreign currencies.[41] By the yardstick of cross-border bank lending, Hong Kong ranks fifth among international financial centres, on account of its importance as a loan syndication centre. Hong Kong-based internationally active banks routinely arrange huge credits for borrowers in the Asia–Pacific region, new syndicated loans in 1996 exceeding $32 billion.[42]

The banking sector has a three-tier structure, comprising licensed banks, restricted licence banks, and deposit-taking companies. Amongst the 175 fully licensed banks, the pre-eminent institutions are the Hongkong Bank (owned by HSBC Holdings) and Standard Chartered Bank, both long-established British banks, the Bank of China, owned by the mainland government, and the indigenous Bank of East Asia. By long-standing tradition, the first three issue Hong Kong's banknotes. The Hongkong Bank has an extra-special place in the territory's financial life, being the biggest bank, the government's principal banker, and where 75 per cent of the population hold accounts.[43]

For much of the 1990s, the Hong Kong banking market was enviably profitable.[44] The principal reasons were:

- rapid growth of the Hong Kong economy, boosted by the dynamic Chinese economy with which it has close ties
- the 'cartel', an arrangement by which the Hong Kong Association

of Banks sets interest rates paid on deposits, enhancing bank margins by keeping rates artificially low

- 'ridiculously low' bad debt levels – 'people just do not default on loans here,' says Stephen Li, of securities house Jardine Fleming[45]
- low interest rates due to the 'peg' between the Hong Kong dollar and the US dollar
- dominance of bank loans over bonds, due to the under-developed bond market

Although the emergence of the Asian bond market is widely predicted to erode the last of these factors, and others may be waning, the Hong Kong banking market remains the most profitable in the region.[46] Hong Kong's banks are ploughing their profits into expansion on the mainland of China, across the border into Guangdong province and beyond.

All the major international investment banks have a presence in Hong Kong. Jardine Fleming, a joint venture between Jardine Matheson, one of Hong Kong's founding trading houses, and UK merchant bank Robert Fleming, is a prominent firm. Its alliance with Ka Wah Bank, the Hong Kong financial arm of China's flagship investment vehicle Citic, promises substantial access to mainland business.[47] Peregrine Investments, Hong Kong's largest investment bank, was a home-grown investment bank that built up a business with assets of $5 billion and offices in 16 countries,[48] but in January 1998 it filed for liquidation, having suffered massive losses on Indonesian loans and bonds, a casualty of the East Asian financial crisis.

The capital market

Hong Kong's equity market ranks ninth in the world by market capitalisation, eleventh in total turnover, and sixteenth in the number of listed companies. In Asia, it is second only to Tokyo, with capitalisation of US$449 billion at December 1996. And it has been growing rapidly, serving as an important source of funding for companies throughout the Asia–Pacific region but especially from China. Stock Exchange chairman Edgar Cheng, describes Hong Kong as acting as China's international capital market.[49] In the run-up to the 1997 handover, initial public offerings on behalf of Chinese state-owned enterprises raised $5 billion, while so-called 'red chips' – Hong Kong-listed subsidiaries of mainland enterprises or government departments – raised $3 billion.[50] In the 1990s, mainland companies grew from nothing to 15 per cent of market capitalisation. 'The future of Hong Kong's capital markets is China,' says a Hong Kong-based investment banker, predicting the wholesale flotation of Chinese assets on the Hong Kong market.[51]

Yet the China connection is a mixed blessing, since red chips tend to have a high volatility and originate from a weakly regulated environment in which financial malpractice can flourish. Another danger is that 'the increasing use of Hong Kong as the pre-eminent capital market for China could increase the tendency of regulatory authorities there to play a role in regulating mainland companies listed here,' says the managing director of Hong Kong investment bank Indosuez W.I. Carr. 'The biggest risk … is that Hong Kong loses its authority from a regulatory point of view.'[52]

Hong Kong's bond market, by contrast to its equity market, is puny, smaller than every Asian fixed-interest market except Indonesia's and a quarter of the size of Singapore's. 'Bond markets have always been the gap for us in terms of our status as a financial centre,' says Rafael Hui, Hong Kong's secretary for financial services.[53] The principal reason for this has been the Hong Kong government's conservative fiscal policy, which has generated little public debt. Moreover, the traditional prominence of banks relative to securities firms in the Hong Kong system has favoured bank lending over capital market debt instruments.

Although small, the bond market is growing rapidly, issues rising from $3.5 billion in 1989 to $36 billion in 1996.[54] Its expansion has been deliberately fostered by the Hong Kong Monetary Authority (HKMA) to promote Hong Kong as an international financial centre. Helpful developments include the introduction of Exchange Fund notes and bills in 1990, the establishment of an efficient clearing system for debt securities, the launch of the Mortgage Corporation in 1997, and the creation of a mandatory pension fund in 1998. The advent of the national pension scheme will also be a boost for Hong Kong's fund management industry. 'This will be a vital pool of savings and will help counter the attractions of Singapore,' says Andrew Lo, head of the Hong Kong Investment Funds Association.[55]

Money and bullion markets

The Hong Kong money market is an interbank market for short-term funds generally up to six months in duration. All loans are unsecured, so that borrowers are restricted by limits known locally as 'money market dealing lines'.[56] The leading lenders are the big deposit takers, notably Hongkong Bank, Standard Chartered Bank, the Bank of China and its satellites, the Hang Seng Bank and the Bank of East Asia. The principal borrowers are foreign banks, especially American and Japanese banks, deposit-taking companies, and certain large corporations such as Hong

Kong Land or Jardine Matheson. There are ten firms of brokers, but much money-market activity is transacted directly between banks.

The Hong Kong money market comprises five principal instruments:

- negotiable certificates of deposit (NCDs)
- wholesale deposits
- foreign currency deposits – which grew substantially after the abolition of withholding tax in 1982, although Singapore had stolen the lead as the focus of the Asian dollar market (see below) and remains to the fore
- commercial paper
- Exchange Fund bills and notes, Hong Kong's counterparts to treasury bills and notes

Hong Kong is a leading foreign exchange trading centre, ranking fifth in the BIS survey of 1995, up from sixth place in 1992, with an average daily turnover of $90 billion. Unusually for Asia, the Hong Kong foreign-exchange market operates entirely free from exchange controls or other government restrictions, a vital factor in its dynamic development. Besides the banks, market participants include a host of authorised dealers and money changers. More than four-fifths of trades involve foreign currencies other than the Hong Kong dollar, indicating the international orientation of Hong Kong's foreign-exchange market.[57] The main contracts are $US–DM and $US – yen.

The Hong Kong Futures Exchange (HKFE), Hong Kong's financial derivatives exchange, was established in December 1976. During the worldwide stock market crash of October 1987, the HKFE nearly went bankrupt and had to be rescued by the government. Initially, recovery was shaky, but by 1994 turnover had surpassed the pre-crash peak. Trading is dominated by the Hang Seng Index futures contract, which accounts for four-fifths of turnover despite endeavours to promote other contracts. Interest-rate and currencies futures have been slow in developing, as have options. Diversification may be stimulated by an agreement of September 1996 with the New York Mercantile Exchange (NYMEX), which permits HKFE members to trade NYMEX precious metal and energy products contracts through terminals linked to NYMEX's electronic trading system. Looking to the future, HKFE chairman Frank Wing Kwang Shing states that his ambition is 'to develop Hong Kong into the financial hub of China as well as a financial and derivatives centre of the Asia–Pacific region.'[58]

Hong Kong is one of the world's four major gold-trading centres, the others being London, New York and Zurich. It towers over other Asia–Pacific gold markets, accounting for an estimated 75 per cent of the region's turnover. There are three components: a very active international market; a local market; and a futures market. Gold futures were introduced in 1980, being traded on the HKFE.

The Hong Kong Monetary Authority (HKMA)

The Hong Kong Monetary Authority (HKMA), established in 1993, is Hong Kong's de facto central bank. Its functions and objectives are to:[59]

- maintain currency stability
- protect the currency
- determine monetary policy
- promote the safety and stability of the banking system through the regulation and supervision of banks
- enhance the efficiency, integrity and development of the financial system to promote Hong Kong as a financial centre

Hong Kong's currency, the Hong Kong dollar, is pegged to the US dollar at the fixed exchange rate of HK$7.8 to US$1.0. The Hong Kong dollar is freely convertible into other currencies, such convertibility being ensured by the note-issuing mechanism that requires 100 per cent US-dollar backing for the domestic currency.[60] The continued independence of Hong Kong's currency is enshrined in the Sino-British agreement on the Basic Law for the territory despite its return to Chinese sovereignty. Suggestions that the fixed exchange-rate peg might be undermined by international speculators are misconceived, says Joseph Yam, head of the HKMA.[61] The currency issue is covered six times by foreign-exchange reserves, making the peg impregnable, and there is strong local support for a linked and stable exchange rate.

When a speculative assault was launched on the Hong Kong dollar in January 1995, attempting to force a devaluation, the speculators were taught a 'salutary lesson'.[62] The Hong Kong dollar peg survived the regional currency turbulence of 1997. 'A lot of nonsense has been talked about the collapse of the Thai baht possibly spreading to Hong Kong,' barked Nobel Prize-winning American economist Milton Friedman. 'There is all the difference in the world between the two. Hong Kong ... simply stands ready to convert any Hong Kong dollars into US dollars at 7.8 to 1 and vice versa. They can always do that because they have dollar reserves equal to the value of all the Hong Kong currency outstanding.'[63] So long, of course, that the authorities continue to have the will to do so.

The China connection

Since the beginning of Chinese economic reform in 1979, there has been an enormous growth in commerce and investment between China and Hong Kong. By 1996, the value of trade had risen sixtyfold, China becoming Hong Kong's largest trading partner, and the territory's investments on the mainland had reached a total of $68 billion. This intimate involvement with one of the world's most dynamic economic regions has brought enormous benefits and offers great opportunities. Yet the China connection is not without hazards. Political events in China – the Cultural Revolution of 1966–76, the confidence crisis of 1982–83, the Tiananmen Square tragedy of 1989, and the 1996 Taiwan Strait tensions – sent shivers through Hong Kong's markets. Now that Hong Kong is formally part of China, future tensions and upheavals may be more undermining. But all-in-all, says Vincent Cheng, executive director of the regional arm of HSBC Holdings, 'China provides us with far greater opportunities than risks.'[64]

Then there is the challenge from a resurgent Shanghai, which is already China's foremost domestic financial centre. In the 1920s and 1930s, Shanghai was Asia's pre-eminent financial and commercial centre but relinquished this role with the Communist takeover in 1949. Shanghai's bankers and merchants fled south to Hong Kong, contributing to its emergence as a leading international financial centre. Since liberalisation was allowed by Beijing in 1992, Shanghai's local economy has grown by 14 per cent per annum. Such is the construction boom that it is claimed that one-fifth of the world's high-rise cranes are in Shanghai.[65] The new stock exchange building that opened there in summer 1997 has Asia's largest trading floor. By 2001, the city will boast the world's tallest building, the $1 billion Shanghai World Financial Centre.

An ambitious development plan drawn up in 1994 by the Shanghai branch of the Bank of China envisaged Shanghai joining London, New York and Tokyo as a global international financial centre by 2001.[66] It proposed the opening of a gold market, an offshore financial market, the development of a financial futures sector, and the transfer of state enterprise head offices to that city. But the plan fell foul of rivalry between Beijing and Shanghai, and the timetable was quietly ditched. In fact, some argue that politics will protect Hong Kong from competition from Shanghai. 'I doubt that Beijing as the centre for political dominance in China is going to live with one economic centre,' says Hoong Yik-Luen, ING Barings China research head. 'With two, no one dominates and Beijing can call the shots. They can play the game of two cities fighting for favours.'[67]

SINGAPORE

International financial services is an important sector of Singapore's economy, accounting for about 15 per cent of GDP.[68] This is no accident, financial services being deliberately fostered by the newly independent city-state's authorities from 1968. The Singapore government's motives were twofold: first, a sophisticated financial services sector was considered crucial to the success of the planned programme of industrialisation; and second, financial services was targeted as a high-skill, high-earnings sector to be developed in its own right. Singapore's own economic development stimulated demand for the financial sector's services, but with an area of just 646 sq. km. and a population of only 3.1 million the impact was limited. However, because of its early start, Singapore was well placed to act in the 1980s and 1990s as a funding centre for its much bigger regional neighbours, namely Indonesia, Malaysia, the Philippines and Thailand.

Contributory factors in Singapore's success as a financial centre have been its political stability and civic discipline, its skilled and hard-working labour force, its communications (its airport is consistently voted the world's best by business travellers) and the rigour of its regulatory authority. Since the 1980s, Singapore has challenged Hong Kong for the mantle of Asia's second international financial centre after Tokyo. Although it trails Hong Kong by five of the seven indicators in Table 8.4 the gap has been closing. Singapore has benefited from the uncertainty surrounding Hong Kong's future under Chinese rule, a number of businesses hedging their bets by opening operations in Singapore and some even transferring their activities from Hong Kong to Singapore.

Banking

There are three categories of bank: full licence banks, restricted-licence banks, and offshore-licence banks. All three categories are eligible to establish separate bookkeeping units known as Asian currency units (ACUs) in order to participate in the Asian dollar markets (ADM) (see below). There are 13 local commercial banks, of which the largest are DBS Bank and the Oversea-Chinese Banking Corporation – respectively numbers 74 and 87 amongst the world's top 100 banks – the United Overseas Bank, and the Overseas Union Bank. Singapore is host to 185 foreign banks, up from 120 in the early 1990s.[69] Commerzbank, Banque Indosuez and Commercial Union (an insurance company) are some of the major foreign financial firms that have located their regional headquarters in Singapore. There are also around 75 merchant banks that specialise in underwriting, investment management, mergers and acquisitions, and other fee-based activities.

Table 8.4: Singapore as an international financial centre: some indicators

	Volume	World rank
International banking		
Cross-border bank lending[a]		
(Singapore – 1996)	$439 billion	8
Foreign banks present[b]		
(Singapore – 1995) branch, subsidiary, rep. office etc.	185	5
Capital market		
Equity market capitalisation[c]		
(Singapore – 1995)	$148 billion	18
International equities turnover[d]		
(Singapore – 1996)	insignificant	
Asset management		
Institutional equity holdings[e]		
(Singapore – 1995)	na	na
Money markets		
Foreign exchange turnover[f]		
(Singapore – 1995) net daily turnover	$105 billion	4
Derivatives contracts[g]		
(Simex – 1997) average monthly volume	2 million	9

Sources:
[a] IMF, *International Financial Statistics* (Washington D.C., August 1997).
[b] Jao, Y.C., *Hong Kong as an International Financial Centre* (Hong Kong, City University of Hong Kong Press, 1997).
[c] *Emerging Stock Markets Factbook 1996* (Washington D.C., International Finance Corporation, 1996).
[d] *London Stock Exchange Fact File* (London, London Stock Exchange, 1997).
[e] British Invisibles, *UK Financial Trends & World Invisible Trade 1997* (London, 1997).
[f] Bank for International Settlements, *Triennial Survey of Foreign Exchange* (Basle, BIS, 1995).
[g] Liffe, *World Volumes* (London, August 1997).

Monetary Authority of Singapore

The Monetary Authority of Singapore (MAS) was established in 1971 and is Singapore's central bank. Its functions are:

- formulation and implementation of monetary policy and exchange-rate policy

- banker to the government
- financial agent for the government, conducting the issue of all government securities
- provision of re-discount facilities for bills of exchange, as well as general banking facilities, for banks that maintain current accounts, partly to fulfil prudential cash requirements
- regulation and supervision of the financial sector
- promotion of Singapore as an international financial centre through the development of key financial activities

The currency is the Singapore dollar, issued by the Board of Commissioners of Currency of Singapore. It is 100 per cent backed by external assets. The management of the currency is the responsibility of the MAS. The conduct of monetary policy is constrained by the openness of the economy and its international financial linkages. Thus the policy emphasis has been on the management of the exchange rate rather than the domestic money supply or interest rates. Domestic price stability is the primary objective of exchange-rate policy. The currency is managed against a basket of currencies, weighted in accordance with Singapore's pattern of trade and allowed to float within a broad band. Exchange controls were abolished in 1978.

The MAS also acts as the financial sector's regulator, overseeing banks, securities houses, fund managers, the stock exchange, and the Singapore International Monetary Exchange. It has a reputation for being authoritarian, bureaucratic and tough. 'Our primary mission is to enforce the rules,' says MAS deputy managing director, Koh Beng Seng. 'It would be a concern if banks weren't worried about the actions that would be taken if rules are violated. That's a self-enforcing mechanism, if you like.'[70] While sometimes intimidated by the MAS, Western bankers are generally respectful. 'The competence of the MAS,' says a UK banker, 'far exceeds that of their Western counterparts. They're much better than the Bank of England. Okay, it's easier with an economy of only 3.1 million people. But they're outstanding.'[71]

The Asian dollar market (ADM)

Singapore's development as an international financial centre began in 1968 with the establishment of the Asian dollar market (ADM), a wholesale market in offshore currencies modelled on London's eurodollar market. This was effected by the abolition of the withholding tax on foreign currency deposits, a move not emulated by Hong Kong until 1982. It was a deliberate and strategic step on the part of the city-state's economic planners to attract US banks and foster economic develop-ment.[72] 'The idea was first suggested to us by a Bank of America officer,' says Richard Hu, finance minister and head of the MAS, 'who saw the same potential for developing the Asian dollar marketplace as there had been for the eurodollar market. That's when we introduced legislation to allow offshore bank trading in the Asian dollar.'[73]

Encouraged by favourable tax incentives, the ADM grew rapidly, foreign currency assets rising from US$0.39 billion in 1970 to US$439 billion in 1996.[74] Singapore emerged as a leading Asian funding centre – although behind Hong Kong, where foreign assets in 1996 were $608 billion. The highly liquid ADM in Singapore has played a pivotal role in providing funds to fuel the rapid development of the economies of South-East Asia.

Singapore maintains – or attempts to maintain – a strict separation between the Singapore dollar and offshore currencies. 'The Asian (dollar) market is separate from domestic banking,' explains Richard Hu.[75] 'It's an accounting exercise: a bank operates a set of books for the offshore market and one for the domestic market. In principle, we don't allow non-Singapore corporate customers to borrow funds in Singapore dollars unless the end-use is within Singapore – for trade-financing or manufac-turing investments, or for housing development. In other words, we don't allow the Singapore dollar to be used outside Singapore. We want it to be used exclusively or mostly for the development of domestic activities.'[76] However, in practice it is becoming more and more difficult to maintain the separation.

The capital market
With a market capitalisation of US$148 billion, Singapore's stock market ranks fifth amongst Asian capital markets, behind Japan, Hong Kong, Taiwan and Malaysia. Constrained by the relatively small scale of the local economy, initiatives have focused on expanding the exchange's regional role. A foreign board was established on the stock exchange in December 1995, and the following year saw the launch of a Singapore Regional Index that groups local and foreign companies providing a regional reference benchmark.[77] Technically advanced and with improv-ing liquidity, the Stock Exchange of Singapore is well positioned to attract further regional business.

Since the mid-1990s, the MAS has been promoting the development of the fixed-interest market. In 1995, the government actively encouraged government-linked companies to use bond finance. 'But we don't want to promote the markets faster than we can adequately supervise them,' says finance minister Richard Hu. 'Events have proven that we're probably right, given our aversion to market failures in the financial system. Confidence in the system is important.'[78]

The money markets

Singapore's domestic money market has two dimensions, the interbank market and the government securities market.[79] The interbank market operates only in Singapore dollars – the Asian dollar market being the market in foreign currencies. The former is a highly active market in short-term funds, with local banks largely being lenders and foreign banks tending to be borrowers.

The government securities market was fundamentally restructured in 1987, and is now modelled on the US treasury bond market. The reforms were designed to enhance Singapore's competitivness as an international financial centre by broadening the range of fixed-interest investment opportunities for investors and enhancing the liquidity of the secondary market in fixed-interest securities. It was anticipated that this would establish the basis for the development of a corporate debt market.

Singapore is also a leading risk-management centre. Treasury activity has grown as operating costs and political uncertainty have prompted international banks, such as BT Alex. Brown, Credit Suisse First Boston, First Interstate Bank of California and Midland Bank, to shift their regional treasury units from Hong Kong to the city–state.[80]

Foreign exchange and derivatives

Singapore ranks fourth in the world league of foreign-exchange trading centres, with a turnover of $105 billion a day in 1995; it overtook Hong Kong in the early 1990s. Participants in the foreign exchange markets include commercial banks, Asian currency units, investment banks, international money brokers, central banks and corporations. Traditionally, Singapore's foreign-exchange market has been dominated by trading the US dollar against major currencies such as the yen and the Deutschmark, but cross-trades in regional currencies are growing rapidly. Activities encompass spot and forward transactions, as well as arbitrage operations in all currencies.

Time-zone advantage is an important factor in Singapore's success. In the morning, Singapore's foreign-exchange traders deal with counterparts in South-East Asia, Japan, Australia, and New Zealand; in addition, US banks pass on overnight orders for morning execution. In the afternoon, business shifts to transactions with the Middle East and Europe. Activity has been stimulated by the development of financial futures trading in Singapore. Another stimulus has been spillover from the growth of foreign-exchange trading in Tokyo. Intriguingly, the advent of the euro is expected to boost business. 'A lot of European banks,' says finance minister Richard Hu, 'have taken a far greater interest in this part of the world because of the anticipation that, with the introduction of the euro, the amount of intra-European currency trade will drop to zero and hence they want to position themselves in a growth area where there is a lot of volatility.'[81]

The Singapore International Monetary Exchange (Simex), Asia's first financial futures exchange, opened in 1984. To ensure an adequate volume of transactions and liquidity, a link was established with the Chicago Mercantile Exchange (CME). The highly successful CME served as a model for Simex, which adopted its open-outcry trading system and other practices. Spurred by government tax breaks, Simex made rapid strides. By 1997, 18 types of contract were traded – interest rate, stock index, energy, currency and precious metals. It serves a regional and worldwide clientele, 87 per cent of trades deriving from international customers – mostly from the US, Japan and Europe. Users of Simex contracts are mainly banks, fund managers, treasury managers and large pension funds. None of the contracts is based on the local economy and none is denominated in Singapore dollars. The main Simex contracts are for the eurodollar (35 per cent), the euroyen (27 per cent) and the Nikkei 225 (26 per cent). The prominence of Japanese contracts reflects not only the regional importance of Japan but also an entrepreneurial initiative on the part of Simex to provide a bypass to the bureaucratic obstacles to doing derivatives business in Tokyo.[82]

It was Nikkei 225 futures contracts that had been entered into by rogue trader Nick Leeson that brought down Barings in February 1995, thrusting Simex onto the front pages (see chapter 10). The crisis was well handled by the exchange, Baring's position being quickly unwound without disrupting the market. Furthermore, a hard-hitting report ensured that it was the authorities in London rather than in Singapore that shouldered the brunt of the blame for the fall of Barings. Nevertheless, reforms were instigated and the regulatory staff strengthened. 'We would like to ensure that something like this never happens again,' says Elizabeth Sam, the Simex chairman.[83]

Asset management
Asset management grew rapidly in the 1990s in Singapore, and this was largely due to MAS's encouragement and a conjunction of favourable factors: rising personal income (Singapore's income per capita of $24,000

is more than some Western countries); high levels of personal saving; the liberalisation of cross-border capital flows in the region; and the expansion of private banking services catering to high net-worth individuals. Funds under management grew from US$6 billion in 1989 to US$175 billion in 1997,[84] the number of institutions licensed for offshore asset management reaching 161.[85]

Opportunities and aspirations

Singapore's 1997 budget focused on buttressing the city–state's standing as an international financial centre. Singling out financial services for favoured treatment, finance minister Richard Hu delivered a raft of tax incentives for banks, asset managers and currency dealers. He slashed taxes on trade in foreign-currency denominated shares, income earned from managing initial public offerings of companies being listed in foreign currencies, income from foreign-exchange trading, and asset management. Coming just a few weeks after China's resumption of control of Hong Kong, the measures were a timely reminder of Singapore's hospitality for any banks unhappy with the new regime. 'They put out the welcome mat,' says William Philips, chairman of Salomon Brothers' Asia–Pacific operations. 'Singapore is a very good propagandist.'[86]

In a Nutshell

Frankfurt, Paris, Hong Kong and Singapore are leading international financial centres. Each conducts international financial business on a worldwide basis, but on a smaller scale than the global centres of London, New York and Tokyo.

- *Frankfurt* is Continental Europe's foremost financial centre, though lagging London by all indicators. As Frankfurt is the location of the new European central bank, the advent of the single currency, in which the UK is not a participant (at least initially), may allow it to challenge London more effectively.
- *Paris* is a major financial centre, although the volume of business is generally smaller than in London or Frankfurt. The EMU process offers new opportunities to enhance its standing that are being energetically pursued with government support.
- *Hong Kong* is the Asia–Pacific region's second financial centre after Tokyo. A major international banking centre, it is host to more foreign banks than ⇨

any financial centre except London. The transfer of sovereignty to China in July 1997 presents both opportunities and hazards to its continued prosperity.
- *Singapore* has skilfully, under government direction, developed into a major international financial centre challenging Hong Kong. Should political developments undermine Hong Kong's position, Singapore is poised to benefit.

FURTHER READING

Gütz, Ralf-Joachim, and Muller, Johannes *Frankfurt: A Banking and Financial Services Centre* (Frankfurt, Institut für Kapitalmarktforschung, 1990)

Durieux, Gilbert; Serieyssol Michel and Stephan, Patrick *French Financial Markets* (Cambridge, Gresham Books, 1995)

Jao, Y. C., *Hong Kong as an International Financial Centre: Evolution, Prospects and Policies* (Hong Kong, City University of Hong Kong Press, 1997)

Regnier, Philippe, *Singapore: City–state in South-East Asia* (London, Hurst & Co., 1987)

Walter, Norbert, and von Rosen, Rüdiger (eds), *German Financial Markets* (Cambridge, Gresham Books, 1995)

Wilson, J. S. G., *Money Markets: The International Perspective* (London, Routledge, 1993)

Wu, Friedrich, 'The Singapore Financial Centre and its Regional Role in Southeast Asia', *Journal of International Securities Markets*, vol. 6 (Summer 1992)

NOTES AND REFERENCES

In the list below for this chapter, any reference to an author alone should be taken to be a reference to his/her work in 'Further reading' above.

1 Information supplied by the Wirtschaftsförderung (Business and Economic Development Corp.), Frankfurt, 1997
2 Information supplied by the Wirtschaftsförderung (Business and Economic Development Corp.), Frankfurt, 1997
3 'German Banking and Finance', supplement to the *Financial Times*, 9 June 1997
4 *Financial Times*, 1 August 1997
5 *FWB: The Frankfurter Wertpapierbörse* (Frankfurt, Deutsche Börse, 1996)
6 *Financial Times*, 28 November 1997

7 *Deutsche Börse Fact Book 1996*, (Frankfurt, Deutsche Börse, 1997)

8 *FWB: The Frankfurter Wertpapierbörse* (Frankfurt, Deutsche Börse, 1996)

9 *Financial Times*, 29 May 1996

10 'German Banking and Finance', supplement to the *Financial Times*, 9 June 1997; *The European*, 14–20 November 1996

11 *Financial Times*, 18 September 1997

12 *Financial Times*, 8 September 1997

13 *Financial Times*, 9 June 1997

14 *Euromoney*, October 1995

15 'German Banking and Finance', supplement to the *Financial Times*, 9 June 1997

16 *Financial Times*, 14 August 1997

17 *Paris Europlace*, July 1997

18 *The Paris Financial Markets: Your Bridge to Europe, Paris Europlace*, (Paris, Paris Europlace, 1997) 1997

19 *Financial Times*, 27 September 1995 and 10 December 1996

20 *Financial Times*, 10 December 1996

21 *Financial Times*, 16 February 1996

22 *The Paris Financial Markets: Your Bridge to Europe, Paris Europlace*, 1997

23 *Financial Times*, 21–22 June 1997

24 *Financial Times*, 16 February 1996; *Paris Europlace*, July 1997

25 *The Paris Financial Markets: Your Bridge to Europe, Paris Europlace*

26 *Financial Times*, 2 September 1997

27 *Financial Times*, 8 December 1997

28 *Financial Times*, 16 February 1996

29 *Financial Times*, 28 February 1997

30 *Financial Times*, 18 September 1997

31 *Financial Times*, 18 September 1997

32 *Paris Europlace*, July 1997

33 *The Paris Financial Markets: Your Bridge to Europe, Paris Europlace*, p. 11.

34 *Financial Times*, 18 September 1997

35 *Financial Times*, 18 November 1996

36 *Les Echos*, supplement of 3 December 1996

37 Hong Kong Bureau of Census, March 1997

38 Hong Kong Bureau of Census, March 1997

39 Jao, pp. 57–69

40 *Fact Sheet 1997* (Hong Kong, Hong Kong Monetary Authority, 1997)

41 *Fact Sheet 1997* (Hong Kong, Hong Kong Monetary Authority, 1997)

42 *Fact Sheet 1997* (Hong Kong, Hong Kong Monetary Authority, 1997)

43 *Sunday Times*, 22 June 1997

44 *Financial Times*, 27 April 1994 and 9 May 1997

45 *Financial Times*, 14 May 1994
46 *Financial Times*, 9 May 1997
47 *Financial Times*, 2 September 1997
48 *Sunday Telegraph*, 18 January 1998
49 *Financial Times*, 18 September 1997
50 *Financial Times*, 16 June 1997
51 *Financial Times*, 18 September 1997
52 *Financial Times*, 16 June 1997
53 *Financial Times*, 16 June 1997
54 *Fact Sheet 1997* (Hong Kong, Hong Kong Monetary Authority, 1997)
55 *Financial Times*, 20 February 1996
56 Wilson, p. 322
57 Jao, p. 39
58 *Hong Kong Futures Exchange, Annual Report*, 1996
59 *Fact Sheet 1997* (Hong Kong, Hong Kong Monetary Authority, 1997)
60 Jao, p. 60
61 *Financial Times*, 16 June 1997
62 Jao, p. 94
63 *Sunday Times*, 7 September 1997
64 *Financial Times*, 9 May 1997
65 *Financial Times*, 25 July 1997
66 *Financial Times*, 2 July 1991
67 *The Banker*, July 1997
68 *The European*, 5–11 September 1996
69 Jao, p. 31; the FT gives the number as 290 – see the *Financial Times* of 14 July 1997
70 *Euromoney*, February 1997
71 *Euromoney*, February 1997
72 Wu, Friedrich, 'The Singapore financial centre and its regional role in Southeast Asia', *Journal of International Securities Markets*, 6 (1992), p. 199
73 *Euromoney*, February 1995
74 *Euromoney*, February 1995; IMF International Financial Statistics, August 1997
75 *Euromoney*, February 1995
76 *Euromoney*, February 1995
77 *Financial Times*, 18 February 1997
78 *Euromoney*, February 1995
79 Wilson, p. 351
80 Wu, p. 201
81 *Financial Times*, 18 February 1997
82 *Financial Times*, 20 February 1996

83 *Financial Times*, 8 February 1996

84 Wu, p. 202; *Financial Times*, 14 July 1997 (converted at US$1=S1.4)

85 *Financial Times*, 14 July 1997

86 *Financial Times*, 20 February 1996

CHAPTER 9

European Monetary Union and the Euro

INTRODUCTION

Economic and monetary union (EMU) is a major step towards European integration, politically as well as economically. It is the final stage in the creation of the European single market, being the substitution of a single currency – the euro – for national currencies. A common currency means exchange-rate stability amongst participants and a common monetary policy. It necessitates a new set of institutions – notably a European central bank – and common fiscal rules.

All EU members are potentially eligible to join EMU, but to qualify they have to satisfy a set of convergence criteria, defined in the Maastricht Treaty of February 1992, in order that EMU membership may not create undue strains. The EMU timetable adopted at Maastricht envisage the introduction of the euro on 1 January 1999, and the disappearance of national currencies in the EMU bloc in 2002.

Box 9.1: EMU Jargon Busting

Convergence: movement of national economic indicators towards Maastricht targets.
EC: European Community (former name for EU, 1967–92).
ECB: European Central Bank.
ecu: European Currency Unit (name of European currency prior to 1999).
EEC: European Economic Community (original name of EU, 1957–67).
EMS: European Monetary System.
EMU: Economic and Monetary Union.   ⇨

---

euro: name of European single currency to be introduced on 1 January 1999.
European Commission: European Union's secretariat in Brussels.
EU: European Union (name of EC since 1992).
Maastricht: town in the Netherlands, scene of the summit in 1992 at which the Treaty of Maastricht was signed. Often used as shorthand for the treaty.
Stability Pact: agreement to limit fiscal deficits.
Summit: twice yearly meeting of European leaders.

THE ROAD TO ECONOMIC AND MONETARY UNION

The evolution of European economic and monetary union is outlined in Box 9.2 below.

Box 9.2: Countdown to EMU

1957	Treaty of Rome: creation of the EEC.
1969	Hague summit: commitment to EMU.
1972	'The snake': flexible fixed currency agreement.
1979	European Monetary System (EMS) succeeds 'The snake'.
1992	Maastricht summit: agreement to proceed to EMU.
	Stage I of EMU (the stabilisation stage).
1992/93	Exchange-rate mechanism crisis.
1994	Stage II of EMU (the convergence stage).
	Establishment of the European Monetary Institute.
1995	Madrid summit: timetable for EMU agreed.
	New currency named the euro.
1997	Set as the base year for the convergence criteria.
1998	Selection of EMU participants.
	Formation of European Central Bank.
1999	Stage III of EMU (the single currency stage).
	Irrevocable locking of currencies.
	Introduction of the euro for official transactions.
2002	Euro notes and coins introduced.
	National currencies lose the status of legal tender.

The Hague summit and the Werner Report
The Treaty of Rome of 1957, which created the EEC, made no provision

for monetary union. It focused on the creation of a customs union, eliminating trade barriers between the then six member countries and harmonising tariffs in relation to non-members. Progress was such that a dozen years later at the Hague summit of December 1969, the members signed up for an even more ambitious goal – complete economic and monetary union by the end of 1980. A trifle optimistic, as it turned out.

A committee under the chairmanship of Pierre Werner, prime minister of Luxembourg, was established to plan the process, which in October 1970 delivered the Werner Report, a plan for full economic and monetary union. But this ambitious agenda was overtaken by events: the devaluation of the dollar in August 1971, less than a year later, heralded the onset of an era of currency, price and interest-rate instability that made the grand scheme inoperable. But it did result in a new system of semi-fixed exchange rates amongst EEC members.

'The snake': 1972–79

Instead of EMU, Europe got 'the snake'. In contrast to the fixed exchange rates of the Bretton Woods system, European currencies were permitted to vary serpent-like by a maximum of +/−1.125 per cent against each other and +/−2.25 per cent against the US dollar. This arrangement, known as 'the snake in the tunnel', became 'the snake' *tout simple* when the dollar floated in March 1973 and 'the tunnel' disappeared.

The snake, which came into operation in April 1972, had a tortuous history. There were three Deutchmark revaluations, 15 other parity changes, plus a merry-go-round of joinings, leavings and re-joinings. Britain withdrew in 1972, after only six weeks' membership. Italy quit in 1973 and France in 1976, leaving Germany as the dominant member. In 1977, the new president of the European Commission, Roy Jenkins, resurrected the idea of monetary union. His call found support, especially in Germany, which was keen to establish a means of shielding the Deutchmark from the increasingly unstable US dollar. More widely, European politicians wanted to create a stable framework for the conduct of European trade.

The European Monetary System, 1979

At the Bremen summit of June 1978, six of the nine community countries, including France and Italy, subscribed to a proposal to establish a 'zone of currency stability'. This was deemed desirable for several reasons: to reduce inflation, which in some countries was running at unacceptably high levels; to promote currency stability and thus growth and prosperity – exchange rate instability being believed to hamper trade flows and investment; and to promote the gradual convergence of economic policy across the Community, for convergence would promote economic integration – the single market – which would ultimately lead to monetary union.

The European Monetary System (EMS), which gave effect to the Bremen undertaking, came into operation in March 1979. It had four main features:

- Exchange-Rate Mechanism (ERM)
- European Currency Unit (ecu)
- financing facilities
- European Monetary Fund

All currencies that were members of the ERM were linked by a central rate against the ecu, which was a weighted basket of EC currencies. Market rates were permitted to vary by up to +/−2.25 per cent (6 per cent for Italy) against the central rate. A complex set of mechanisms were devised to maintain currencies within the permitted bands, but if a problem proved persistent, realignment of the central rate was a last resort.

There were 37 realignments in the years 1979–92, notably in 1983 and 1985. But then the system settled down, and from January 1987 to August 1992 there were no realignments at all. This was the context in which the Maastricht Treaty, an agreement to proceed to a European single currency, was signed in February 1992. It was assumed that the stability of the ERM and the convergence of inflation rates and interest rates amongst EMS members would continue. But the ink scarcely had time to dry before the ERM was beset by a crisis.

The ERM crisis of 1992–93

The timetable of the rise and fall of the ERM is shown in Box 9.3. By the summer of 1992, the ERM included all 12 European community members, and four other countries had linked their currencies to the ecu. But in September 1992, the system was buffeted by unprecedented speculative pressure. Two important currencies, sterling and the lira, left the ERM while others devalued. Currency turbulence continued through the winter of 1992 and the spring of 1993. Finally, in August 1993, even stronger speculation against the fixed floor and ceiling limits forced a widening of the fluctuation bands from +/−2.25 per cent to +/−15 per cent, a relaxation so drastic that membership scarcely impinged on policy. But by now, post Maastricht, it was the convergence criteria that were acting as the external discipline on governments.

Box 9.3: The rise and fall of the ERM

Rise

March 1979	EMS begins.
March 1983	General realignment.
July 1985	General realignment.
January 1987	Belgium, Germany, the Netherlands realign.
June 1989	Spain joins ERM.
October 1990	UK joins ERM.
October 1990	Norway links to the ecu.
April 1991	Sweden links to the ecu.
June 1991	Finland links to the ecu.
April 1992	Portugal joins ERM.
June 1992	Cyprus links to the ecu.

Crisis of 1992–93

1992

June 2	First Danish Maastricht referendum: majority 'no'.
July 16	Bundesbank hikes discount rate.
September 8	Finland floats the markka.
September 13	Italy devalues the lira.
September 16	UK withdraws from ERM.
September 16	Italy withdraws from ERM.
September 16	Spain devalues peseta by 5 per cent.
September 20	French Maastricht referendum: majority 'yes'.
November 19	Sweden floats krona.
November 22	Portugal and Spain devalue by 6 per cent.
November 30	Irish overnight lending rate raised to 100 per cent.
December 10	Norway floats the krone.

1993

January 10	Ireland devalues punt by 10 per cent.
May 13	Spain devalues by 8 per cent.
May 13	Portugal devalues by 6.5 per cent.
May 18	Second Danish Maastricht referendum: majority 'yes'.
July 23	Banque de France forced to hike overnight rate.
August 2	ERM bands widened to +/−15 per cent (except DM-guilder band that remained +/−2.25 per cent).

The IMF's analysis of the causes of the ERM crisis of 1992–93 was that relatively high rates of inflation in some countries and the lack of compensating realignments since 1987 had resulted in overvaluation of the official exchange-rate parities of the lira, sterling, escudo, peseta and krona. The other factor was the perception in the financial markets of the inconsistency between the downward direction of interest rates, required to relieve the depressed levels of economic activity in many European countries, and the upward direction of rates required by Germany to contain the inflationary pressures resulting from unification.[1]

The European Commission in contrast placed the blame for the crisis on an assault by international currency speculators. Foremost amongst their number was George Soros, whose funds made a profit of $1 billion by speculating against sterling and forcing it out of the ERM. Soros, the Hungarian-born head of the Quantum hedge fund, was by no means bashful about wreaking such havoc or making such profits. But, as he explained to a journalist, the opportunity arose only because Britain's position was untenable: 'If it hadn't been untenable, our "ganging up on it" wouldn't have pushed Britain out of the ERM. ... we were not the only ones playing, and the process would have unfolded more or less the same way even if I had never been born.'[2]

From the summer of 1993, the ERM continued as a looser and less rigid association of currencies. In July 1995, the central rates of the peseta and escudo were devalued. Austria, Sweden and Finland joined the EMS upon becoming members of the EU. Italy was re-admitted in 1996 after lengthy negotiations.

The Maastricht Treaty and economic and monetary union

French and Italian dissatisfaction with German domination of the EMS prompted the establishment of a committee chaired by European Commission president Jacques Delors to prepare a plan for monetary union. The Delors Report was discussed at the Madrid summit of June 1989, and its proposals became the basis of the Maastricht Treaty.

The Maastricht Treaty instigated a three-stage process for the achievement of European economic and monetary union:

- Stage I: 1979–93 (the stabilisation stage). Stabilisation of exchange rates in the ERM (subsequently disrupted by the crisis of 1992–93).
- Stage II: 1 January 1994 to 31 December 1998 (the convergence stage). Economic convergence through the achievement of a common set of 'convergence criteria'. The establishment of an institutional framework to meet the economic, political and

administrative requirements of EMU.
- Stage III: 1 January 1999 onwards (the single-currency stage). Introduction of a single currency, initially as a set of fixed exchange rates but from 2002 in the form of a new single currency, subsequently named the euro.

The treaty was adopted at the Maastricht Summit of December 1991, signed in February 1992, and ratified by referendums in France and Ireland and, at second attempt after an initial rejection by the electorate, in Denmark.

Convergence criteria and new institutions

Monetary union means the surrender of two of the principal instruments of economic management and adjustment by national economies: the interest rate and the exchange rate. With a single currency, there is a single interest rate, set by a European central bank. Moreover, there is no opportunity for devaluation of the currency to restore competitiveness. In order for EMU to stand a chance of working, it is essential for the economies and economic policies of participants to achieve a degree of convergence prior to entry. The achievement of a set of 'convergence criteria' was the agenda for Stage II over the years 1994–98.

The convergence criteria specified in the Maastricht Treaty were:

- *inflation* not exceeding 1.5 per cent above the average inflation of the three lowest members
- *an interest rate* not exceeding 2 per cent above the average of the three members with lowest inflation
- *government debt as a per cent GDP* at a maximum of 60 per cent
- *government deficit as a per cent of GDP* at a maximum of 3 per cent
- *ERM membership* for two years
- *an independent central bank*

The institutional developments programmed for Stage II were:

- *Monetary Committee* Its mandate is to monitor member states' budgetary performance and progress towards the convergence criteria. It reports to the Council of Ministers or the European Commission on its own initiative. Membership comprises two representatives of each state and two from the Commission.
- *European Monetary Institute (EMI)* The embryonic European Central Bank (ECB) (see below and Chapter 5). Located in Frankfurt, the

EMI began in January 1994. The first president was Alexandre Lamfalussy, former head of the Banque de France. He was succeeded in 1997 by Wim Duisenberg, a Dutchman who was a former finance minister and head of the Dutch central bank.

The Stage III institutional developments are:

- *European Central Bank (ECB)*   The ECB succeeded the EMI in 1998. It is a highly 'independent' institution, directed by a Governing Council comprising an executive board and the governors of the national central banks. The executive board is composed of 'persons of standing and professional experience in monetary or banking matters'. The term of office is eight years, and is not renewable. The ECB has the sole right to authorise the issue of banknotes within the EU, but it shares the process of issue with the national central banks. Member states may issue coins, subject to ECB approval.
- *European System of Central Banks (ESCB)*   The ESCB comprises the ECB and the central banks of the member states. It is governed by the decision-making bodies of the ECB, including the governors of the national central banks. Its primary objective is the maintenance of price stability. To this end it: defines and implements the monetary policy of the EU; conducts foreign-exchange operations; holds and manages the official reserves of the member states; promotes the effective operation of payment systems; and contributes to the prudential supervision of credit institutions and the stability of the financial system.

UK and Danish opt-outs

The UK and Denmark were not prepared to make a commitment to participate in Stage III at the time of the Maastricht Treaty. They were accorded 'opt-outs' – perhaps better called 'opt-ins' – whereby they deferred the decision to join a single currency.

Introduction of the euro

After much conjecture and controversy, it was announced at the Madrid meeting of the European Council in December 1995 that the new European currency would be called the euro. A detailed three-phase agenda for the introduction of the euro was set out:

- *Phase A: May 1998* Naming of the countries to participate in EMU at the start.

- *Phase B: 1 January 1999* Launch of EMU through the irrevocable locking of the conversion rates of the participating currencies with the euro and the assumption of responsibility for the single monetary and exchange-rate policy by the European System of Central Banks.
- *Phase C: 1 January 2002* The spread of the single currency to all means of payment, marking the completion of the process of introducing the single currency. National currencies will be abolished and the euro will be the sole legal tender in the EMU area.

DEBATE ABOUT EMU

In the opt-out countries of the UK and Denmark, there has been a lively controversy about the pros and cons of EMU. In other countries, for different and disparate reasons, EMU has been regarded as more desirable than alternative monetary arrangements, and debate has been more muted. But as doubts gathered about the extent to which some countries were fudging their convergence criteria statistics, questions were raised about the wisdom of proceeding prematurely. In Germany, and even in France, attention began to be paid to the costs and risks of the enterprise, taking the bloom off the federalist fantasy of boundless benefits.

Arguments for EMU

1 EMU promotes trade and eliminates transaction costs
It is argued that exchange-rate volatility discourages international trade because of exchange-rate risk incurred by importers and exporters. The elimination of this uncertainty will promote trade amongst EMU participants. A single currency will also increase price transparency permitting consumers to compare prices in different places boosting competition, exchange and efficiency.

The countries of the EU constitute the world's foremost trade bloc. As its currency, the euro will become one of the main exchange and reserve currencies, on a par with the dollar and the yen. EMU members will increasingly be able to conduct import and export transactions with non-members in euros, eliminating their exposure to exchange risk. Furthermore, a stable euro, based on the collective European economy, will foster global currency stability and thus world trade.

The cost of exchanging currencies is a burden upon traders and travellers. The European Commission estimates that about 0.4 per cent of European GDP – ecu 20–25 billion – is consumed by such foreign exchange transactions. It makes the point by citing a traveller who sets off in one EU country with £100. He visits every other member country, changing his money into the local currency every time. Without having made a single purchase, he arrives home with only £50 in his pocket because of the cost of conversion.[3]

Nevertheless, although small firms may perhaps be discouraged from participating in international trade because of the exchange-rate risk, the bulk of trade is conducted by large corporations that are able to use sophisticated financial instruments to hedge the risk reasonably cheaply. Likewise, while the cost of currency conversion may be considerable for holidaymakers, bulk buyers get much better rates. As regards European Commission's woeful tale about the traveller, the governor of the Bank of England comments, 'anyone who travels throughout the European Union exchanging all his currency as he goes deserves to pay for the privilege – particularly in the age of the plastic card!'[4]

2   EMU increases price stability and lowers interest rates

Price stability – in other words, low or no inflation – is generally held to be economically beneficial. This is because any disruption of the price mechanism inflicts costs that diminish welfare. Based on an independent European Central Bank whose 'primary objective' is price stability, the institutional arrangements for EMU are the best available guarantee of low inflation.

Stable prices plus financial market confidence in the institutional arrangements of EMU mean lower interest rates. The low rate of inflation under EMU will dampen inflationary expectations, constraining infla-tionary price and wage behaviour. In this non-inflationary environment, governments will be able to run their economies at higher levels of output, and hence lower levels of unemployment, than would otherwise be the case without running the risk of inflation.

However, it should be remembered that the claims that EMU will deliver lower inflation are untested. In order for it to do so, it is critical that members meet, and continue to meet, the convergence criteria. Moreover, the fledgling ECB may prove to be less than perfectly adept in monetary management.

3   Single European capital market

The euro will trigger the formation of a single European capital market.

This will rival the scale of the US dollar financial markets and should develop a similar profusion of instruments and innovations. This will benefit borrowers and lenders, not just in Europe but worldwide.

4 EMU promotes investment and growth

Cheaper money through lower interest rates ought to mean higher investment. Moreover, in a non-inflationary environment producers can concentrate on 'real' challenges, such as raising the productivity of labour and capital. Thus EMU may give rise to increases in the quality as well as the quantity of investment, enhancing economic growth. It is also argued that countries participating in EMU will be more attractive than non-members as locations for inward investment because of the absence of currency risk.

It is nevertheless a fact that, despite being outside the ERM except fleetingly in 1990–92, the UK has been the EU's biggest recipient of inward investment. Plainly other factors were more important than exchange stability in the determination of those investment decisions, which has a bearing on the pro-EMU argument.

5 Public finances and EMU

The EMU convergence criteria require governments to restrict total public debt to 60 per cent of GDP and the fiscal deficit to 3 per cent of GDP. These formal targets impose a rigorous and beneficial economic discipline, which cannot be relaxed by incumbent governments to foster their re-election prospects. Thus the disruptive electoral boom–bust cycle is banished.

It should be noted that point 2 against EMU (below) counters this argument to some extent.

6 European integration

EMU constitutes the completion of the single market, and is thus a major step in the evolution of European integration. It means the instigation of a single monetary policy. The logical corollary is a co-ordinated fiscal policy amongst participants, plus a considerable degree of tax harmonisation. It thereby implies an enhanced role for a central European economic authority – akin to the US Treasury – to co-ordinate economic policy and to even out income discrepancies. This would be a big stride towards a federal government of Europe.

Arguments against EMU

1 Loss of exchange rate as an adjustment mechanism
The surrender of the exchange rate as an instrument of economic management has important implications. Devaluation, which, as recent UK experience illustrates, can be a beneficial adjustment mechanism, is no longer possible. Balance of payments imbalances become a regional problem requiring different solutions.

The US illustrates the problems and mechanisms of adjustment to economic shocks in a large monetary union. Say, for example, the price of oil quadruples, as happened in 1973–74. In Texas, an oil producing state, it's boom time. Output and employment increase, and thus so do taxes paid to the federal government. In Michigan, home to 'rust belt' manufacturing industries, companies having to pay more for fuel become uncompetitive and jobs are lost. Tax revenues fall, and unemployment payments rise. Thus the federal government receives greater taxes from Texas and pays out more benefits in Michigan. Around 40 per cent of the relative changes in income between the two states will be evened out in this way.

The other familiar adjustment mechanism in the US is the migration of labour – in the above example workers could move from Detroit to Huston.

In Europe, the effects of a shock that benefits one region but adversely affects another could not easily be evened out in the absence of exchange-rate adjustment. Neither of the adjustment mechanisms that operate in the US would work as well. With the resources of the EU restricted to 1.2 per cent of GDP (rising to 1.27 per cent after 1999), and mostly committed to agricultural support, the scope for income redistribution around the EMU block is very limited.

As regards labour mobility, in Europe this is restricted by language, culture, and a host of bureaucratic hurdles. The relative immobility of labour is realised by the European Commission, which comments that regional labour mobility is 'neither feasible, at least not across language barriers, nor perhaps desirable.'[5] The most likely outcome is higher unemployment in the stricken regions.

2 Loss of monetary policy as an instrument of economic management
In addition to the loss of control over the exchange rate, EMU means the surrender of monetary policy. Henceforth, there will be a single interest rate determined by the ECB. The rate will be set to deliver price stability over the EMU bloc as a whole. Inevitably, this single rate will be less

appropriate – too high or too low – for some countries at some time than nationally determined rates.

The transfer of monetary policy to the ECB elevates price stability, its 'primary objective' as defined by treaty, above other goals of economic management. The priority accorded to the control of inflation in the EMU institutional arrangements has been criticised by politicians and economists more concerned about the reduction of unemployment and economic growth.

In the absence of a nationally determined exchange rate or interest rate, fiscal policy becomes the principal lever of national economic management to address national needs. But because governments don't have to worry about the impact of their conduct on the currency or the cost of borrowing, the temptation exists for fiscal laxity. To avert such irresponsibility, the Dublin summit of December 1996 adopted a Stability Pact by which governments pledged support for a permanent adoption of the convergence criterion of keeping budget deficits below 3 per cent of GDP.

Germany wanted automatic and massive fines for violations of the 3 per cent benchmark, except in extreme recessions – a 'recession pact', as *The Economist* dubbed the proposals.[6] But French arguments for a more lenient system allowing countries to plead 'exceptional circumstances' and for fines to be decided at least partly by politicians on the day instead.[7] Nonetheless, the Stability Pact constitutes a significant constraint upon EMU participants' ability to operate counter-cyclical fiscal policy in a recession.

3   Sovereignty and the democratic deficit

Opponents claim that EMU means the surrender of economic sovereignty. Another objection is that it involves the transfer of economic policy from democratically elected governments to an unelected, unrepresentative body, the ESCB. Indeed, it is argued that EMU constitutes a major step in deepening the 'democratic deficit' that blights the EU. Diminishing electoral control over decision-making is not only anti-democratic, but potentially undermines popular support for the EU.

However, membership of the EU itself means the surrender of sovereignty, so joining EMU is a matter of degree not principle. Furthermore, it is questionable how much economic sovereignty nations really have in the modern global economy. In a world without controls on the movement of capital, no government is able to pursue economic policies that flout what the financial markets regard as credible.

As regards the 'democratic deficit', many EU countries had independent or semi-independent central banks prior to Maastricht, and others are moving towards independence. So the transfer of monetary policy to the ESCB is not a shift away from democratic control, which has been ceded anyway to central banking technocrats. Moreover, as an institution established by treaty agreed by the government of members states, the authority of the ESCB is rooted in the democratic process.

4 Adaptation costs

The cost of physical adaptation to the euro will be substantial, placing a considerable burden both on participant and non-participant EU countries and cancelling some of the benefits of a single currency – in the short term at least. In 1996, the European Banking Federation estimated the conversion bill for Europe's banks at ecu 8–10 billion, equivalent to 1–2 per cent of the banks' operating costs spread over three or four years.[8] Another estimate put the cost at £50 billion ($83 billion), or 2 per cent of a single year's EU GDP. To put these numbers in perspective, it has been predicted that the elimination of foreign-exchange costs in EMU would add 0.33 per cent a year to EU GDP. Thus, the transition costs wipe out six years' worth of anticipated additional growth.[9]

5 The fudge risk

Enthusiasm among European politicians for their countries to qualify for EMU has led to fudging the figures for the convergence criteria – most notoriously the transfer of Ff37 billion of France Telecom's pension fund assets to the government to reduce the level of public debt and a controversial (and unsuccessful) proposal of creative accounting on the part of Germany to reduce public debt by revaluing the country's gold reserves. A euro grounded on strict adherence to the convergence criteria reflecting genuine progress in economic integration will present problems a-plenty, but a common currency based on fudged figures would be inherently unstable and fraught with danger (see section below).

It must nevertheless be realised that there is never a perfect time for any project as bold and problematic as EMU. The political momentum that prompted Europe's leaders to press for EMU sooner rather than later might just carry it through.

6 European integration

EMU is the 'trojan horse' of European federalism, leading logically to the strengthening of European federal government. This is anathema to anti-federalists.

EMU – pro or con?

The transition to EMU has costs and risks. However, once established, a single currency would lead to cost reductions that would boost welfare. But some of these economic efficiencies can be achieved in other ways, and there is a danger that the system will produce increased and persistent regional unemployment. On economic grounds alone, the benefits do not overwhelm the costs.

So the answers to the question 'Pro or con?' depends on a subjective political judgment as to whether the creation of a United States of Europe is desirable or undesirable. The introduction of the single currency is driven by politics, not economic necessity. But successful implementation depends very much on getting the economic and financial arrangements right.

The first wave

In May 1998, it was decided that 11 of the 15 EU members had slimmed their budget deficits enough and made sufficient progress on the other convergence criteria to meet the requirements for joining Europe's new single currency. The first wave comprises Austria, Belgium, Finland, France, Germany, Ireland, Italy, Luxembourg, the Netherlands, Portugal and Spain. Locking their exchange rates, they agreed to co-operate on monetary policy until 1 January 1999, when the European Central Bank assumes responsibility and applies a single monetary policy to all of them.

Denmark, Sweden and the UK, though qualifying for the euro according to the convergence criteria, decided to defer entry to the single currency. Greece missed by a mile. In the UK's case, membership had been ruled out until at least 2002 on the grounds of the non-convergence of the UK and European business cycles. Ironically, the meeting that decided on membership was chaired by the British prime minister, as it was Britain's turn for the EU presidency.

Intrinsic to the 'wide band' euro is the problem that the short-term interest rate imposed by the single monetary policy will be inappropriate for some members. In mid-1998, a core group of countries; comprising Austria, Belgium, France, Germany and Luxembourg were recovering from several years of sluggish growth. For them, a short-term interest rate lower than the EU average of around 4 per cent was appropriate. But another set of countries, Ireland, Italy, Portugal and Spain were growing rapidly, with pressure on wages and property prices. For these periphery countries a relatively high and restraining short-term interest rate was appropriate. Since room for manoeuvre in fiscal policy – adjusting taxes or government spending – was strictly constrained by the convergence criteria, the introduction of the euro and the accompanying single monetary policy seemed destined to cause pain and discontent somewhere.

The determination of the powerful and highly independent ECB to establish its anti-inflationary credentials, militated towards the adoption of a relatively restrictive monetary policy. In the longer run, as European economic cycles converge the dilemma should abate. Indeed, one of the functions of the single currency is to bring Europe's economies more closely into cyclical alignment.

The impact of the euro on European financial markets and banks was the subject of a study by the Bank for International Settlements that was published in May 1997.[10] The study argued that the introduction of the euro would have an immediate and direct impact on European bond markets, stimulating the growth of a much larger and more liquid securities market in Europe. The switch away from bank debt to bond debt on the part of European corporations would curb demand for bank lending. Coming on top of competitive and other pressures, it might be the trigger to a widespread restructuring of the European banking industry (see Chapter 3).

EMU AND AFTER

David Lascelles, a distinguished financial journalist and banking expert, has written a speculative scenario, *The Crash of 2003: An EMU Fairy Tale*, of how the EMU process might develop. His fictional but carefully considered and not implausible story unfolds in the following way:

1999

EMU starts on time in 1999 with seven first-wave participants: Austria, Belgium, France, Germany, Ireland, Luxembourg and the Netherlands. The launch of the euro takes place thanks to a 'flexible' interpretation of the convergence criteria, overlooking even Belgium's massive public debt-to-GDP ratio and vast unfunded pension liabilities. In fact, on a strict interpretation of the Maastricht criteria most of the first-wave participants would have been disqualified.

Participants and non-participants alike incur heavy adjustment costs for the conversion of contracts, cash-point machines etc.

The ECB, up and running since 1998, takes a robust approach to its 'primary objective' of maintaining price stability, setting interest rates cautiously high. Starting strong, the euro countries attract inflows of international capital and the euro appreciates. European politicians expect EMU to reduce unemployment, but in fact the strength of the euro and the level of EMU interest rates exacerbate the problem.

2000–02

Italy and Spain join EMU in the second wave.

A Wall Street stockmarket crash (or some other external shock) sends European bourses tumbling. Cutbacks in spending by impoverished and nervous consumers trigger the onset of a recession within the EMU bloc. The recession is exacerbated by the operation of the Stability Pact, which prevents governments from taking counter-cyclical fiscal measures, deepening the downturn and sending unemployment soaring. Jobless-ness and austerity lead to riots in France and rising support for the neo-fascist *Front National*, putting pressure on politicians. But remedial actions are blocked by the EMU institutional structure.

With social disorder and political extremism on the increase, politi-cians begin to put national concerns before monetary union. France wants reforms to diminish discontent. Germany is wary of changes that will burden German taxpayers. The UK, Denmark and Sweden become more and more resolutely hostile to membership of the single currency.

Disagreements between France and Germany over EMU reform undermine market confidence in the euro. The euro slumps against the US dollar. Speculative pressure on the euro becomes intense.

2003

At a crisis summit in Brussels in January 2003, the French propose the creation of an EMU Treasury, on the model of the US Treasury, that would take over the funding of members' debts. But this means ceding to the EMU Treasury the authority to control the indebtedness of EMU members and to raise taxes to fund the centralised debt, elevating monetary union to federal government.

Germany refuses to go along with the French plan, which effectively makes German taxpayers underwrite the debts of other EMU members. France withdraws from EMU and re-establishes the franc. Italy, Spain and Ireland do likewise. Reconversion from the euro to national currencies imposes further large costs.

The ERM – now comprising Germany, Luxembourg, Belgium, the Netherlands and Austria – nevertheless continues. It is now, in all but name, an expanded Deutschmark bloc. Economic disruption is substan-tial and expensive, but the European single market survives and continues to function.

Recrimination embitters relations amongst Europe's politicians, and progress towards political union suffers a major setback. Ironically, the federalist enthusiasts for EMU have achieved the very opposite of what they wanted.

Epitaph

Purporting to be written from the vantage point of July 2003, Lascelles' epitaph for EMU reads:[11]

> EMU was a well-intentioned but premature strategem. It aimed to raise European union to new levels. But it was driven by political imperatives which ignored the full practical implications, and in the end, those imperatives were not sufficiently powerful to see it through economic problems that were evident from the outset.

Lascelles himself calls his scenario a 'fairy tale'. It remains to be seen whether the conventional fairy-tale ending, 'And they all lived happily ever after,' is a fitting finale to the EMU story.

In a Nutshell

European economic and monetary union (EMU) is a process that has been going on since the 1970s. By the Maastricht Treaty of 1992, the members of the European Union committed themselves to the introduction of a single currency – the euro – in 1999. To qualify for the euro, countries were required to meet a set of economic convergence criteria by 1998.

The single currency requires new institutional arrangements, notably a European central bank. A forerunner institution, the European Monetary Institute, was established in Frankfurt in 1994. A fully fledged European Central Bank came into being in 1998.

The single currency potentially confers the benefits of reducing exchange-rate risk and transaction costs, and lower inflation and interest rates for some countries. The costs are the loss of the interest rate and exchange rate as tools of economic management. It remains to be seen whether the euro can be introduced successfully and survive the economic and political pressure of adjustment.

FURTHER READING

Currie, David, *The Pros and Cons of EMU* (London, EIU, 1997)

Giovannini, Alberto, and Mayer, Colin (eds), *European Financial Integration* (Cambridge, Cambridge University Press, 1991)

Issing, Otmar, *Europe: Political Union through Common Money?* (London, IEA, 1996)

Johnson, Christopher, *In with the Euro, Out with the Pound: the Single Currency for Britain* (London, Penguin, 1996)

Lascelles, David, *The Crash of 2003: An EMU Fairy Tale.* (London, Centre, 1996)

Economic and Monetary Union (Brussels, European Commission, 1996)

McCauley, Robert N., and White, William R., *The Euro and European Financial Markets*, BIS Working Paper No. 41 (Basle, 1997)

Temperton, Paul (ed), *The Euro* (Chichester, John Wiley, 1997)

NOTES AND REFERENCES

In the list below for this chapter, any reference to an author alone should be taken to be a reference to his/her work in 'Further reading' above.

1 IMF, *World Economic Outlook*, October 1993

2 Soros, George, *Soros on Soros: Staying Ahead of the Curve* (Chichester, John Wiley, 1995)

3 *Economic and Monetary Union* (European Commission, Brussels, 1996)

4 Speech at the Association of French Bankers, 31 January 1995

5 European Commission Report, Paris 31 January 1995

6 *The Economist*, 14 December 1996

7 *The Economist*, 21 December 1996

8 *Euromoney*, September 1996

9 Lascelles, p. 13

10 McCauley and White

11 Lascelles, p. 26

CHAPTER 10
Financial Scandals

INTRODUCTION

Financial scandals are as old as financial markets. Indeed, recent scandals seem small compared with episodes of the past such as the South Sea Bubble of 1720 that revolved around speculation in the shares of a company that had purchased the privatised UK national debt. But today's liberalised markets and the globalisation of financial flows offer new and unprecedented opportunities for misdemeanours. Greed and incompetence – often together – being human perennials, it is safe to predict that there will be many more financial scandals in future, despite the best endeavours of compliance officers and regulators.

Table 10.1 lists some of the most notorious financial scandals since the mid-1980s.

SAVINGS AND LOAN

In the 1980s, the newly deregulated savings and loan industry – America's equivalent of British building societies – experienced a wave of plundering and recklessness on the part of managements secure in the knowledge that the federal government's deposit-insurance legislation would make good any losses by depositors. The outcome was a raft of failures that landed taxpayers with a bail-out bill estimated in 1990 as likely to amount to $500 billion, meaning $2,000 for every American.

IVAN BOESKY AND MICHAEL MILKEN

Ivan Boesky, a leading Wall Street arbitrageur, and Michael Milken, inventor of the junk bond and a key figure at investment bank Drexell Burnham Lambert, made millions by buying shares of takeover targets based on illegal insider information. Both received prison sentences, in 1987 and 1990 respectively, but they kept most of their gains.

Table 10.1: Recent financial scandals

Scandal	Date of scandal	Nature of scandal	Location
Savings and Loan	1980s/90s	$500 billion tax-payer bail-out of bent or bad managements	US
Ivan Boesky and Michael Milken	1986	Insider trading in shares of Wall Street takeover targets	US
Guinness	1987	£258 million illegal share-price support scheme in UK takeover	UK
Barlow Clowes	1988	Theft of investors' money by fund manager	UK
Lloyd's of London	1980s/90s	£8 billion losses and questionable conduct by insiders	UK
BCCI	1991	$20 billion bank fraud	International
Robert Maxwell	1991	Pension fund plundering	UK
Tangentopoli	1992	Bribery and corruption in business and politics	Italy
Pensions mis-selling	1993	£4 billion professional negligence and lack of redress	UK
Pyramid finance schemes	1990s	Get-rich-quick scams in Eastern Europe	Russia/Albania etc.
Barings	1995	$1.3 billion unauthorised trading losses and bank failure	UK/Singapore
Daiwa Bank	1995	$1.1 billion unauthorised trading losses	US/Japan
Sumitomo Corporation	1996	$3 billion unauthorised trading losses	Japan/US
Morgan Grenfell Asset Management	1996	Investment fund mismanagement	UK
Sokaiya extortion	1997	Payments to gangsters by Japanese banks and brokers	Japan

GUINNESS

....

The Guinness scandal in the UK was about illegal share purchases with the aim of supporting the price of Guinness shares during a bitter and highly publicised takeover battle for whisky maker Distillers. It was an episode that undermined faith in the City's traditional self-regulatory system and gentlemanly fair play.

Ernest Saunders, appointed managing director of Guinness in 1982, had ambitious plans to turn the sleepy brewing group into a major player in the international drinks industry. Assisted by strategic consultants Bain & Co., he devised a plan to grow and reposition the company through a series of acquisitions. The takeover spree began modestly in June 1984. A year later, Guinness launched a hostile bid for Scottish whisky producer Arthur Bell, which it won at a price of £370 million. Then came the big one – Distillers.

Distillers was also a whisky maker, the flagship of the independent Scottish whisky industry. In December 1985, the Argyll Group, a UK supermarket multiple, made a hostile bid for Distillers worth £1.87 billion. Guinness successfully courted the Distillers directors, who threw their support behind its counter-bid, worth £2.2 billion. The fight for control of Distillers was on – a robust bout that witnessed unprecedented public-relations trickery and illegal takeover tactics. When Argyll upped its bid to £2.3 billion, Guinness responded with £2.35 billion ($3.8 billion).

The Guinness offer to Distillers shareholders comprised part cash, part Guinness shares. The higher the price of Guinness shares, the more enticing its offer became. Correspondingly, any fall in the Guinness share price made its offer less attractive. A 'concert party' was put together to sustain the Guinness share price by purchases in the stock market, the participants being indemnified against losses by secret undertakings from Guinness. This was illegal. But it was also effective – on 18 April 1986, an ecstatic Saunders announced to the City that he had control of 50.7 per cent of Distillers shares. With the help of £258 million ($425 million) in improper share purchases, Guinness had won the City's most acrimonious takeover battle.[1]

The euphoria didn't last long. Almost immediately, there was an ugly row when Saunders reneged on undertakings given to win the support of the Distillers directors. Then, in December 1986, inspectors from the Department of Trade and Industry began probing, initially investigating some minor irregularities but then more serious matters following plea-bargaining revelations to the American Securities and Exchange Commission by disgraced Wall Street arbitrageur Ivan Boesky, a member of the concert party. Heads rolled at Morgan Grenfell, Guinness's principal merchant bank, and at other advisers and associates. Saunders himself was arrested in May 1987, and sacked by Guinness.

In August 1990 – after a trial lasting 107 days – Ernest Saunders and three co-defendants were found guilty of theft, conspiracy, and false accounting. They went to jail. However, two subsequent group trials of further persons allegedly involved in the share purchase concert party collapsed. Saunders protested a miscarriage of justice, but his appeals in the UK were unsuccessful.

BARLOW CLOWES

The Barlow Clowes scandal was about the theft of £150 million ($250 million) from the supposedly risk-free bond funds run by investment management firm Barlow Clowes. The principal villain, Peter Clowes, received a ten-year prison sentence in 1992.

BANK OF CREDIT AND COMMERCE INTERNATIONAL (BCCI)

The BCCI scandal was the biggest bank fraud in history, costing depositors and investors at least $5 billion and, according to Manhattan district attorney Robert Morganthau, as much as $20 billion.[2] It also involved the laundering of large sums of money on behalf of international drug dealers.

The BCCI was founded in 1972 by Pakistani businessman Agha Hassan Abedi and associate Suraleh Naquvi as an international bank focusing on serving Muslim and third-world clients who felt neglected by Western banks. Abedi's backers were mostly fellow Muslims, notably the sheikh of Abu Dhabi, but also included the giant Bank of America, which took a 30 per cent shareholding that was intended to enhance the new bank's prestige. Abedi's management culture was a novel, and distinctly wacky, cocktail of Muslim mysticism, third-world idealism, and cynical materialism. Senior management seemed more interested in soul searching than credit control: on one occasion, Abedi startled executives by explaining that, 'the reason why I was late is that as I was leaving I met God in the corridor and I had to talk to him. I had to bring his feelings to you.'[3] Staff meetings resembled revivalist gatherings, ordinary members of the 'BCCI family' – many of them deferential fellow Shia Muslims – voicing tearful adulation of 'Agha Sahib'. But the boss was no ascetic, revelling in his private jet, a fleet of cars, and shopping expeditions. BCCI was more like a cult than a bank, and prayers proved a poor substitute for sound business practice.

BCCI expanded rapidly. Between 1972 and 1991, the capital base grew from $2.3 million to $23 billion. By then, it had 420 offices around the world and a presence in 70 countries. Britain was an important country of operations, a British banking licence being obtained in 1973, and by 1978 there were 45 UK branches. Although registered in Luxembourg, London was BCCI's international operating headquarters.

Abedi was eager to establish a presence in the US, but this was impossible under US banking legislation because of the Bank of America shareholding. So BCCI entered the US illegally through frontmen, who first acquired control of the National Bank of Georgia and then in the late 1970s the larger First America Bank. It was with a sigh of relief that Bank of America sold its BCCI stake in 1980.

A driving force behind the rapid growth of BCCI's balance sheet was the quadrupling of oil prices in 1973–74, providing Arab oil producers with plenty of money to put on deposit. On the lending side, the expansion was achieved with little regard to the quality of business. Dangerously large exposures were made to favoured companies and individuals, violating prudent banking practices. An inquiry in 1978 revealed that loans to the Gulf Group, a Pakistani shipping company, totalled $185 million, three times the bank's capital and thirty times the prudent maximum exposure to a single client.[4] Although BCCI's published results showed ever-rising profits, by the late 1970s the bank was suffering an alarming level of bad debts.

Reality was not reflected in BCCI's accounts because the losses were concealed in a Cayman Islands subsidiary, a bank within a bank known internally as 'the dustbin', safe from regulatory scrutiny.[5] From the outset, BCCI's complex structure – registered in Luxembourg, headquartered in London, and operating across the world with numerous tax haven offshoots – was designed to prevent outsiders from gaining an accurate view of what was going on at the bank. Two prestigious firms of auditors were used, but neither of them had access to the whole picture. As the losses mounted, the accounts became more and more phoney, and Abedi was obliged to resort to increasingly reckless ways of keeping the bank afloat so as not to be found out.

Big and bold 'proprietary trading' – trading using the bank's own capital geared up with borrowings, in other words large-scale gambling – was Abedi's answer. But BCCI's traders lost money by the bucketful – $849 million between 1982 and 1986 – and the situation slipped from débâcle to disaster. The bank only kept going by its creative accounting and the massive misappropriation of depositors' funds. Abedi desperately needed new sources of revenue and deposits. So he became banker to Latin America's drug barons, a clientele who were happy to pay handsomely for international money-laundering services.

Panama fell under the sway of General Manuel Noriega, the head of the Panamanian intelligence services, following the death of the president in an air crash in 1981. In 1982, Noriega opened an account with BCCI's Panama City branch through which he routed the pay-offs he was receiving from the Colombian cocaine cartels for allowing them to use Panama as a transit point. Soon, the drug barons themselves were using BCCI's services to launder their proceeds. Similar services were provided for other drug dealers by BCCI in Hong Kong and Abu Dhabi. Investigations after the bank's collapse revealed a rogues' gallery of shadowy clients – not only narcotics dealers but also black-market foreign-exchange operators, arms traders, intelligence agencies (most famously Colonel Oliver North) and assorted terrorists. One deal, bizarrely, even financed the purchase by Arab terrorists of Israeli-built weapons.

In 1987, the head of BCCI's Miami branch made the mistake of offering the bank's money-laundering services to an undercover US customs agent. A customs service 'sting' operation resulted in a fine of $14.8 million and jail for four employees in 1989. Subsequent investigations by the US and UK authorities revealed the bank's criminal culture and found 'evidence of massive and widespread fraud'. BCCI was closed down by concerted action in a number of countries, led by the Bank of England, in July 1991.

The BCCI fraud ruined many small businessmen around the world. The biggest loser of all was Abedi's backer, the sheikh of Abu Dhabi. Recriminations abounded about negligence on the part of the various regulatory authorities and the bank's accountants, and whether the process by which the bank had been shut down had exacerbated the losses of depositors. Small depositors eventually recovered about 35 per cent of their money, although they had to wait until 1998 to do so.[6] Abedi and Naqvi were indicted in the US but could not be extradited. Abedi's death in 1995 put him beyond the law; 13 BCCI executives were convicted of fraud in Abu Dhabi.

The BCCI scandal demonstrated how criminally-minded international bankers could outwit regulators and accountants with national remits. BCCI, with its Luxembourg registration, London headquarters, Middle-Eastern shareholders and worldwide operations was regulated by everyone and no one. The need for closer co-operation was an urgent lesson for the major central banking authorities. The US also took unilateral action, amending its International Banking Act of 1978 to bolster the Federal Reserve's authority over foreign bank operations.

ROBERT MAXWELL

The Robert Maxwell scandal involved the collapse of that individual's UK-based publishing business and the theft of perhaps £730 million ($1.2 billion) from its pension funds.[7] Robert Maxwell, perpetrator of the fraud, was found drowned in 1991 and, four years later and after the most expensive trial in British history, his sons were acquitted of any wrongdoing. Subsequently, the extortionate fees charged by the lawyers and accountants handling the receivership became a scandal within a scandal: the High Court judge handling the matter called the fees 'profoundly shocking' and said, 'I find it shameful that a court receivership should produce this result.'[8]

TANGENTOPOLI

Italy's Tangentopoli scandal was about bribery and corruption amongst politicians and businessmen, to the tune of an estimated £2.6 billion ($4.2 billion) per year from the mid-1980s to the early 1990s.[9] A wave of arrests began in 1992, and by mid-1993 more than 2,500 eminent figures had been investigated. Several committed suicide.[10]

LLOYD'S OF LONDON

In the late 1980s and early 1990s, the insurance market Lloyd's of London ran up losses of £8 billion ($13.2 billion) due to a succession of natural disasters, a massive rise in US pollution liabilities, and managerial failures. Some of the 'names' – the 34,000 individuals whose assets traditionally back Lloyd's – won negligence cases based on the questionable conduct of market insiders and refused to pay their share of the losses. Eventually, in August 1996, a £3.2 billion settlement – the UK's largest ever out-of-court settlement – was agreed between Lloyd's and the names, and a recovery plan was set in motion.[11]

PENSIONS MIS-SELLING
....

In the four years following the UK government's introduction of new personal pensions in 1988, an estimated half-a-million people near retirement age and perhaps two million younger people were wrongly advised to leave their employer's pension scheme by greedy and unscrupulous personal pension salesmen.[12]

Despite instructions from the appropriate financial services regulator in 1994, the pensions industry did little to compensate victims of mis-selling. As a result, 44 firms, including household names, were fined during 1996 for delays in case reviews. Despite the penalties, by mid-1997 only 5 per cent of cases had been cleared up and Helen Liddell, Economic Secretary to the UK Treasury, decided to 'name and shame' the laggards.[13] 'No one gets off the hook where mis-selling of personal pensions may have occurred,' she says. 'Every firm must get on with reviewing cases and provide redress where it is due. ... It is a public scandal that these people have had to wait so long for help.'[14]

It was estimated that compensation to victims would cost pensions providers £4 billion, and some put the figure as high as £8 billion.[15]

PYRAMID FINANCE SCHEMES
....

The impoverished and financially unsophisticated peoples of the former Soviet Union and Eastern Europe were sitting ducks for unscrupulous promoters of get-rich-quick pyramid finance schemes, which operated on the same basis as a chain letter. In Albania, more than $1 billion – one-third of gross domestic product – was invested in such schemes; their collapse wiped out seven out of ten Albanian families of their savings provoking riots there in the spring of 1997.[16]

BARINGS
....

The Barings scandal of 1995 was about the bankrupting of a prestigious London merchant bank by losses of £830 million ($1.3 billion) run up by derivatives trader Nick Leeson in the bank's Singapore office.

Barings, established in 1762, was Britain's oldest merchant bank and a highly esteemed firm – the UK's Queen Elizabeth II was a customer. Like other banks, Barings expanded proprietary trading in financial products in the 1980s and 1990s as the margins on other businesses were squeezed by competition. Such trading could be highly profitable, but it was also very risky, as Barings learnt to its cost.

Nick Leeson, from Watford in the UK, left school at 18 with qualifications in English and History but a fail in Maths. He worked for a couple of banks in menial capacities, and then joined Barings and became a trader. Leeson took readily to trading. 'We admired Nick because he had almost no fear,' said another Singapore trader. 'It was like watching someone juggling hand-grenades, but we always thought if he dropped one he would blow just himself up.'[17]

In April 1992, aged 25, Leeson was posted to Singapore. He took with him his new wife, Lisa, and left behind £3,000-worth of unpaid county court judgments, tokens of his careless attitude to other people's money. Singapore suited Leeson. Soon he was earning £200,000 plus bonuses, had a flat in a fashionable suburb, and drove a Porsche and a Mercedes. The only cloud on the horizon was that his trading wasn't going so well, and although regarded by his bosses as a star performer, he was, in fact, running up losses that he was covering up. He could do so because he was able improperly to influence the back office – the accounts department that supposedly monitored his trades and positions – where his wife worked. He took to falsifying client documentation, pretending to London that he was trading on behalf of clients whereas in fact he was taking positions on behalf of the bank.

Leeson observed that futures and options contracts based on the Nikkei 225 index, Japan's leading share index, on the Osaka stock exchange traded at a premium to identical contracts on the Singapore exchange. By capturing the difference – in effect buying in Singapore and selling in Osaka – there was money to be made. The profit on each trade was minute, but if done on a large scale, the operation could be very lucrative. He was also convinced that the Nikkei would rise, generating a capital gain as well as the arbitrage profit. To insure against the possibility that prices would move against him, Leeson claimed to have hedged his position with another set of trades, assurances that turned out to be, as a colleague put it with restraint, 'a stream of unadulterated falsehoods.'[18]

Leeson built up a large and largely unauthorised position in Nikkei 225 futures contracts in early January 1995. Then the Kobe earthquake of 17 January 1995 sent Japanese share prices tumbling. More convinced than ever that Japanese shares were undervalued, he doubled his exposure to $7 billion in the days after the earthquake. The scale of Leeson's commitments required huge margin calls – deposits against potential losses required by financial exchanges. Some £500 million – more than half the bank's capital – was forwarded by London in early 1995. But, at last, senior management was beginning to ask what Leeson was up to. On 24 February 1995, an audit was ordered of his operations and it became clear that Barings had incurred massive losses. The Bank of England was informed, the governor Eddie George being whisked back from a skiing holiday without ever touching the snow.

Over the weekend 27/28 February 1995, the Bank of England and City firms endeavoured to put together a rescue package to recapitalise Barings and keep it going. Their task was bedevilled by the nature of the commitments Leeson had entered into, the open-ended futures contracts meaning that the level of eventual losses depended upon the level of the Nikkei on the settlement day, 10 March 1995. Not even the world's richest man, the Sultan of Brunei, was prepared to take on the risk. With the failure of the rescue attempt, administrators were appointed to oversee the stricken bank's affairs. They quickly came to terms with Dutch bank ING, which acquired Barings, plus its liabilities, for a nominal £1.

Back in Singapore, the Leesons had disappeared, Nick leaving a note on his desk for his colleagues reading 'I'm sorry'. 'Where's Leeson?' ran the joke in City wine bars. 'Wandering about in the jungle having lost his bearings.' After a few nights in exotic resort hotels, Leeson boarded a flight to Frankfurt, where he was arrested. Extradited to Singapore, he found himself in court.

The prosecution accused Leeson of cheating and lying, covering his tracks using a secret account (Error Account No. 88888), fictitious names, falsified documents and falsehoods. It was established that by the end of 1994, before betting the bank on the Nikkei 225, he had run up hidden losses of £50 million ($79 million). He was sentenced to six-and-a-half years in jail. The case received worldwide media attention and Leeson became a celebrity. The rights to his autobiography were sold for £500,000, and television personality David Frost is producing a film.

Barings' senior management emerged from the episode looking staggeringly foolish, the UK Chancellor lambasting 'the total collapse of management control'. Those who had failed to supervise Leeson lost their jobs, and others retired. The Bank of England was also criticised for 'a lack of vigour' in overseeing Barings, prompting the response that there was no way it could have prevented Barings' failure, given deliberate deception by Leeson and lax management controls. Overall, the episode highlighted the hazard posed by a 'rogue trader' in modern financial markets, where perilous positions can be built up very rapidly. It was a danger soon to be further illustrated by the Daiwa Bank and Sumitomo Corporation scandals.

DAIWA BANK

The Daiwa Bank scandal was about losses totalling $1.1 billion incurred through unauthorised trades in US Treasury bonds by dealer Toshihide Iguchi in Daiwa Bank's New York branch.

Japanese born, Iguchi studied psychology at Southeast Missouri State University and then stayed in the US working as a car salesman. Impressively fluent in English, he joined Daiwa in New York in 1976. He was able and hard-working, and his dedication was respected and rewarded. Hired as an administrative clerk, he was given the opportunity to work in the dealing room trading US Treasury bonds. Iguchi had a flair for dealing, and rose rapidly through the ranks. In 1979, he was given responsibility for the back-office processing of trades, as well as continuing to be a dealer – a similar set-up to Leeson's in Singapore, and with similarly unfortunate consequences. He was promoted again in 1986, being made head of government bond trading, the New York branch's most profitable department.

Iguchi's nightmare began in 1984 when he made a $200,000 trading loss. Hoping to win the money back, he covered up the deficit. But luck had walked out on him – to the tune of losses averaging $400,000 per working day over 11 years. In July 1994, no longer able to take the pressure, he sent a 30-page confession to the president of Daiwa Bank, explaining how he hid the trading losses by selling securities deposited by the bank's clients. He concealed these sales by hiding the confirmation documents and using duplicate order forms in such a way as to enable him to trade without detection by Daiwa or the US Federal Reserve, the bank's US regulator.

Remembered by college contemporaries as shy and courteous, Iguchi became more and more irascible as his secret took its toll. His marriage was a casualty, and his colleagues suffered too. 'He was famous for his quick temper, banging down the phone if you couldn't quote him a price fast enough,' commented a fellow Japanese bond dealer.[19] Usually, Japanese bank staff are given three-year postings in overseas branches, but Iguchi was recruited locally and was not one of the bank's mainstream employees. And he never took a holiday – he couldn't for fear that someone would stumble upon his stupendous losses. That was how he was able to hide the deficits for so long.

Iguchi was arrested and prosecuted for forgery and falsifying records. He received a four-year jail sentence in December 1996. He presented his version of events in a book, *The Confession*, (Bungei Shonju, 1997) published in 1997, blaming the US and Japanese regulatory authorities for negligence in not detecting his activities earlier, thereby allowing him to go on running up losses. Over 11 years, he had executed 30,000 unauthorised transactions, massively exceeded his trading limits, hidden trade confirmation documents and forged statements – and nobody noticed. 'Like not noticing there is an elephant in the living room,' commented a stupefied Wall Street banker.[20]

The manager of Daiwa Bank's New York branch was also indicted, charged with conspiring to cover-up Iguchi's losses from the US regulators. In fact, the US authorities were furious at the way Daiwa Bank's senior management handled the episode, waiting for two months before informing them. The scandal cast doubts upon the competence of the US regulators and upon New York's reputation as a tightly regulated financial centre. The regulators pointed out that they had warned Daiwa twice about Iguchi's dual responsibilities, but the bank had done nothing. Furthermore, the bank had gone ahead with a pending $500 million share issue, making no mention of Iguchi's losses. When these facts became public knowledge, Daiwa Bank shares slumped 7 per cent.

The US regulators decided to make an example. Daiwa Bank's entire US operations were closed down, and federal prosecutors issued a criminal indictment of 24 counts, including conspiracy to defraud the Federal Reserve. In January 1996, Daiwa sold its US assets to Sumitomo Bank for the 'fire-sale' price of $65 million. The legal case was settled with the payment of a fine of $340 million, the largest ever recorded. 'This record fine demonstrates that we take the rules seriously,' remarked US Attorney General, Janet Reno.[21]

SUMITOMO CORPORATION

Yasuo Hamanaka is the world's most disastrous trader, losing $3 billion – more than Leeson and Iguchi put together – on his dealings for Sumitomo Corporation.

Hamanaka was head of copper trading in Tokyo at the leading Japanese trading company Sumitomo Corporation. Nicknamed 'Mr Five

Per Cent' – the proportion of world copper stocks he was reputed to control – or, more sinisterly, 'The Hammer', he was a formidable figure in the base metals market. When news of his dismissal hit the market in June 1996, the price of copper dropped 25 per cent.

Hamanaka's troubles began in 1985, with a small but humiliating trading loss that he covered up. Over the next 11 years, he made unauthorised trades in order to try to recoup the deficit, but instead ran up further losses. His undoing came when he and some confederates, under intense pressure to produce profits, squeezed the copper market and pushed up prices. Recognising a rigged market, US hedge funds piled in to profit from a price fall. The hedge funds won, and Hamanaka's losses soared. The débâcle caused Sumitomo Corporation to declare a loss for the first time in 77 years.

Hamanaka was able to conceal the losses for so long because of the trust-based Japanese management style. To all appearances, he was a model salary-man, the sort who gave the company's name first and his own afterwards. He wore a sober blue suit, lived in a quiet suburb and liked swimming with his family. Being highly experienced and well respected, he was allowed to handle his own paperwork, and so his irregularities went undetected by colleagues or regulators. Hamanaka confessed only when an investigation into copper prices brought his misdemeanours to light. In court in Tokyo, he pleaded guilty to charges of fraud and forgery.

MORGAN GRENFELL ASSET MANAGEMENT (MGAM)

The MGAM scandal of autumn 1996 concerned the conduct of fund manager Peter Young, who made improperly large investments in risky unquoted high-tech shares and obscured his doings by routing transactions through a labyrinth of holding companies in Luxembourg. His conduct cost Young his job and MGAM's parent, Deutsche Bank, £230 million ($380 million) in compensation to the funds he managed.[22]

SOKAIYA EXTORTION

Sokaiya is a Japanese form of extortion, perpetrated on companies by *yakusa* gangsters through the disruption of their annual general meetings. To protect themselves from awkward revelations, Japanese bankers and brokers illegally pay off these blackmailers. The revelation of illegal *sokaiya* payments by leading securities house Nomura led to the resignation of Japan's finance minister Ryutaro Hashimoto in 1991.

In spring 1997, a new *sokaiya* scandal erupted in Japan. The official explanation is that it arose from the Ministry of Finance's endeavours to clean up corporate ethics ahead of Japan's Big Bang (see Chapter 7), which will allow much more competition from foreign banks. But others have suggested that the impetus came from politically ambitious officials in the Tokyo prosecutor's office.[23] Again, it was Nomura that was in the eye of the *sokaiya* storm and the Japanese government, headed by new prime minister Ryutaro Hashimoto, ordered a crackdown.[24]

All four major Japanese securities houses were found to have made *sokaiya* payments, as was Japan's second-largest bank Dai-Ichi Kangyo Bank. By winter 1997, 58 senior bank executives had resigned, including the chairman, president and entire board of Nomura, the chairman of Daiwa Securities, and the chief executive of Nikko Securities. There had been 32 arrests for making payments to racketeers, and the former chairman of Dai-Ichi Kangyo Bank had committed suicide. 'Imagine the chairmen of Goldman Sachs, Merrill Lynch, Morgan Stanley, and Salomon Brothers resigning because their firms were discovered making payments to the Mafia. That is the scale of the scandal now overwhelming Japan's four brokers,' wrote the *Financial Times*.[25]

Undermined by the *sokaiya* scandal and by hidden trading losses, Yamaichi Securities, Japan's fourth-largest securities house, collapsed in November 1997 (see Chapter 4). Nomura was punished by being required to stop trading for its own account, banned from underwriting issues of public bonds until the end of 1997, and ordered to suspend equity trading for a week. The other firms faced similar penalties. And prison awaits some executives.

In a Nutshell

Financial scandals are a perennial feature of financial markets. Fifteen prominent financial scandals of the late 1980s and 1990s are listed in Table 10.1. The list is full of 'firsts', such as the Savings and Loan scandal being the biggest tax-payer bail-out, the BCCI scandal being the biggest bank fraud, and the Sumitomo Corporation scandal being the biggest trading loss. But sooner or later, these records will be broken by new scandals.

FURTHER READING

Adams, James Ring, and Frantz, Douglas, *A Full Service Bank* (London, Simon & Schuster, 1992)

Bailey, Fenton, *The Junk Bond Revolution: Michael Milken and the 'Roaring Eighties'* (London, Mandarin, 1992)

Fay, Stephen, *The Collapse of Barings* (London, Arrow, 1996)

Gunn, Cathy, *Nightmare on Lime Street: Whatever Happened to Lloyd's of London?* (London, Smith Gryphon, 1993)

Jaffa, Sam, *Safe as Houses: The Schemers and Scams behind some of the World's Greatest Financial Scandals* (London, Robson, 1997)

Widlake, Brian, *The Serious Fraud Office* (London, Little, Brown, 1995)

NOTES AND REFERENCES

In the list below for this chapter, any reference to an author alone should be taken to be a reference to his/her work in 'Further reading' above.

1 'The Guinness Report', *Financial Times*, 28 November 1997

2 *The Observer*, 8 September 1991; Jaffa, p. 237

3 *The Observer*, 8 September 1991

4 Jaffa, p. 243

5 *The Observer*, 1 September 1991

6 *Financial Times*, 7 July 1997

7 Jaffa, p. 220

8 *Financial Times*, 11 July 1997

9 *Financial Times*, 16 March 1993

10 *New York Times*, 24 July 1993

11 *Financial Times*, 1 September 1996

12 *Financial Times*, 25 June 1997

13 *The Times*, 16 November 1996; *Financial Times*, 10 July 1997

14 *The Sunday Telegraph*, 21 September 1997

15 *Financial Times*, 9 July 1997

16 *Financial Times*, 4 March 1997; The Economist, 9 May 1998

17 *Sunday Times*, 5 March 1995

18 Jaffa, p. 47

19 *Financial Times*, 27 September 1995

20 Jaffa, p. 296

21 Jaffa, p. 305

22 *Financial Times*, 7 and 8 September 1996 and 25 September 1997

23 'Asia in crisis', *Financial Times*, 14 January 1998
24 *Daily Telegraph*, 30 August 1997
25 *Financial Times*, 1 October 1997

APPENDIX
Leading International Banks

ABN-Amro Holding NV
Foppingadreef 22,
P.O. Box 600,
1000 AP Amsterdam, The Netherlands.
Tier-one capital: $16,098m. Capital rank: 8.
Total assets: $341,396m. Assets rank: 15.
Proportion of business overseas: 49.3%.
Staff: 66,200.

The Netherlands' biggest commercial bank, formed by the merger
of two Dutch banks in 1990. Since the merger it has expanded globally
through a patchwork of small acquisitions, becoming the biggest foreign
bank in both the US and Japan. No other bank has such a diversity of
banking businesses, from auto leasing in Brazil, to retail banking in the
US, and Eurobond lead-management. It has a presence in 70 countries.

ANZ Banking Group
100 Queen Street,
Melbourne,
Victoria 3000, Australia.
Tier-one capital: $4,971m. Capital rank: 73.
Total assets: $90,009m. Assets rank: 89.
Proportion of business overseas: 42.0%.
Staff: 39,700.

ANZ Banking Group operates in 41 countries besides its domestic
market in Australia and New Zealand. A network of niche banking
operations provide trade finance and commercial banking services

throughout the Asia Pacific region. This is complemented by an active presence in the major global financial centres.

Banca Commerciale Italiana
Piazza della Scala, 6,
20121 Milan,
Italy.
Tier-one capital: $5,327m. Capital rank: 68.
Total assets: $115,448m. Assets rank: 70.
Proportion of business overseas: 43.6%.
Staff: 22,000.

One of the larger Italian commercial banks. Italy's most international bank, with a presence in 43 countries.

Banco Bilbao Vizcaya
Gran Via 1,
48001 Bilbao,
Spain.
Tier-one capital: $6,288m. Capital rank: 51.
Total assets: $131,069m. Assets rank: 59.
Proportion of business overseas: 43.5%.
Staff: 44,000.

Spain's largest and most international bank undertakes a full range of commercial bank activities and asset management. The international network comprises 908 offices in 34 countries, notably in Portugal and Latin America where it has an important presence.

Bank of Tokyo-Mitsubishi
7-1, Marunouchi 2-chome,
Chiyoda-ku,
Tokyo 100, Japan.
Tier-one capital: $23,323m. Capital rank: 2.
Total assets: $647,781m. Assets rank: 1.
Proportion of business overseas: 33.5%.
Staff: 23,500.

The world's biggest bank by assets, formed by the merger of the Bank of Tokyo and Mitsubishi Bank in 1996. Founded as Japan's specialist foreign exchange bank 50 years ago, the Bank of Tokyo has had a long-standing presence in international markets with more than 70 offices overseas. Half of the bank's revenues derive from its overseas operations.

BT Alex. Brown
One Bankers Trust Plaza,
New York, NY 10006,
USA.
Tier-one capital: $5,929m.* Capital rank: 56.*
Total assets: $120,235m.* Assets rank: 66.
Proportion of business overseas: 49.5%.*
Staff: 15,000.*
*Bankers Trust only, before merger with Alex. Brown.

BT Alex. Brown was formed in 1997 by the merger of Bankers Trust New York Corporation, one of the largest US commercial banks specialising in the provision of wholesale banking services to corporations, governments, institutions and wealthy individuals, and Baltimore-based investment bank Alex. Brown. Bankers Trust's international network comprises 80 offices in 50 countries.

Canadian Imperial Bank of Commerce (CIBC)
Commerce Court,
Toronto, Ontario M5L 1A2,
Canada.
Tier-one capital: $6,310m. Capital rank: 50.
Total assets: $141,936m. Assets rank: 54.
Proportion of business overseas: 44.0%.
Staff: 41,600.

Canada's most international bank. CIBC divides its activities into two parts: the Personal and Commercial Bank, largely for domestic clients; and CIBC Wood Grundy. The latter conducts the corporate and investment banking operations, providing integrated financial solutions for clients worldwide.

Chase Manhattan Corporation
270 Park Avenue,
New York, NY 10017,
USA.
Tier-one capital: $21,095m. Capital rank: 4.

Total assets: $336,099m. Assets rank: 17.
Proportion of business overseas: 33.6%.
Staff: 65,000.

Until recently the largest US bank, Chase Manhattan has two main businesses – global wholesale banking and regional and domestic commercial banking. Chase's wholesale clients include leading multinational corporations, governments and wealthy individuals. The regional client-base comprises 25 million individuals and households.

Citicorp

399 Park Avenue,
New York, NY10043,
USA.
Tier-one capital: $20,109m. Capital rank: 5.
Total assets: $281,018m. Assets rank: 27.
Proportion of business overseas: 59.6%.
Staff: 85,000.

With 1,130 branches and 50 million customers in 98 countries, Citicorp has the most extensive global banking network. 'No other financial institution,' it declares, 'has our ability to serve customers around the world and around the clock.' In 1998, Citicorp announced a merger with Travelers Group, owner of Salomon Brothers.

Compagnie Financière de Paribas

3, rue d'Antin, BP 141,
75078 Paris Cedex 02,
France.
Tier-one capital: $10,765m. Capital rank: 26.
Total assets: $290,720m. Assets rank: 25.
Proportion of business overseas: 55.6%.
Staff: 9,000.

France's foremost investment bank, which is also a leading provider of specialist financial services to corporations and individuals. Expanding globally from a strong European base, Paribas is active in 60 countries. It specialises in corporate banking, capital markets activities and financial services.

Crédit Lyonnais Group

19 boulevard des Italiens,

75002 Paris,
France.
Tier-one capital: $7,757m. Capital rank: 41.
Total assets: $310,040m. Assets rank: 22.
Proportion of business overseas: 52.5%.
Staff: 57,000.

State owned Crédit Lyonnaise is one of the biggest French banks. It has an international presence in more than 70 countries. It supplies a wide range of commercial banking products and services to retail clients and small firms mostly in France, and to major corporations, governments and institutions worldwide. The French government's massive bail-out of Crédit Lyonnais' losses has been controversial.

Credit Suisse Group
Nüschelerstrasse 1,
P.O. Box 669,
8021 Zurich, Switzerland.
Tier-one capital: $11,611m. Capital rank: 22.
Total assets: $389,300m. Assets rank: 11.
Proportion of business overseas: 74.2%.
Staff: 34,800.

Swiss-based Credit Suisse Group is one of the largest international financial services groups in the world. The group comprises four business units: Credit Suisse, Credit Suisse Private Banking, Credit Suisse First Boston and Credit Suisse Asset Management, each geared to the requirements of specific customer groups and markets.

Dai-Ichi Kangyo Bank
1-5, Uchisaiwaicho 1-chome,
Chiyoda-ku,
Tokyo 100, Japan.
Tier-one capital: $15,162m. Capital rank: 12.
Total assets: $433,860m. Assets rank: 6.
Proportion of business overseas: 26.1%.
Staff: 18,000.

Dai-Ichi Kangyo is one of Japan's leading commercial banks. It also has a well-established presence in North America and Europe and extensive representation in the Asia–Pacific region. The Dai-Ichi Kangyo network comprises 77 offices in 31 countries and 52 cities around the world.

Daiwa Securities Company
6-4 Otemachi 2-chome,
Chiyoda-ku,
Tokyo 100, Japan.
Tier-one capital: $7,000m.
Total assets: $108,000m.
Staff: 11,600.

Daiwa Securities Company is the second largest of Japan's major securities brokerage houses. Its global activities include securities brokerage, trading, underwriting, strategic advice, product development and structured finance. Its network comprises 123 offices in Japan and operations in 35 locations overseas.

Deutsche Bank
Taunusanlage 12,
60262 Frankfurt-am-Main,
Germany.
Tier-one capital: $18,517m. Capital rank: 4.
Total assets: $336,099m. Assets rank: 2.
Proportion of business overseas: 46.5%.
Staff: 148,400.

Germany's largest bank, and one of the world's leading financial institutions operating in more than 50 countries. Besides extensive commercial and corporate banking operations in Germany and elsewhere, it has a global investment banking business focused on London and in 40 other offices around the world.

Dresdner Bank A.G.
Jürgen-Ponto-Platz 1,
60301 Frankfurt-am-Main,
Germany.
Tier-one capital: $9,325m. Capital rank: 29.
Total assets: $355,605m. Assets rank: 13.
Proportion of business overseas: 43.0%.
Staff: 46,000.

Germany's second largest bank, with nearly 1,600 branches operating in more than 70 countries. Commercial banking business is headquartered in Frankfurt, while global investment banking services offered under the brand name Dresdner Kleinwort Benson are based in London.

Flemings
25 Copthall Avenue,
London EC2R 7DR,
UK.
Tier-one capital: $1,206m.
Total assets: $132,663m.
Staff: 7,000.

Flemings is one of the few remaining independent UK investment banks. It has offices in 40 countries and is especially strongly represented in the Asia–Pacific region.

Goldman Sachs
85 Broad Street,
New York, NY 10004,
USA.
Tier-one capital: $6,293m.
Total assets: $152,045m.
Staff: 10,000.

Goldman Sachs is the only remaining partnership amongst the global investment banks. It provides a full range of investment banking activities on the basis of five operating divisions: investment banking; fixed income; equities; currency and commodities; and asset management. Goldman Sachs has 34 offices in 20 countries.

HSBC Holdings
10 Lower Thames Street,
London EC3R 6AE,
UK.
Tier-one capital: $25,716m. Capital rank: 1.
Total assets: $401,686m. Assets rank: 10.
Proportion of business overseas: 62.8%.
Staff: 130,000.

The world's largest bank by tier-one capital and one of the most international. It provides consumer, commercial and investment banking services and insurance under long-established names in the Asia–Pacific region, Europe, the Americas, the Middle East and Africa. Subsidiaries include Midland Bank in the UK and Marine Midland in the US. It has more than 5,000 offices in 78 countries.

ING Group

Strawinskylaan 2631,
P.O. Box 810,
1000 AV Amsterdam, The Netherlands.
Tier-one capital: $7,609m. Capital rank: 42.
Total assets: $178,614m. Assets rank: 46.
Proportion of business overseas: 33.0%.
Staff: 58,000.

Dutch universal bank ING Group conducts commercial banking, investment banking, asset management and insurance. It is a leader in the development of integrated financial services, offering personal and corporate customers a comprehensive range of financial services. It undertakes banking activities in 57 countries, especially in Europe and Asia, and insurance activities in 28.

JP Morgan

60 Wall Street,
New York, NY 10260–0060,
USA.
Tier-one capital: $11,469m. Capital rank: 23.
Total assets: $222,026m. Assets rank: 37.
Proportion of business overseas: 50.9%.
Staff: 15,500.

US-based JP Morgan is a leading global financial firm that meets the financial needs of business enterprises, governments, financial institutions and governments worldwide. It advises on corporate strategy and structure, raises capital, makes markets in a range of financial instruments and undertakes asset management. It operates in 33 countries.

Lehman Brothers

3 World Financial Center,
New York, NY 10285,

USA.
Tier-one capital: $3,874m.
Total assets: $128,596m.
Staff: 7,500.

Lehman Brothers has for many years been a leading Wall Street brokerage house and investment bank. It has a global presence, with offices in 22 countries. In 1996, 59 per cent of revenues were generated by activities in the Americas, 29 per cent from Europe and the Middle East, and 12 per cent from Asia–Pacific.

Merrill Lynch
North Tower,
World Financial Center,
New York, NY 10281–1332, USA.
Tier-one capital: $6,892m.
Total assets: $213,016m.
Staff: 54,000.

Merrill Lynch has long been America's foremost retail securities broker. In the 1980s and 1990s, it developed a major investment banking capability and global reach. It is one of the world's leading and most dynamic investment banks, operating in 45 countries.

Morgan Stanley Dean Witter
1285 Broadway,
New York, NY 10036,
USA.
Tier-one capital: $6,538m.*
Total assets: $196,446m.*
Staff: 45,000.
*Morgan Stanley only, before the merger with Dean Witter.

US-based Morgan Stanley has for many years been a leading global securities firm and investment bank, offering a complete range of sophisticated financial services to governments, corporations, institutions and individuals worldwide. The 1997 merger with retail broking and credit card business Dean Witter Discover created a formidable financial conglomerate. The combined firm operates from 409 offices located in 22 countries around the world.

National Australia Bank
500 Bourke Street,
GPO Box 84A,
Melbourne, Victoria 3001, Australia.
Tier-one capital: $8,042m. Capital rank: 38.
Total assets: $123,952m. Assets rank: 64.
Proportion of business overseas: 46.7%.
Staff: 52,900.

National Australia Bank is an international financial services group conducting commercial banking operations in five countries – Australia, UK, Ireland, New Zealand, and the US – and a network of branches and representative offices throughout Asia.

National Westminster Bank
41 Lothbury,
London EC2P 2BP,
UK.
Tier-one capital: $11,914m. Capital rank: 20.
Total assets: $314,716m. Assets rank: 21.
Proportion of business overseas: 47.3%.
Staff: 71,000.

The National Westminster Bank is engaged in a wide range of banking, financial and related activities in the UK and 34 other countries. In recent years it has retrenched in international and investment banking and focused on its core commercial domestic banking activities.

Nomura Securities
1-9-1, Nihonbashi 1-chome,
Chuo-ku,
Tokyo 103, Japan.
Tier-one capital: $17,363m.
Total assets: $120,149m.
Staff: 11,000.

Nomura Securities is Japan's leading securities house and investment bank. Its activities encompass securities brokerage, trading, investment banking and commercial banking in global markets. Nomura's revenues are derived from commissions, underwriting and distribution, net gain on trading, and interest and dividends. It has offices in 27 countries.

Salomon Smith Barney
Seven World Trade Center,
New York, NY 10048,
USA.
Tier-one capital: $4,857m.
Total assets: $194,881m.
Staff: 8,500.*
*Salomon Brothers only before merger with Smith Barney.

Leading US investment bank Salomon Smith Barney is the outcome of the 1997 merger between Salomon Brothers, a pre-eminent global trading, market-making and investment banking firm, and brokerage house Smith Barney, owned by Travelers Group, one of America's largest financial services groups. Besides a major presence in the US, it has a network of 30 subsidiaries and affiliates on four continents. In 1998, a merger was announced with Citicorp.

Schroders
120 Cheapside,
London EC2V 6DS,
UK.
Tier-one capital: $1,553m.
Total assets: $17,110m.
Staff: 5,000.

Schroders is a leading international investment bank, merchant bank, and asset management group. It is one of the few remaining independent UK merchant banks. It is represented in 45 cities in 32 countries around the world.

Société Générale
29 Boulevard Haussmann,
75009 Paris,
France.
Tier-one capital: $10,735m. Capital rank: 27.
Total assets: $339,996m. Assets rank: 16.
Proportion of business overseas: 46.8%.
Staff: 45,000.

Société Généralé is the largest private sector French bank with 2,000 branches in France and 500 offices in over 70 countries worldwide. It is organised in three divisions, Retail Banking, which is mainly in France,

International and Finance, and Resources and Services. The International and Finance division services some 500 multinational corporations, 4,000 institutional investors and 1,300 banks.

Standard Chartered Bank
1 Aldermanbury Square,
London EC2V 7SB,
UK.
Tier-one capital: $3,890m. Capital rank: 94.
Total assets: $71,554m. Assets rank: 109.
Proportion of business overseas: 74.3%.
Staff: 25,000.

UK-based Standard Chartered Bank is an international bank which focuses its activities on Africa, the Middle East and Asia, operating in every Asia–Pacific country except North Korea. It is the most international of all banks, having almost three-quarters of its assets based overseas.

Swiss Bank Corporation
Aeschenplatz 6,
CH-4002 Basel,
Switzerland
Tier-one capital: $10,264m. Capital rank: 28.
Total assets: $267,339m. Assets rank: 29.
Proportion of business overseas: 64.6%.
Staff: 26,800.

Swiss Bank Corporation is a Swiss universal bank, conducting commercial banking in Switzerland, private banking for wealthy individuals around the world, investment banking through SBC Warburg Dillon Read, and asset management through SBC Brinson. In 1997 it announced a merger with fellow Swiss bank Union Bank of Switzerland to form a formidable global financial grouping.

Union Bank of Switzerland
Bahnhofstrasse 45,
8021 Zurich,
Switzerland.
Tier-one capital: $15,743m. Capital rank: 10.

Total assets: $324,756m. Assets rank: 19.
Proportion of business overseas: 71.0%.
Staff: 28,600.

Union Bank of Switzerland is a Swiss universal bank, conducting commercial banking in Switzerland, private banking for wealthy individuals, international investment banking and asset management. It has 48 overseas offices. In 1997 it announced a merger with fellow Swiss bank Swiss Bank Corporation to form a formidable global financial grouping.

Sources: annual reports and accounts of firms. 'Capital rank' refers to tier-one capital (shareholders' equity) amongst commercial banks. 'Assets rank' refers to balance sheet assets amongst commercial banks. Both are derived from *The Banker*, July 1996. The proportion of business overseas is derived from *The Banker*, February 1998.

INDEX